Security, Conflict and Cooperation in the Contemporary World

Series Editors
Effie G. H. Pedaliu
LSE Ideas
London, UK

John W. Young
University of Nottingham
Nottingham, UK

The Palgrave Macmillan series, Security, Conflict and Cooperation in the Contemporary World aims to make a significant contribution to academic and policy debates on cooperation, conflict and security since 1900. It evolved from the series Global Conflict and Security edited by Professor Saki Ruth Dockrill. The current series welcomes proposals that offer innovative historical perspectives, based on archival evidence and promoting an empirical understanding of economic and political cooperation, conflict and security, peace-making, diplomacy, humanitarian intervention, nation-building, intelligence, terrorism, the influence of ideology and religion on international relations, as well as the work of international organisations and non-governmental organisations.

More information about this series at
http://www.palgrave.com/gp/series/14489

Grace Livingstone

Britain and the Dictatorships of Argentina and Chile, 1973–82

Foreign Policy, Corporations and Social Movements

Grace Livingstone
Centre of Latin American Studies
University of Cambridge
Cambridge, UK

Security, Conflict and Cooperation in the Contemporary World
ISBN 978-3-030-08666-4   ISBN 978-3-319-78292-8   (eBook)
https://doi.org/10.1007/978-3-319-78292-8

© The Editor(s) (if applicable) and The Author(s) 2018
Softcover re-print of the Hardcover 1st edition 2018
This work is subject to copyright. All rights are solely and exclusively licensed by the Publisher, whether the whole or part of the material is concerned, specifically the rights of translation, reprinting, reuse of illustrations, recitation, broadcasting, reproduction on microfilms or in any other physical way, and transmission or information storage and retrieval, electronic adaptation, computer software, or by similar or dissimilar methodology now known or hereafter developed.
The use of general descriptive names, registered names, trademarks, service marks, etc. in this publication does not imply, even in the absence of a specific statement, that such names are exempt from the relevant protective laws and regulations and therefore free for general use.
The publisher, the authors and the editors are safe to assume that the advice and information in this book are believed to be true and accurate at the date of publication. Neither the publisher nor the authors or the editors give a warranty, express or implied, with respect to the material contained herein or for any errors or omissions that may have been made. The publisher remains neutral with regard to jurisdictional claims in published maps and institutional affiliations.

Cover credit: © Homer W Sykes/Alamy Stock Photo and © mirjanajovic/Getty Images

Printed on acid-free paper

This Palgrave Macmillan imprint is published by the registered company Springer International Publishing AG part of Springer Nature
The registered company address is: Gewerbestrasse 11, 6330 Cham, Switzerland

"The book is constructed by pioneering research of outstanding quality. It places British foreign policy of the 1970s in a quite new and questionable light."
—David Rock, *Emeritus Professor of History, University of California, USA*, author of *Argentina 1516–1987: From Spanish Colonization to Alfonsín*

"Grace Livingstone provides a brilliantly original analysis of UK-Latin American relations prior to the Falklands conflict. Her investigations into recently released archives yield many important insights into the often murky fields of arms sales, the politics of oil, and violations of human rights. Livingstone also develops original and illuminating theoretical perspectives on her subject. Scholarly, compelling and intellectually sophisticated, this book is outstanding."
—John Dumbrell, *Emeritus Professor of Government, Durham University, UK*

"Meticulously researched, well-written and very convincing, this book is an authoritative account of the making of British foreign policy towards the military regimes of Argentina and Chile. It is an indispensable study of how both Conservative and Labour governments tried to balance the competing forces attempting to influence the policy-making process. I cannot recommend it too highly."
—Alan Angell, *Emeritus Fellow, St Antony's College, Oxford, UK*

"In this major new study, Grace Livingstone contrasts the way in which British Governments treated the military dictatorships in Chile and Argentina during the 1970s and 1980s, examining the conflicts between ministers and officials, and the role of public opinion. It is an absorbing read which illuminates some dark corners of British foreign policy."
—Andrew Gamble, *Professor of Politics, University of Sheffield, UK*

"This is an exhaustive exploration of British National Archives covering Pinochet's coup in Chile in 1973 and the Argentine coup of 1976 leading to the South Atlantic conflict in 1982. The resulting book provides a detailed analysis of British foreign policy-making towards Chile and Argentina in the Cold War years. The focus is on the diverging and contrasting attitudes of both Labour and Conservative governments when dealing with Chile and Argentina. All in all, this book is a must read for those interested in international relations, in the making of British foreign policy, and in understanding the context that led to the 1982 conflict."
—Celia Szusterman, *The Institute for Statecraft, UK*

"Grace Livingstone's work marks an important contribution to the study of British policy toward Latin America. Examining the informal networks of a wide range of actors, from civil servants and politicians to business leaders and interest groups, it demonstrates how the social class of officials influenced the policymaking process."

—Aaron Donaghy, *EU Marie Skłodowska-Curie Global Fellow, Harvard University, USA*

"Grace Livingstone's meticulous and detailed work to unearth and document the execrable position of the FCO, its desk officers, section heads and embassy staff, is wonderful. This book takes us behind the scenes to see how Foreign Office ambassadors and civil service respond to and seek to mould the policies of governments—nowhere more so than in their response to the 1973 military coup in Chile. Conservatives wanted business as usual, Labour wanted an ethical foreign policy. Human rights campaigners wanted something stronger. Here, in telegrams and briefing memos, you can see how it all played out. Grace Livingstone has added a vital and previously missing component to our understanding of the period."

—Mike Gatehouse, *former joint-secretary of the Chile Solidarity Campaign*

Contents

1	Introduction: Making Friends With the Junta	1
2	Chile 1973–1982	35
3	Welcoming Pinochet's Coup (1973–1974)	45
4	Ethical Foreign Policy? Labour Versus the Foreign Office (1974–1979)	57
5	Tea with a Dictator: Mrs. Thatcher and the General (1979–1982)	85
6	Chile Conclusion	115
7	Argentina 1976–2 April 1982	121
8	Business as Usual: Arming the Junta (1976–1979)	129
9	Oil, the Islands and the Falklands Lobby (1976–1979)	161
10	Befriending 'Common or Garden' Dictators (1979 to 2 April 1982)	181

11	Antarctica, Oil and Leaseback: Britain's Strategic Interests in the Falklands (1979 to 2 April 1982)	205
12	Conclusion	233
Appendix A		241
Appendix B		243
Appendix C		249
Bibliography		253
Index		271

List of Tables

Table 9.1	Anglo-Argentine negotiations on the Falkland Islands 1966–1982	163
Table 9.2	British oil exploration around the Falkland Islands since 1982	170
Table 10.1	British interests in Argentina in 1981 according to the FCO	184
Table 10.2	British arms sales to Argentina 1967–1982	195
Table 10.3	Major defence items agreed by British ministers for sale to Argentina 1980–1982 which were either not bought by that country or were not delivered	196
Table 11.1	Anglo-Argentine talks on the Falkland Islands 1979–1982	207
Table 11.2	The Falkland Islanders and British citizenship	225

CHAPTER 1

Introduction: Making Friends With the Junta

While researching this book I interviewed a former minister in the Thatcher government. As we sat in his private members club, sipping tea and balancing biscuits on delicate china saucers, he told me that British ministers had given little thought to the human rights abuses being committed by the Argentine dictatorship in the years before the Falklands war. It was the Cold War he reminded me. I was surprised and impressed by his frankness, but when I wrote to him afterwards asking for permission to cite his exact words, he refused and instead supplied me with an anodyne quote which bore little relation to his previous remarks.

Interviewees can be unreliable sources for historians. It is hard for anyone to remember accurately events from decades before. Politicians, especially, can be prone to embellish or omit facts to ensure that they are remembered in the best possible light. But after a war, the temptation to embroider or erase is particularly great. It is therefore vital that we go back to the contemporary records to find out what government ministers and officials actually said at the time.

Using the newly-opened British government papers at the National Archives, this book looks at Britain's relations with the Argentine dictatorship that came to power in 1976. It not only gives the most complete picture of British arms sales to the regime, providing evidence that ministers violated their own guidelines on human rights, but also outlines the political and military links between Britain and the junta. Neither Labour nor Conservative governments imposed any sanctions on the Argentine

© The Author(s) 2018
G. Livingstone, *Britain and the Dictatorships of Argentina and Chile, 1973–82*, Security, Conflict and Cooperation in the Contemporary World, https://doi.org/10.1007/978-3-319-78292-8_1

military government before the invasion of the Falkland Islands in 1982. Both governments promoted trade and sold military hardware that was later used against British forces.

In contrast, the Labour governments of Harold Wilson and James Callaghan (1974–1979) imposed a series of measures against the regime of General Augusto Pinochet in Chile that represented an early example of an 'ethical' foreign policy—an arms embargo, a refugee programme, the cutting of export credits and the withdrawal of the British ambassador. These measures were overturned when Margaret Thatcher's Conservative government came to power in 1979. While the British labour movement barely noticed the coup in Argentina in 1976, it had been horrified when Hawker Hunter planes bombed the Chilean presidential palace on 11 September 1973. Thirty years later, the Chilean coup still aroused passionate divisions among British politicians. Speaking to the Labour Party conference in 1999, Tony Blair confessed that he found General Pinochet 'unspeakable', while Peter Mandelson, an architect of New Labour, which sought to eradicate naïve leftism from the party's ideology, declared that it would be 'gut-wrenching' if the former Chilean dictator evaded extradition to Spain.[1] Former Prime Minister Margaret Thatcher and her ex-chancellor Norman Lamont, meanwhile, spoke out in defence of Pinochet as a 'friend of Britain'.

The opening of the archives has also made it possible to investigate whether the British government had economic or strategic reasons for retaining sovereignty over the Falkland Islands—a longstanding debate between Argentine and British academics and politicians. While the documentary record suggests that fear of a domestic political outcry over 'selling-out' the Islanders was the primary reason British politicians failed to reach a sovereignty deal with Argentina in this period, the evidence presented here shows that the British government and British oil companies were very interested in exploiting the oil in the waters around the Islands and that whenever cabinet ministers discussed the Falklands dispute, securing Britain's access to the hydrocarbon and other marine resources was part of the calculations. This book also presents exclusive evidence that, during the Falklands War, ministers feared that losing the Islands could set a precedent for Britain's territorial claim in Antarctica.

But this is not a history of the Falklands dispute, nor is it simply an account of Britain's relations with two South American dictatorships; it is an investigation into the making of foreign policy. Taking an inter-disciplinary approach, it assesses the factors that influence policy-makers and considers the role of private companies and banks, politicians and party ideology, and the media. It gauges the extent to which human right groups, solidarity campaigns and other social movements can have an impact on policy.

The attitudes of British diplomats and officials are also looked at closely. British diplomats welcomed the coups in both Chile and Argentina and sought to dissuade Labour ministers from taking any type of sanction against the military regimes. In this Cold War period, they were profoundly suspicious of radicalism both at home and abroad. British business leaders shared these attitudes and were critical of any policies that might 'sour the atmosphere' for those who wished to invest or trade with these dictatorships. This book examines the narrow social background of British officials and traces the informal social networks between diplomats, officials, business leaders, and other influential figures such as newspaper editors, peers and Conservative politicians. It argues that theoretical approaches to foreign policy-making should not ignore the social class of state officials nor the social context in which they operate. Similarly, when analysing how social movements can influence policy, it is important to consider the existing biases of policy-makers and their informal links to the private sector or other influential societal groups.

One of the central themes of this work is the extent to which elected politicians have the freedom to implement policy and how far they are constrained by external factors: the agency-structure debate. One of the main divisions among international relations theorists is between those who focus on relationships between states and those who think it important to look at how decisions are made within states. Informed by foreign policy analysts who seek to 'open the black box' of the decision-making process, this study looks closely at how policy is made.[2] While acknowledging that policy-makers may be constrained by systemic factors, it accepts that there is, in Christopher Hill's words, a 'decisional space' in which politicians can choose between different policy options or, as Gaskarth has put it: 'The British government retains the capacity to make political choices and these decisions have important effects.'[3] It accepts too, as Carlsnaes notes, that neither the individual (the national politician) nor the structure (the international area) is an immutable separate entity: each continually influences and shapes the other.[4] The book is based on the premise that the state remains a legitimate focus of study for understanding international relations, despite the growth of transnational organisations, such as multinational corporations or international non-governmental organisations (NGOs). Certainly, during the period under study—the 1970s and 1980s—and to a large extent today, nation states retain a capacity to shape the rules of the international game, formulating policies on key areas such as trade, tax and immigration.[5]

A politician may have the freedom to make foreign-policy choices within the constraints of international circumstances, but there is another aspect of the agency-structure debate that is looked at more closely in these pages and that is the extent to which a politician is able to pursue his or her chosen policies in the face of bureaucratic opposition from the civil service. Or to put it another way, it asks who makes policy: the democratically-elected politician or the appointed official? David Vital, for example, once suggested that the very excellence of the Foreign Office bureaucratic machine, its efficiency and its competence, made its influence so formidable that the role of any Cabinet or Foreign Secretary could become marginal.[6] The question has been of particular interest to the left wing of the Labour party which, from Harold Laski and Stafford Cripps in the 1930s to Richard Crossman and Tony Benn in the 1960s and 1970s, has long held the suspicion that a conservative civil service will seek to undermine left-wing governments.[7] Crossman's diaries were one of the sources of the BBC TV comedy *Yes Minister*, which portrayed Machiavellian civil servants as the real power behind the throne.

Foreign Office documents show that Foreign and Commonwealth Office (FCO) officials welcomed the overthrow of the socialist president of Chile, Salvador Allende, and were critical of British activists and Labour politicians who campaigned against the coup. Thus, the election of a Labour government determined to take radical measures against the Pinochet regime provides an opportunity to examine the power of the elected politician versus the bureaucrat. The governments of Edward Heath and Margaret Thatcher shared with the Foreign Office a similar attitude towards the Pinochet regime, so there was little debate or antagonism between politicians and officials on policy towards Chile and there is therefore little scope to examine the power of the politician against the bureaucratic machine during those Conservative administrations.

In the case of Argentina, Labour did not seek to introduce tough sanctions against the junta, so once again there was less conflict in the policy-making process, although whenever Labour politicians did consider taking measures on human rights, the Foreign Office advocated moderation, warning of the risks to commercial and political relations. The politician versus bureaucrat debate does arise in the context of Argentina, however, as some British politicians and historians have accused the Foreign Office of pursuing, in an underhand manner, policies that were aimed at transferring the sovereignty of the Falkland Islands to Argentina, against the wishes of both Labour and Conservative governments. This claim is explored and judged to be unfounded.

One of the central propositions of this book is that the attitudes of British diplomats and state officials reflected, at least in part, their social class: their upbringing, education, their socio-economic and cultural status, and the social circles in which they moved. Theorists of Foreign Policy Analysis—the sub-set of international relations which has looked most closely at the decision-making process—have considered many attributes that might affect the decisions of policy-makers, including their psychology, their belief systems and the political culture in which they operate. Much useful work has been done on the functioning of bureaucracies, their structures, inter-departmental rivalries and the nuances of group dynamics.[8] But social class is a factor that has been overlooked.[9]

The 'critical' approach to foreign policy-making proposed by Dunne, Hadfield and Smith, which emphasises the need to look at both agency and structure, and advocates a theoretically-informed reading of the primary sources, could allow for the class background and informal social networks of state officials to be considered; however the case studies in their collection have not done so.[10]

There is a neo-Gramscian critique of international relations, following the work of Robert Cox, which introduces the idea of class and class conflict into the field of international relations; however, this work has been largely theoretical, rather than empirically or historically based, and it focuses on the international level rather than the national decision-making process.[11] Marxist-inspired dependency theorists, meanwhile, did seek to study class formation in both the metropolis and the periphery, but the state and decision-making were not their main focus of study.[12] If it is accepted, however, that national governments have the power to shape the framework within which countries interact and within which private companies operate, then the study of the decision-making process is a crucial question for those interested in power and social class. And by taking account of the *social* context in which these decisions are made, we can begin to identify the individuals or societal groups which have most influence on policy—accepting, of course, that these state-societal relations will vary in different historical periods and from country to country.

The Foreign Office has long drawn its recruits from a narrow stratum of society. Originally recruited from the aristocracy, by the end of the nineteenth century, officials were increasingly being drawn from the class which Cain and Hopkins have described as 'gentlemanly capitalists', consisting of landowners and rich professionals from the fields of finance, law or other services who had re-invested in land and through their wealth, inter-marriage and public-school education had been elevated into the social elite.[13] This southern-centred elite, which dominated the ancient universities, the civil service, the armed forces, the church, the City and the major professions, was socially separate from, and may have looked down upon, the manufacturing magnates of the great northern cities such as Manchester and Liverpool. However, after the Second World War, the financial and industrial elites became more socially intertwined, as the City became more involved in financing large scale industry, as corporations became more important wealth creators than individuals, as productive manufacturing businesses came under the control of banks, and as industrialists themselves invested in land and adopted the lifestyle of the 'gentlemanly capitalists'.[14] One illustration of this social transformation is the change in careers of Oxford graduates: in 1917 no graduate went into industry or commerce (all were employed in education or public service), whereas by 1958, as many as 50% found employment within industrial or commercial firms.[15]

Labour party intellectual Harold Laski memorably described the Foreign Office in the 1930s as a 'nest of public school singing birds', and throughout the twentieth century, the proportion of recruits who attended fee-paying schools remained high, despite the reforms following the Fulton Report of 1968, which aimed to make it easier for people from humbler backgrounds to reach top jobs in the diplomatic service.[16] In the period 1950–1954, 83% of recruits to the Foreign Office had attended private school. Ten years later, the proportion had fallen to 68%; but the figure for the top-ranking posts was higher: more than 80% of ambassadors and senior FCO officials in 1961 had attended fee-paying schools (and these public-school educated ambassadors took all the most prestigious postings, such as Paris, Berlin and New York).[17] Even by 1993, 66% of the fast-track entrants to the FCO—those destined for the top posts—had attended public school.[18] They were also overwhelmingly male: in 1991, only 3.4% of the top grades in the

FCO were women, which added to the clubbish nature of the Foreign Office.[19] A survey conducted for this book of diplomats dealing with policy towards Argentina and Chile in the 1970s and 1980s found that more than 75% had attended fee-paying schools.[20] Most Foreign Office officials were also graduates of Oxford or Cambridge; in 1966, 84% of successful applicants for the diplomatic service came from these two universities; by 1989, this had fallen only slightly to 73%.[21] When a senior diplomat claimed in 1977 that recruitment to the Diplomatic Service was wide open, Labour MP Neville Sandelson retorted: 'Like the Ritz'.[22]

While few deny that FCO officials are recruited from a narrow social base, Theakston and others have argued that it is hard to draw a straightforward connection between diplomats' class backgrounds and their views.[23] Certainly, a number of caveats need to be made. Working class Jim Callaghan got on better with FCO officials than the young middle-class upstart David Owen, although Callaghan did make sure he distributed Labour Party manifestos to FCO staff on becoming Foreign Secretary.[24] Similarly trade unionist Ernest Bevin—who liked to boast that he was educated 'in the hedgerows of experience'—was well-respected, even loved, by the FCO, while aristocrat Tony Benn was always highly suspicious of the civil service.[25] So clearly social class—particularly that of a single individual—cannot be the only indicator of a person's views and cannot be the only indicator worth evaluating.

There was also a range of views among FCO officials, although this remained within a narrow spectrum from conservative to conservatively moderate and all new recruits imbibed the ethos of gentlemanly capitalism that permeated the institution. But, the Foreign Office always kept a certain autonomy; diplomats prided themselves on seeing the 'overall picture' and certainly did not act as the 'arm' of the business-owning class. In fact, other government departments, such as the Ministry of Defence sales section, had a much closer relationship with the private sector, sometimes acting as virtual lobbyists for arms companies and chafing against any restrictions on sales opportunities. The Departments of Energy and Trade also had close links with the oil and manufacturing companies. To some extent, the FCO saw itself as an arbitrator between departments and these bureaucratic rivalries—or differences of institutional perspective—are explored throughout the work.

It should also be emphasised that Foreign Office attitudes evolved during the nineteenth and twentieth centuries as the social composition of recruits changed. Otte, who accepts that the mindset of officials did reflect their social class and, in particular, their public-school education, concluded in his study of the nineteenth-century: 'Foreign Office Mind' that it was elitist, non-intellectual, had a strong code of honour and a belief in public service. While it understood that security underpinned Britain's status in the world, it concentrated on political aspects of policy and did not narrowly reflect the financial or commercial interests of the class from which it came.[26] Jones too emphasises the nineteenth-century British diplomat's reluctance to become a direct advocate of British merchants and bankers in Argentina.[27] The Foreign Office 'mind' may have changed again in the late twentieth century as the recruitment base widened and Britain's manufacturing sector shrank. But this study suggests that in the decades following the Second World War, the Foreign Office shared the business community's outlook that trade and investment should be promoted regardless of the nature of the recipient regime, and shows that many diplomats—and businessmen—thought military governments were beneficial for British business because they brought stability. Did this view reflect the class outlook of diplomats? A number of objections may be made. Firstly, most of the population shared the view that promoting British exports was in the national interest; it was the hegemonic view, and certainly Labour ministers—particularly the ministers for employment, trade and industry—argued vigorously for trade with the Argentine military regime. Another objection is that it was the job of the Foreign Office to promote trade. At least since the nineteenth century, one of the aims of British foreign policy had been to ensure security for British trading interests. It was a short step from protection to promotion and the Committee on Overseas Representation (the Duncan Committee) in 1969 specifically urged diplomats to promote British business abroad, leading to complaints that ambassadors were to become little more than 'travelling salesmen'.[28] In this post-war period, it was a central objective of successive British governments to avoid balance of payments deficits and the dangers to sterling that these could bring. Securing contracts to protect British manufacturing jobs was also an important concern.

In the case of Chile, however, when a class-conscious trade union movement at the height of its militancy in the 1970s, backed by Labour politicians, demanded action against the Pinochet regime, there was a clear difference between the outlook of Foreign Office officials and the labour movement, and this may be attributed to differing class outlooks. The Foreign Office favoured stability over radicalism, criticising the chaos under Allende and predicting that the Pinochet regime would be better for British business. The FCO was staunchly anti-Communist in this Cold War period; many officials were critical of human rights campaigners and Chile Solidarity activists, suspecting that they had underlying 'political' motives, by which they meant left-wing or pro-Communist objectives. The Foreign Office believed that Britain's commercial interests should be put above ethical considerations and were against ending arms sales, cutting export credits and withdrawing the British ambassador.

There was less of a clash of views between the labour movement and Whitehall in the case of Argentina, because the left had not taken up Argentina as a cause in the same way. The Labour Party regarded Peronism as akin to fascism and did not mourn the overthrow of the corrupt and repressive government presided over by Juan Perón's widow. Chile, on the other hand, was viewed as a clear-cut case of a democratically-elected socialist being ousted by a fascist dictator. Nevertheless, the pro-business attitude of the Foreign Office can be seen in its consistent advocacy of closer commercial ties with the Argentina junta, despite the growing awareness of the gross human rights abuses being perpetrated by the regime. Indeed, in the absence of a strong lobby, the de facto policy of the Foreign Office towards all the military regimes of South America, including Argentina, Brazil, Uruguay and Paraguay, was to impose no sanctions and to continue to promote trade, including arms sales. Britain had a particularly strong relationship with the military regime of Brazil, inviting dictator General Ernesto Geisel on a state visit in 1976 and providing the Brazilian armed forces with British military training manuals.[29]

Henry Fairlie, the *Spectator* journalist who coined the phrase 'the Establishment' wrote: 'By its traditions and its methods of recruitment the Foreign Office makes it inevitable that the members of the Foreign Service will be men...who "know all the right people".'[30] Using primary sources, this study traces the informal social networks between Foreign Office officials and business leaders, financial executives, newspaper editors and some Conservative politicians. They were often members of the same private clubs—such as the Athenaeum in Pall Mall or the Carlton in St. James's Street—and they attended the same seminars, lunches and drinks parties in Belgravia. Business executives had numerous informal channels of access to the Foreign Office; officials regularly reported conversations with representatives of—for example BP,

Rothschild or GEC—whom they had met at a function or had spoken to on the phone. This elite often shared a common social and educational background, having attended the same universities and fee-paying schools, and bought property in similarly wealthy parts of cities or affluent villages. They often had common cultural interests, reading the same newspapers or following the same sports, such as horse racing or cricket. These repeated informal and semi-formal encounters therefore had a dual role, reinforcing existing social and political affinities, as well as giving private sector representatives direct access to policy-makers.

Ambassadors and embassy staff in Chile and Argentina socialised in an even more tightly-knit social milieu, comprising the British business community, many of whom were virulently right wing and in favour of military rule, along with upper-class Argentines and Chileans, including military officers. Embassy functions, drinks funded by private companies, polo matches, dinner parties, as well as the more formal tasks of hosting trade missions or meeting Argentine or Chilean government officials, were all part of the British diplomat's life in South America. The common upbringing and education, socio-economic status and social connections, may not have been the only factors determining the views of Foreign Office officials, but there is a strong case for arguing they contributed to the convergence of views between the Foreign Office and Britain's financial and commercial elites. Certainly, the Foreign Office, as an institution, articulated a conception of the 'national interest' which reflected the interests of the dominant industrial, financial, professional and landed groups of post-war Britain.

The term elite has been used loosely in this work to describe individuals who hold economic or political power, including the executives of large private companies and financial institutions, people who hold great personal wealth or land, government ministers, influential back-benchers, peers, the monarchy, editors of influential broadsheets, magazines and broadcasting companies, and those populating the higher ranks of the civil and foreign service, the military, the judiciary and the Church of England. The language of elites sits uneasily with that of class, the two coming from distinct intellectual traditions. Certainly, elite is not used here with any of the normative connotations of the early elite theorists, Mosca and Pareto, who saw elitism as both inevitable and necessary in all societies.[31] But viewing the elite as the people within a class who are most active in public life, or who act on behalf of powerful economic sectors, is not necessarily incompatible with a class-based analysis.[32]

It is not suggested here that members of the elite coordinated their actions in a conspiratorial way, rather that the elite shared an anti-egalitarian, pro-business outlook in this post-war period, which in foreign-policy terms translated into the promotion of British manufacturing and financial interests abroad.

However a simple binary opposition between the class outlook of the labour movement and that of the pro-business elite—while useful to describe differing perspectives on the Pinochet regime—has not been found adequate to describe the political debates on the Falkland Islands during the 1970s and 1980s, not least because the trade union movement and the Labour Left had no coherent position on the sovereignty dispute. Political divisions on the Falklands, particularly during the Thatcher years, are best ascribed to splits within the elite and these are analysed in the final chapter of this book.

Social Movements and Policy-Making

This study also looks at the circumstances in which non-parliamentary campaigning groups can be successful. It explores why the Chile Solidarity Campaign had a much wider appeal than the groups lobbying for human rights in Argentina. It also considers the impact of the Falkland Islands Committee, an organisation that campaigned for the rights of Falkland Islanders. The two political science approaches that look most closely at how social movements can influence policy-making are political process theory, which uses the concept of 'political opportunity structures', and the veto-player/gate-keeper approach, which is derived from game theory.[33] The merit of these approaches is that they examine the nature of the governing structures and do not just consider the characteristics of the campaigning organisations. In Guigni's terms, both the 'external' and 'internal' are considered.[34] While there are a number of factors which help determine the success of a social movement, including the clarity of its message, the breadth of its appeal and its tactics and strategies, it is arguably crucial for a lobbying organisation to have some sort of leverage over key policy-makers (or 'gate-keepers'). So, for example, the Chile Solidarity Campaign successfully persuaded the Labour government to impose sanctions on the Pinochet dictatorship because it not only had the support of sympathetic ministers, but also had institutional links to the government through both the party and the trade unions. Its leverage was particularly strong because Labour held only a small majority, then a minority, of seats in parliament. The Chile campaign had less influence on the Thatcher administration because it had no supporters in cabinet and no institutional links to the governing Conservative party, which had a large majority in parliament.

But neither political process theory nor the gate-keeper approach analyses the social context in which policy is made, so do not consider the potential biases of state officials stemming from their social class or their informal social networks. Political process theorists have considered a range of variables, including the relative repressiveness of a regime, its openness to new actors and the multiplicity of power centres within in it.[35] Some have adopted a narrower focus on institutional arrangements and compare features such as: federalism versus centralism, the electoral system, the relationship between the legislature, executive and judiciary and availability of referenda.[36] But the role of state officials and their biases has not been considered. The veto-player approach *has* considered the role of unelected officials, suggesting that they will have more autonomy when there are more key policy-makers (veto-players), because as the number of veto-players increases, the chain of command becomes less clear and officials may play ministers off against each other.[37] There is no attempt, however, to discern the preferences or motives of officials; unsurprisingly because in game theory all actors are divorced from their social context and are ultimately reducible to quantifiable variables.

The actions of state officials may not always be the factor which determines whether a social movement is successful. However, overlooking the social matrix in which officials operate risks underestimating the resistance to campaigners' demands from the state machinery and the subtle ways in which officials try to dissuade ministers from taking action. In the case of a weak lobby group, such as the Argentina human rights campaign, the result was that no sanctions were imposed and business links with the military regime were pursued. Even in the case of a strong campaign, such as Chile, policy-making was a constant process of negotiation between FCO officials, who advised caution, and ministers, who were in turn under pressure from their base. While the Labour government did succeed in introducing a policy that was radically different from that of its Conservative predecessors, officials successfully persuaded ministers against taking the most extreme measures demanded by activists such as the breaking of existing arms contracts with the Pinochet regime. Meanwhile, the Falkland Island Committee, which had the support of influential figures such as peers, high-ranking former military officers and business leaders, had enhanced social access to policy-makers; for example its supporters hosted private dinners and drinks parties for FCO officials and the campaign's secretary belonged to the same private club as the head of the FCO's Falkland Island Department (see Chapter 5). This informal social nexus, complemented its more traditional lobbying techniques such as writing to MPs. By taking an inter-disciplinary approach, using the methods of a social historian and reading the primary sources critically, this study aims to show that officials cannot be regarded as neutral players and that their attitudes and social networks must be taken into account when analysing decision-making in government.

INFORMAL EMPIRE

'And so behold! The New World established and if we do not throw it away, ours', proclaimed Foreign Secretary George Canning in 1825.[38]

Britain became the dominant economic power in Latin America in the nineteenth century until it was superseded by the United States from 1900 onwards. Britain controlled almost a third of Latin America's trade in 1870 and, by 1913, 50% of all foreign investment in Latin America came from Britain.[39] Even these figures mask the greater relative economic weight Britain had in the Southern Cone economies of Brazil, Chile and Argentina, where British companies and investors built railways, held controlling shares in banks and public utilities, had large holdings of government bonds and bought substantial amounts of land. In Chile, British companies controlled the lucrative nitrate-mining industries, while in Argentina they dominated the banks, transport industry and import trade. In both Argentina and Chile, there was often a convergence of interests between the British and Latin American landed elite, who favoured free trade and welcomed foreign investment. The British did not create this elite—it was a legacy of Spanish colonialism—but they did help to strengthen it and ensure that it remained dominant for longer than might otherwise have been the case.

The British dominance of the economy of Latin America, and in particular Argentina, has led to a debate about the extent to which Britain profited at the expense of Latin Americans and distorted Latin America's development path. Robinson and Gallagher argued that Argentina was part of Britain's 'informal empire', exploited economically like a colony but through informal means.[40] Some historians, such as H. S. Ferns, rejected this argument on the grounds that the relationship was mutually beneficial to Britain and Argentina.[41] But while there may have been a convergence of interests between the Argentine elite and the British in the nineteenth century, it was clearly an asymmetrical relationship. British investment in Argentina reached a peak in 1913 of 10% of total British overseas investment—a not insignificant figure for a country that was not even a colony—but in Argentina, it had far greater weight, representing 60% of all inward investment.[42]

D.C.M. Platt and others attacked the concept of an 'informal empire' on the basis that it was not the British state that was investing or interfering in Latin America, but British firms. Platt argued that business imperialism should be the focus of study and that the impact of British investments in each country or sector should be examined to see whether or not they were detrimental to indigenous interests.[43] So Colin Lewis, for example, maintained that British investment in the railways was beneficial for Argentine economic development and that the counterfactual argument that Argentine development would have been more balanced without the British could not be proven.[44] Charles Jones, on the other hand, argued that although state imperialism did not exist because the British state did not encourage or help investors overseas, British banks did ultimately undermine the authority of the Argentine state.[45] A new generation of historians have looked at the cultural impact of British involvement in Latin America placing greater emphasis on the subjectivity of experiences.[46]

British influence in Latin America declined in the twentieth century. In 1870, Latin Americans bought 32% of their imports from British merchants; by 1950 this had fallen to just 6.5%.[47] But the concept of an 'informal empire' has some relevance to this study in helping to explain the disjuncture between the attitudes of Britons and Argentines—for example, among politicians, journalists and members of the public—towards the Falklands dispute. While in Argentina, there is a strong historical memory of British 'imperialism' among nationalists on the right and left of the political spectrum, in Britain there is little awareness of Britain's 'imperial' past in Argentina.

Although the concept of 'informal empire' was intended to encompass Britain's relationship with all of Latin America, the vast majority of the scholarship has focused on Argentina and there is less work on Anglo-Chilean relations.[48] Perhaps this is unsurprising given that by the turn of the twentieth century, British trade and investment, which had been quite evenly distributed between Latin American countries in the 1860s, was overwhelmingly concentrated on Argentina. But as Miller points out, 'what looked marginal to the British could be central to a small Latin American country.⁴⁹ From a Chilean perspective, the British were the dominant foreign presence in the second half of the nineteenth century and remained Chile's most important trading partner until 1914. In 1895, 74% of Chilean exports went to Britain and almost half its imports came from there.⁵⁰ Despite the potential for anti-imperialist resentment, however, the image of the British imperialist has not become such a potent hate-figure in modern Chile as it has in Argentina. This is partly because the ongoing dispute over the Falklands Islands has been a source of nationalist anger in Argentina throughout the twentieth century. But it also stems from the fact that British economic dominance lasted longer in Argentina than in Chile. It lingered throughout the 1930s, in large part due to the Roca–Runciman pact which gave Britain preferential treatment in the Argentine market, whereas in Chile, British influence was eclipsed by the United States after the First World War. Chilean progressives therefore directed their ire at 'Yankee imperialists' rather than the British in the twentieth century, while the Chilean elite 'the English of Latin America', remembered the Anglo connection with rose-tinted nostalgia. Pinochet, of course, had a fondness for old England; during the days before he was arrested in London in 1998, he had shopped at Burberry, lodged at a Park Lane hotel and dined at Fortnum and Mason.

BRITAIN AND LATIN AMERICA IN THE 1970S AND 1980S

Latin America was a low priority for Britain after the Second World War. The Duncan Report of 1969 defined it as an 'outer area of concentration' for policy-makers and Britain recognised that the region was a US sphere of influence.⁵¹ Foreign Office reviews of British policy in Latin America in 1975, 1978 and 1982 saw British interests as primarily economic, combined with the geopolitical desire to keep Latin American countries on the 'right side' during the Cold War. These interests were identified as:

1. Latin America as a source of raw materials
2. Latin America more visible at the UN and international fora
3. Technological advances of Argentina and Brazil, particularly steps towards nuclear power
4. Latin America as an export market
5. Latin America as a capital hungry area.⁵²

These themes were strikingly similar to those highlighted by Victor Perowne, the head of the South America Department at the Foreign Office in his 1945 paper 'The Importance of Latin America': (i) Raw materials; (ii) British investment in Latin America; (iii) Latin America as an export market; (iv) The significance of Latin America for US strategic interests; (v) The prospect of Latin American nations emerging with a distinct identity in the new world order.[53]

After the Second World War, British politicians and policy-makers frequently lamented Britain's loss of economic influence in Latin America and periodically launched export drives, but Britain's overall share of the Latin American market continued to fall, until by 1988, it was just 1.2%.[54] There was one industry, however, in which Britain secured a significant share of the Latin American market: the arms industry. During the 1970s, Britain was the second-largest provider of armaments to South America, supplying 25% of the total, compared with 29% for the United States, the market leader.[55] It was such a lucrative market that the Foreign Office came under strong pressure from the Departments of Trade and Industry, the Ministry of Defence's sales department and from British companies to allow arms trading with the military regimes of the Southern Cone, despite human rights concerns and the potential threat to the Falklands.

British investment in the region, despite suffering an overall decline over the twentieth century, experienced a mini boom in the 1970s—British net outward investment flows to Latin America rose from 1.9% of total British outward investment in 1970 to 8.2% in 1977—and a number of British banks found themselves dangerously exposed when the Latin American debt crisis broke in 1982.[56] Although investment in Chile fell during the Allende years, by 1981, Chile and Argentina were among the top three destinations for British investment and exports within Latin America.[57]

Latin America, Human Rights and Solidarity Campaigns

While Latin America was a low priority for British policy-makers in the post war period, there was a growing public interest in the region. The Cuban revolution sparked interest in Latin America among British progressives and Che Guevara became an icon to the student radicals of 1968. Meanwhile, the Latin American literary 'boom' of the 1960s brought worldwide fame to authors such as Gabriel García Márquez, Mario Vargas Llosa and Carlos Fuentes. The growing cultural and academic interest was reflected in the Parry Report of 1962, which assessed the state of Latin American studies in British universities and led to the creation of five specialist Latin American studies centres in Oxford (1964), London (1965), Cambridge (1966), Liverpool (1966) and Glasgow (1967). Academics founded the Society for Latin American Studies in 1964. The *Latin American Newsletter* was established in 1967 to provide specialized news to the growing audience, while the quantity and quality of mainstream media reporting on Latin America increased, culminating in the 1980s in numerous documentaries on the region, particularly after the creation of Channel Four.[58]

British governments in the 1970s and 1980s faced an array of pressure groups trying to influence policy on Latin America. The Chile solidarity movement was the largest and most successful, encompassing a broad array of trade unions, political parties, human rights groups, religious organisations, student groups and refugee organisations. The Argentina campaign was much smaller, consisting mainly of human rights groups, individuals with a prior interest in Argentina, and exiles. Revolt and repression in Central America in the late 1970s and early 1980s led to the creation of a new generation of solidarity organisations, including the Nicaragua Solidarity Campaign and the El Salvador and Guatemala Committees for Human Rights. The Latin America Bureau, a publishing house funded by NGOs, was founded in 1977 to 'raise public awareness on social, economic, political and human rights issues in Latin America, especially in relation to British involvement in the region'. It provided an alternative nexus of human rights campaigners, progressive academics, journalists and Labour politicians, which rivalled the traditional institutions for Anglo-Latin interchange such as Canning House, whose members tended to be diplomats and notables from the worlds of banking and commerce.[59]

ETHICAL FOREIGN POLICY

The British labour movement had a history of internationalism and had, in the past, been inspired by international events such as the defence of the Spanish republic against Franco—a cause to which events in Chile were often compared. There was also a long tradition of humanitarian organisations taking up the cause of subjugated peoples overseas. After the Second World War, however, in most Western countries, the number of NGOs seeking to influence foreign policy proliferated and they acquired a growing legitimacy among the public, press and politicians.[60] The idea that human rights should play a part in foreign policy considerations became more widespread following the Universal Declaration of Human Rights (1948), the European Convention of Human Rights (1953) and the creation of rights-based lobbying organisations such as Amnesty International (1961).

The 1974–1979 Labour governments' policies towards the Pinochet regime can be seen as an early attempt at an 'ethical foreign policy', although the term is anachronistic as it did not become common usage until the announcement in 1997 by British Foreign Secretary Robin Cook that New Labour's foreign policy would have an 'ethical dimension'. Britain had only imposed peacetime sanctions on a foreign government for 'ethical' reasons twice before, and in both of these cases, the UK had come under strong pressure from the United Nations to do so. Harold Wilson's Labour government (1964–1970) applied sanctions on the British colony of Rhodesia in 1965, when Ian Smith unilaterally declared independence for a white minority regime, and after the UN Security Council had urged Britain to take the strongest possible action. The Wilson government also imposed an arms embargo on South Africa in 1964, but this followed the UN Security Council's 1963 call for all states to impose voluntary arms embargoes. Britain's sanctions against the Pinochet regime were unilateral and not a result of pressure from the UN. While campaigners were less successful in persuading the British government to impose sanctions on Argentina, they nevertheless convinced the Labour government in 1979 to introduce guidelines on weapon sales, which advised against the sale of arms that could be used for internal repression. Such a formula had only been used once before (on South Africa in 1961) but became increasingly common in later years. These measures can be seen as part of a growing trend by governments, in Britain and internationally, to consider the human rights impacts of overseas policies.

In the United States, President Jimmy Carter's (1977–1981) advocacy of human rights as a foreign policy goal transformed the international debate and ensured that ethics became part of the rhetoric of policy-making. Trans-national human rights campaigns on South Africa and Chile, as well as other Latin American countries, also helped to ensure that during the 1970s the language of human rights became an integral part of international politics.[61] It is noteworthy that both Labour foreign secretary David Owen and the Conservative MP Richard

Luce (who went on to become a minister in the FCO), published books on human rights and foreign policy in the 1970s, while Labour MP Stan Newens initiated a debate in parliament on 'foreign policy and morality'.[62]

During the Cold War, both superpowers used the issue of rights to discredit the other, which led politicians from opposing sides to distrust the motives of their opponents; in Britain, for example, Conservative and Labour attitudes towards the abuses of the Pinochet regime often divided along Cold War lines. Nevertheless, these international discussions cemented the idea that human rights could be a legitimate element of foreign policy.[63] Academic work on ethics and foreign policy has grown dramatically since the 1990s.[64] Chandler and Heins date the rising interest in ethical foreign policy from the end of the Cold War, suggesting that the collapse of faith in broader explanatory frameworks, such as Marxism or modernization theory has led to a demand from the public for ethical action from governments.[65]

But while the language of 'ethics' has become more widespread in government, the dilemmas of weighing economic, geopolitical and strategic concerns against human rights issues remain as sharp as ever. Just as the most contentious aspect of Labour's 1970s Chile policy was the decision not to break contracts to supply warships and submarines to the Pinochet regime, so Cook's ethical policy fell into disarray when his government honoured agreements to deliver Hawk jets to Indonesia, which had invaded the former Portuguese colony of East Timor in 1975. Similarly, Britain's prioritising of economic and strategic interests over human rights in its attitude toward the Argentine and Brazilian dictatorships in the 1970s, has clear echoes in British policy towards Saudi Arabia or Yemen in recent years. But the new global architecture of human rights laws and institutions—from the European Court of Human Rights (1959, sitting permanently from 1998) and the Inter-American Court of Human Rights (1979) to the UN Office of the High Commissioner for Human Rights (1993)—as well as the public's acceptance of ethics as a legitimate or even necessary facet of foreign policy, allows social movements and civil society to apply pressure on governments at multiple levels in both the domestic and international arenas. The campaigns on Chile—and to a lesser extent Argentina—were an important early step in the construction of these new institutional and conceptual frameworks for global human rights governance.[66]

Europe and the United States

Chile, then, was an international cause. Across Europe, broad and popular solidarity movements were formed. Of the 200,000 political exiles who fled the Pinochet regime, a half to a third settled in Western Europe.[67] The highest numbers of refugees settled in France, Sweden, Italy, and—after the death of General Francisco Franco in 1975—Spain. The overthrow of the democratically elected government in Chile revived memories of the anti-Fascist struggle in Europe during World War II and parallels were drawn with the anti-dictatorial cause both in Spain, and in Portugal, where civil and military resistance to the repressive Estado Novo erupted into revolution in 1974. The parties of the left and centre in Europe had strong sympathy for the opponents of Pinochet; the socialist prime minister of Sweden, Olof Palme, was a particularly prominent critic of dictatorships in Latin America. Meanwhile Italy, governed by Christian Democrat prime ministers during the 1970s, became the main place of refuge for the leaders of Chilean Christian democracy. Even in countries not governed by the centre left, the large socialist and communist parties, and their affiliated trade unions, pressured their governments to welcome Chilean refugees. France, which had a tradition of welcoming people fleeing political persecution, was headed by centre-right president Valéry Giscard D'Estaing (1974–1981). His government granted thousands of Chileans asylum—by 1983, up to 15,000 Chileans were residing in France.[68] The Chilean coup profoundly affected the thinking of some European politicians. It convinced the Italian Communist Party leader, Enrico Berlinguer, of the need for compromise with other parties and played a part in his conversion to Euro-communism: the idea that European communist parties should not follow a 'line' from Moscow but adopt positions suited to their national circumstances. Chilean political parties based their exiled headquarters in Europe: the Socialist Party in Berlin, the Christian Democrats in Rome and the Communist Party in Moscow. Rome was also the base for Chile Democrático, the coordinating body of Popular Unity parties set up to liaise with solidarity movements around the world, while the Chilean trade union confederation, the *Central Única de Trabajadores* (CUT) had its office in Paris. Chilean leaders were, in turn, influenced by the moderating arguments of European social democracy and Euro-communism; these convinced them of the need to create the broad cross-party alliance, the *Concertación*, which went on to govern Chile after the fall of Pinochet.[69]

The British Labour party was aware of the groundswell of anti-Pinochet feeling across Europe and this reinforced its desire to take a strong stance on Chile. Labour politicians kept in touch with European opinion through the Socialist International. The Foreign Office too kept a close eye on the positions taken by other European governments. Britain joined the European Economic Community (EEC) in 1973, a decision that was ratified in a referendum in 1975. Before advising the British government on any policy decision on Chile, FCO officials considered what the other nine members of the EEC were doing.

The coup in Argentina, however, did not generate large solidarity movements in Europe. Just as activists in Britain had been confused by the complex Argentine political scene, not easily explicable along Cold War lines, so too in Europe there was a lack of awareness of events in Argentina, at least until the late 1970s, when the Mothers of Plaza de Mayo began to draw the world's attention to mass disappearances.

British politicians and officials also watched carefully the changes in United States policy towards Chile and Argentina between 1973 and 1982. President Richard Nixon (1969–1974) and his secretary of state Henry Kissinger had sought to foment a coup against Allende and had heavily funded his opponents. Nixon and his successor Gerald Ford (1974–1977) were allies of the Pinochet regime, providing economic aid and technocratic advisors, while the CIA worked closely with the Chilean security and intelligence services. However, when a Senate investigation in 1974 revealed US attempts to undermine Allende, the US Congress began to place restrictions on US aid and, in 1976, imposed a complete ban on arms sales. Following the assassination of a Chilean former diplomat in Washington, President Jimmy Carter cut all military and economic aid to the regime and reduced the US diplomatic mission in Chile, but these sanctions were lifted when Republican Ronald Reagan came to office in 1981.

US policy towards Argentina followed a similar trajectory: the Nixon administration welcomed the 1976 coup, Henry Kissinger telling the Argentine foreign minister in October 1976, 'Look, our basic attitude is that we would like you to succeed'.[70] On coming to office, Carter imposed a ban on military and economic aid, which was overturned by the Reagan administration. This neoconservative-influenced administration had a close relationship with the Argentine military regime; President Reagan welcomed junta leader Roberto Viola as an official guest to Washington and during his administration the US military worked closely with the Argentine armed forces, training anti-communist paramilitary groups in Central America.

The Foreign Office were anxious to 'keep in step' with the United States when considering, for example, when to recognise a new government or whether to impose sanctions. But there is no archival evidence to suggest that the United States sought unduly to influence British policy towards the Pinochet regime, or the Argentine junta, before the invasion of the Falklands Islands. After 2 April 1982, as has been well documented, the Reagan administration sought to avert a conflict between its two allies: Britain and the Argentine military regime.[71]

BRITAIN, ARGENTINA AND CHILE

There is a large and rich body of scholarship on British relations with Latin America in the nineteenth century. There is, however, far less material on the twentieth century and very little on the years following the Second World War. Rory Miller's seminal study of British-Latin American relations in the nineteenth and twentieth century ends its narrative in the 1940s.[72] Victor Bulmer-Thomas's *Britain and Latin America: A Changing Relationship* (2008) is one of the few publications covering the more recent period.[73] All academic books on Chilean-British relations focus on the nineteenth century or the years preceding the First World War. Journalist Andy Beckett has written one of the few books on Britain's relations with Chile in the twentieth century, an evocative book based on secondary sources and interviews.[74] There are no archival-based studies of Britain's relationship with the Pinochet regime, although the arrest of the former dictator in London in 1998 prompted the publication of numerous texts on the legal implications of the Pinochet case.[75] There is also a growing academic interest in the Chile Solidarity Campaign and Chilean exiles in Britain.[76] This book, however, is the only work that uses primary material from the newly-opened British government archives to examine British-Chilean relations in the period 1973–1982.

The literature on Argentine-British relations extends further into the twentieth century reflecting the longer-lasting British influence in that country, but there are almost no accounts that go beyond Juan Perón's first administration (1946–1955).[77] There is a vast literature on the Falklands war and a sizable body of work devoted to the origins of the conflict, but no academic study focused on Britain's relationship with the Argentine junta of 1976–1982. Very few books on the origins of the Falklands conflict are based on official British government sources, which have only recently opened in line with the thirty-year rule. *The Official History of the Falklands Campaign Volume 1: The Origins of the War* (2005) by Lawrence Freedman, who had early access to the official sources, is an indispensable account of the British government's position on the Falklands dispute in the years preceding the war.[78] Aaron Donaghy's *The British Government and the Falkland Islands, 1974–1979* (2014) argues convincingly that the Wilson and Callaghan governments took a more robust approach to the defence of the Falklands than the Conservatives.[79] The primary material examined for this book supports Donaghy's conclusion that James Callaghan and David Owen kept a more watchful eye on defence deployments in the South Atlantic than did Margaret Thatcher's ministers. The *Falkland Islands Review* (1983), the report of the official inquiry into the causes of the war chaired by Lord Franks is also an invaluable account of the British government's actions in the years before the war, based on government papers and testimonies, and its text is far more critical of ministers than its anodyne conclusion would suggest. [80]

This is a study of British policy-making and is therefore based on British primary sources. The Argentine official archives for the period covering the military dictatorship, 1976–1982, have largely remained closed and substantial amounts of material may have been destroyed. In 2015, however, the Argentine government announced the release of thousands of documents relating to the dictatorship, which will be a rich seam for future research. This book has, nevertheless, referred to a wide variety of Argentine secondary sources.[81]

This book aims to give a much fuller account of Britain's relations with the Argentine military regime than any earlier study, and to place Anglo-Argentine relations in the context of British policy towards the other Southern American dictatorships. It does not attempt to provide a detailed account of the origins of the Falklands war, which has been well covered elsewhere. It does, however, look closely at the attitudes of British business towards the Falklands dispute, an area that has been insufficiently studied. It also considers whether Britain had strategic, economic and commercial interests in the South Atlantic, a suggestion that has been discounted in much of the British literature, but overplayed in many Argentine accounts.

Among the British academics who downplay strategic and economic factors is the war's official historian, Lawrence Freedman, who concludes: 'Other than possible oil resources... the strategic and economic value of the Falklands to Britain was minimal...For Britain, it was the people who lived on the Islands.'[82] Similarly George Boyce writes: 'There was...no selfish economic or strategic British interest in the Falklands', while Hastings and Jenkins say the Islands 'were never of any great strategic importance—certainly not before the advent of coal-powered vessels', but do not mention any subsequent strategic interests.[83] Many popular British histories simply ignore the question of British strategic interests.[84] A small number of British works do note strategic or economic interests including those by Klaus Dodds, Robert Miller and Martin Middlebrook.[85]

Most accounts by British politicians claim that the Falklands were of little strategic value, with the exception of those by Margaret Thatcher and Tony Benn. Thatcher wrote in her autobiography that 'the islands had obvious strategic importance', and during the Falklands war she attempted to win US support by emphasising their strategic role to President Reagan.[86] Tony Benn, who was energy secretary during the 1970s and witnessed oil companies' interest in Falklands oil, wrote in his diary on the outbreak of the Falklands conflict on 2 April 1982: 'The real interest there is oil'.[87]

But it was more common for politicians to dismiss their strategic value. Barbara Castle, for example, reported in her diary a cabinet conversation in 1968: 'It was Jim Callaghan who asked solemnly whether the Falkland Islands were any use to us. Apparently none at all but there would be one of those absurd parliamentary rows if we were to try and disembarrass ourselves of them.'[88] The foreign secretary at the time of the Argentine invasion in 1982, Lord Carrington, assessed that the Islands had 'no vital strategic or economic interest for Britain', and his junior minister at the Foreign Office, Richard Luce, suggested that there was 'no direct British interest in the Falklands, but a responsibility for the 2000 subjects who were mainly of British origin'.[89]

In contrast, many accounts by Argentine academics, journalists and politicians suggest that Britain retains the Falkland Islands for strategic and economic reasons, highlighting, in particular, their location as a gateway to Antarctica and the access they provide to the oil, mineral and marine resources in South Atlantic waters.[90] As the Argentine ambassador told Nicolas Ridley in 1981: 'The Argentine man in the street was convinced that the UK was interested solely in the oil potential.'[91] While some Argentine works are highly polemical, others, such as Monica Pinto's balanced survey of Anglo-Argentine interest in hydrocarbons around the Falklands, provide useful research that should be integrated into British accounts.[92] Lowell Gustafson also gives a useful overview of negotiations about oil, but both accounts are limited by the source material available in the 1980s.[93]

This book accepts the traditional British interpretation that domestic factors are key to understanding the British government's failure to reach an agreement with Argentina over the sovereignty of the Falkland Islands. However, it provides archival evidence that the British government and British companies were interested in the oil around the Falklands, and that officials were keen to preserve their access to Antarctica, indicating that strategic and economic concerns did play a role in the British government's deliberations over the Islands in the years before the war.

Political scientists are critical of purely 'factual' accounts and historians, too, try to explain events rather than simply relate 'what happened'. While this book has attempted to take a theoretically-informed analytical approach to explaining Britain's engagement with Argentina and Chile, it also sees value in bringing into the public domain new empirical material such as the details of export licences for armaments approved by the British government for sale to the Argentine dictatorship—including bomber planes, battle tanks and armoured cars—or the fact that the head of the Argentine navy met the head of the British navy in Britain four years before the Falklands war. Sadly, a complete picture of British official actions may never be possible because, as a Freedom of Information Request by this author has revealed, 322 FCO files on British relations with Argentina between the years 1976 and 1982—including files on military visits and arms sales—have been permanently destroyed by the British government.[94]

Notes

1. Andy Beckett, *Pinochet in Piccadilly: Britain and Chile's Hidden History* (London: Faber and Faber, 2002), p. 6. 'Gut-wrenching' quote from 'Jack Straw and General Pinochet', *The Economist*, 3 December 1998.
2. Richard Snyder, H.W. Bruck and Burton Sapin, *Decision Making as an Approach to the Study of International Politics* (New York: Free Press of Glencoe, 1962). See also Valerie Hudson, *Foreign Policy Analysis: Classic and Contemporary Theory* (Maryland: Rowman & Littlefield, 2014) p. 4.

3. Christopher Hill, *The Changing Politics of Foreign Policy* (London: Palgrave Macmillan, 2003), p. 294; Jamie Gaskarth, *British Foreign Policy* (Cambridge: Polity Press, 2013), p. 2.
4. Walter Carlsnaes, 'The Agency-Structure Problem in Foreign Policy Analysis' in Walter Carlsnaes and Stefano Guzzini, *Foreign Policy Analysis*, Vol. 4 (London: Sage, 2011), pp. 165–199.
5. On globalisation and foreign policy-making, see Chris Alden and Amnon Aran, *Foreign Policy Analysis: New Approaches* (Abingdon, Oxon: Routledge, 2012).
6. David Vital, *The Making of British Foreign Policy* (London: George Allen and Unwin, 1968), p. 98.
7. Kevin Theakston, *The Labour Party and Whitehall* (London: Routledge, 1992); Tony Benn, 'Obstacles to Reform', in Ralph Miliband, Leo Panitch and John Saville (eds.), *The Socialist Register 1989* (London: Merlin Press, 1989); G.D.H. Cole, 'Reform in the Civil Service' in *Essays in Social Theory* (London: Macmillan, 1950); Stafford Cripps, 'Parliamentary Institutions and the Transition to Socialism' in Cripps et al., *Where Stands Socialism Today?* (London: Rich & Cowan, 1933); Richard Crossman, *The Diaries of a Cabinet Minister, Volume 1* (London: Hamish Hamilton & Jonathan Cape, 1975); Harold Laski, *The Labour Party and the Constitution* (London: Socialist League, 1933); and Ralph Miliband, *Capitalist Democracy in Britain* (Oxford: OUP, 1984).
8. For a history of FPA see Valerie Hudson, 'The history and evolution of foreign policy analysis' in Steve Smith, Amelia Hadfield and Tim Dunne (eds.), *Foreign Policy: Theory/Actors/Cases* (Oxford: OUP, 2012); Chris Alden and Amnon Aran, *Foreign Policy Analysis: New Approaches* (Abingdon, Oxon: Routledge, 2012).
9. Hill, *The Changing Politics*, p. 240.
10. Steve Smith, Amelia Hadfield and Tim Dunne (eds.), *Foreign Policy: Theory/Actors/Cases* (Oxford: OUP, 2012), p. 5. Their critical approach to foreign policy builds on the work of Colin Hay and Paul Williams.
11. Robert Cox and Timothy Sinclair, *Approaches to World Order* (Cambridge: CUP, 1996); Andreas Bieler, Werner Bonefeld, Peter Burnham and Adam David Morton (eds.), *Global Restructuring, State, Capital and Labour: Contesting Neo-Gramscian Perspectives* (London: Palgrave Macmillan, 2006); Adrian Budd, *Class, States and International Relations* (London: Routledge, 2013); and Richard Wyn Jones (ed.), *Critical Theory and World Politics* (Boulder: Lynne Rienner, 2000).
12. See Fernando Henrique Cardoso and Enzo Faletto, *Dependency and Development in Latin America* (Berkeley: University of California Press, 1979).

13. P.J. Cain and A.G. Hopkins, 'Gentlemanly Capitalism and British Expansion Overseas I. The Old Colonial System, 1688–1850', *Economic History Review*, 39 (1986), 501–525; P.J. Cain and A.G. Hopkins, 'Gentlemanly Capitalism and British Expansion Overseas II: New Imperialism, 1850–1945', *Economic History Review*, 40 (1987), 1–26; P.J. Cain and A.G. Hopkins, *British Imperialism 1688–2000* (London: Pearson, 2001).
14. Cain and Hopkins, *British Imperialism*, pp. 620–621.
15. Author's analysis of Oxford University Careers Data. University of Oxford Appointment Committee Reports, 1917–2004. See Appendix A.
16. Laski quote from G.D.H. Cole (ed.), *Plan for Britain* (London: Routledge & Sons Ltd., 1943), p. 119. 'Committee on the Civil Service (Fulton Committee)', 1968, The National Archives (TNA): CAB/168/105.
17. Data for 1950–1954 and 1960–1964, from FCO sources, cited in Moorhouse, *The Diplomats*, p. 59. The 1961 figure from Anthony Sampson, *Anatomy of Britain* (London: Hodder and Stoughton, 1962), p. 304.
18. Ruth Dudley Edwards, *True Brits* (London: BBC Books, 1994), p. 91.
19. Ibid., p. 98.
20. See Appendix B.
21. John Dickie, *Inside the Foreign Office* (London: Chapmans, 1992), p. 17.
22. Ibid., p. 19.
23. Kevin Theakston, 'New Labour and the Foreign Office', in Richard Little and Mark Wickham-Jones, *New Labour's Foreign Policy: A New Moral Crusade* (Manchester: Manchester University Press, 2000), p. 118; Geoffrey Fry, 'The British Diplomatic Service: Facts and Fantasies', *Politics* (1982) 4–8; Simon Jenkins and Anne Sloeman, *With Respect, Ambassador: An Inquiry into the Foreign Office* (London: BBC Books, 1985), pp. 105–106; and Hill, *The Changing Politics*, p. 241.
24. Theakston, 'New Labour', p. 113.
25. Bevin quoted in Sampson, p. 313.
26. T.G. Otte, *The Foreign Office Mind: The Making of British Foreign Policy 1865–1914* (Cambridge: CUP, 2011).
27. Charles Jones, '"Business Imperialism" and Argentina, 1875–1900: A Theoretical Note', *Journal of Latin American Studies*, 12 (1980), 437–444 (p. 442).
28. *Report of the Review Committee on Overseas Representation* by Sir Val Duncan (London: HMSO, 1969) [The Duncan Report]; 'Travelling salesman' remark made by the Marquess of Lansdowne: *Hansard*: House of Lords Debate, 19 November 1969, Vol. 305, cc917–1055.
29. H.E. Affleck-Graves, Capt. R.M., to DS5, RM7/14/5, 13 August 1976, TNA: DEFE 24/1416.

30. Henry Fairlie, 'Political Commentary', *The Spectator*, 22 September 1955.
31. Gaetano Mosca, *The Ruling Class* (New York: McGraw-Hill, 1939); Vilfredo Pareto, *The Mind and Society* (New York: Harcourt-Brace, 1935). See also James Burnham, *The Managerial Revolution* (New York: Putnam, 1942); Charles Wright Mills, *The Power Elite* (New York: Oxford University Press, 1966); W.L. Guttsman, *The British Political Elite* (London: MacGibbon & Kee, 1968); and Geraint Parry, *Political Elites* (Colchester: ECPR Press, 2005) [orig. pub. 1969].
32. Works that combine an analysis of elites and class include, David Lane, *Elites and Classes in the Transformation of State Socialism* (London: Transaction Publishers, 2011); Ralf Dahrendorf, *The Modern Social Conflict* (New Brunswick NJ: Transaction, 2007) and P.J. Cain and A.G. Hopkins, *British Imperialism 1688–2000* (London: Pearson, 2001).
33. Veto players is a term coined by George Tsebelis and is an analysis derived from game theory. The term 'gate-keepers' is used by Joshua Busby who thinks it better describes the role of key policy-makers who can facilitate legislation, but not necessarily veto it. George Tsebelis, *Veto Players: How Political Institutions Work* (New York: Princeton University Press, 2002); Joshua Busby, *Moral Movements and Foreign Policy* (Cambridge: CUP, 2010), p. 60.
34. Marco Giugni, 'How Social Movements Matter' in Marco Giugni, Doug McAdam and Charles Tilly (eds.), *How Social Movements Matter* (Minneapolis: University of Minnesota Press, 1999), pp. xix–xx. See also Margaret Keck and Kathryn Sikkink, *Activists Beyond Borders: Advocacy Networks in International Politics* (New York: Cornell University Press, 1998); David Skidmore and Valerie Hudson, 'Establishing the Limits of State Autonomy: Contending Approaches to the Study of State-Society Relations and Foreign Policy-Making' in Skidmore and Hudson, *The Limits of State Autonomy* (Boulder: Westview Press, 1993), pp. 1–22.
35. These variables are taken from Charles Tilly and Sidney Tarrow, *Contentious Politics*, 2nd Edition (Oxford: Oxford University Press, 2015), p. 59. For foundational work on Political Opportunity Structures see Herbert Kitschelt, 'Political Opportunity Structures and Political Protest: Anti-nuclear Movements in Four Democracies' *British Journal of Political Science*, 16 (1) (1986), 57–85; and Doug McAdam, John McCarthy and Mayer Zald (eds.), *Comparative Perspectives on Social Movements* (Cambridge: CUP, 1996).
36. Hein-Anton van der Heijden, 'Globalization, Environmental Movements and International Political Opportunity Structures', *Organization and Environment*, 19 (1) (2006), 28–44; Hanspeter Kriesi et al., *Social Movements in Western Europe. A Comparative Analysis* (Minneapolis: University of Minnesota Press, 1995).

37. George Tsebelis, *Veto Players: How Political Institutions Work* (New York: Princeton University Press, 2002), pp. 235–239.
38. Leslie Bethell, *George Canning and the Independence of Latin America* (London: The Hispanic and Luso Brazilian Council, 1970).
39. Victor Bulmer-Thomas, *British Trade with Latin America in the Nineteenth and Twentieth Centuries* (London: ILAS, University of London, Occasional Papers No. 19, 1998), p. 8.
40. John Gallagher and Ronald Robinson, 'The Imperialism of Free Trade' in *Economic History Review*, 6 (1953), 1–15 (p. 13).
41. H.S. Ferns, *Britain and Argentina in the Nineteenth Century* (Oxford: Clarendon Press, 1960); H.S. Ferns, 'Argentina: Part of an Informal Empire' in Alistair Hennessy and John King, *The Land that England Lost: Argentina and Britain, a Special Relationship* (London: British Academic Press, 1992), p. 60.
42. 10% figure from Rory Miller, *Britain and Latin America* (London: Longman, 1993), p. 5 and 60% figure from Alistair Hennessy, 'Argentines, Anglo-Argentines and Others' in Hennessy, *The Land that England Lost*, p. 10.
43. D.C.M. Platt, 'Further Objections to an 'Imperialism of Free Trade', Economic History Review, 26 (1973), 77–91; D.C.M. Platt, *Finance, Trade and Politics in British Foreign Policy, 1815–1914* (Oxford: Clarendon Press, 1968); and D.C.M. Platt (ed.), *Business Imperialism, 1840–1930, An Inquiry Based on British Experience in Latin America* (Oxford: Clarendon Press, 1977).
44. Colin Lewis in Platt, *Business Imperialism*, p. 427; Colin Lewis in Hennessy, *The Land that England Lost*.
45. Charles Jones in Platt, *Business Imperialism*; Charles Jones, '"Business Imperialism" and Argentina, 1875–1900: A Theoretical Note', *Journal of Latin American Studies*, 12 (1980), 437–444 (p. 442).
46. See Matthew Brown (ed.), *Informal Empire in Latin America: Culture, Commerce and Capital* (Oxford: Blackwell, 2008).
47. Bulmer-Thomas, *British Trade*, p. 8 and Miller, *Britain and Latin America*, p. 246.
48. Works on Chilean-British relations which do not necessarily accept the informal empire approach but consider the evidence include Harold Blakemore, *British Nitrates and Chilean Politics 1886–1896* (London: Athlone Press, 1974); Juan Ricardo Couyoumdjian, *Chile y Gran Bretaña: Durante la Primera Guerra Munidal y la Postguerra: 1914–1921* (Santiago: Editorial Andrés Bello, 1986); Robert Greenhill, 'The Nitrate and Iodine Trades 1880–1914' and Linda and Charles Jones and Robert Greenhill 'Public Utility Companies' both in Platt, *Business Imperialism*; John Mayo, *British Merchants and Chilean Development 1851–1886* (Boulder, CO: Westview

Press, 1987); and Thomas O'Brien, *The Nitrate Industry and Chile's Crucial Transition 1870–1891* (New York: New York University Press, 1982).
49. Miller, *Britain and Latin America*, p. 13.
50. Couyoumdjian, p. 27.
51. *The Duncan Report*, 1969.
52. Cited in Robert Graham 'British Policy Towards Latin America' in Bulmer-Thomas, *Britain and Latin America*, p. 61.
53. Ibid., p. 55. See also 'Bones of Contention in Latin America', memorandum by Victor Perowne, FCO, 22 April 1943, A3479/3479/51, TNA: FO371/33929.
54. Miller, *Britain and Latin America*, p. 246.
55. Frank Barnaby, 'Latin America and the Arms Trade', in *Britain and Latin America* (London: LAB, 1979), p. 67.
56. David Atkinson, 'Trade, aid and investment since 1950' in Bulmer-Thomas, *Britain and Latin America*, p. 115.
57. Ibid., p. 113.
58. Gerald Martin, 'Britain's Cultural Relations with Latin America' in Bulmer-Thomas, *Britain and Latin America*, p. 32.
59. *Britain and Latin America* (London: LAB, 1979), inside cover page.
60. Hill, *The Changing Politics*, p. 269. See also Peter Willets (ed.), *Pressure Groups in the Global System: The Transnational Relations of Issue-Orientated Non-Governmental Organizations* (London: Frances Pinter, 1982).
61. Samuel Moyn, *The Last Utopia: Human Rights in History* (London: Belknap, 2010); Flood, Patrick James, *The Effectiveness of UN Human Rights Institutions* (Westport, CT: Praeger, 1998).
62. David Owen, *Human Rights* (London: Jonathan Cape, 1978); Richard Luce and John Ranelagh, *Human Rights and Foreign Policy* (London: Conservative Political Centre, 1977). *Hansard*: 'Foreign Policy and Morality': HC Deb., 9 February 1976, Vol. 905, cc35–99.
63. For more on superpowers' use of the concept of human rights during the Cold War, see Dilys Hill, *Human Rights and Foreign Policy* (Basingstoke: Macmillan, 1989) and R. J. Vincent, *Human Rights and International Relations* (Cambridge: Cambridge University Press, 1986).
64. Karen Smith and Margot Light (eds.), *Ethics and Foreign Policy* (Cambridge: Cambridge University Press, 2001); William Walldorf, *Just Politics: Human Rights and the Foreign Policy of the Great Powers* (London: Cornell University Press, 2008); Richard Little and Mark Wickham-Jones, *New Labour's Foreign Policy: A New Moral Crusade* (Manchester: Manchester University Press, 2000); and Jamie Gaskarth, 'Interpreting Ethical Foreign Policy: Traditions and Dilemmas for Policy Makers', *The British Journal of Politics and International Relations*, 15 (2013), 192–209.
65. David Chandler and Volker Heins, *Rethinking Ethical Foreign Policy* (London: Routledge, 2006).

66. Thomas C. Wright, *State Terrorism in Latin America: Chile, Argentina and International Human Rights* (Lanham, MD: Roman & Littlefield, 2007); Patrick William Kelly, 'The 1973 Chilean coup and the origins of transnational human rights activism', *Journal of Global History*, 8 (1) (2013), 165–186.
67. Thomas C. Wright and Rody Oñate Zúñiga, 'Chilean Political Exile', *Latin American Perspectives*, 34 (4) (2007), 31–49.
68. Nicolas Prognon, 'France: Welcoming Chilean Exiles' in Kim Christiaens, Idesbald Goddeeris and Magaly Rodríguez García (eds.), *European Solidarity with Chile, 1970s–1980s* (Frankfurt: Peter Lang, 2014), pp. 187–207.
69. Peter Read and Marivic Wyndham, 'Eurocommunism and the Concertación: Reflections on Chilean European Exile', 1973–1989, *Journal of Iberian and Latin American Research*, 21 (1) (2015), 116–125.
70. Grace Livingstone, *America's Backyard* (London: Zed Books, 2009), p. 69, citing US State Department Memorandum of Conversation, 7 October 1976.
71. Grace Livingstone, 'British and US policy towards Argentina before and during the Falklands/Malvinas War', paper presented at the 2013 Congress of the Latin American Studies Association, Washington DC. See also: Richard Aldous, *Reagan and Thatcher: The Difficult Relationship* (London: Arrow, 2012); Louise Richardson, *When Allies Differ: Anglo-American Relations during the Suez and Falklands Crises* (New York: St. Martin's Press, 1996).
72. Miller, *Britain and Latin America*.
73. Bulmer-Thomas, *Britain and Latin America*.
74. Beckett, *Pinochet*.
75. Reed Brody and Michael Ratner, *The Pinochet Papers: The Case of Augusto Pinochet in Spain and Britain* (The Hague: Kluwer Law International, 2000); Madeleine Davis (ed.), *The Pinochet Case, Origins, Progress and Implications* (London: Institute of Latin American Studies, 2003); and Ariel Dorfman, *Exorcising Terror: The Incredible Unending Trial of General Augusto Pinochet* (London: Pluto Press, 2002).
76. Alan Angell, 'International Support for the Chilean Opposition, 1973–1989: Political Parties and the Role of Exiles', in Laurence Whitehead (ed.), *International Dimensions of Democratization* (Oxford: OUP, 2001); T. Kushner and K. Knox. 'Refugees from Chile: A Gesture of International Solidarity' in K. Knox and T. Kushner (eds.), *Refugees in an Age of Genocide* (London: Frank Cass, 1999); Jasmine Gideon, 'Health and Wellbeing among Chilean exiles in London', Birkbeck College, 2015 https://ageingandmigration.files.wordpress.com/2013/10/gideon-ageing-and-migration-pp.pdf; Paola Bayle, '*La Diáspora de una Población Calificada: el Exilio Académico Chileno en el Reino Unido*', unpublished

doctoral thesis, Universidad Nacional de Cuyo, Argentina, 2010; Michael D Wilkinson, 'The Chile Solidarity Campaign and British Government Policy towards Chile, 1973–1990', *European Review of Latin American and Caribbean Studies*, 52 (1992), 57–74; and Ann Jones, *No Truck with Chilean Junta* (Canberra: Anu Press, 2014).

77. Alistair Hennessy and John King, *The Land That England Lost: Argentina and Britain: A Special Relationship* (London: British Academic Press, 1992). This excellent collection includes three essays on the post-war period.
78. Lawrence Freedman, *The Official History of the Falklands Campaign*, Vol. 1 (London: Routledge, 2005).
79. Aaron Donaghy, *The British Government and the Falkland Islands, 1974–1979* (Basingstoke: Palgrave Macmillan, 2014).
80. *Falkland Islands Review*, Report of a Committee of Privy Counsellors, Chairman: The Rt Hon The Lord Franks (London: HMSO, 1983).
81. Books the author has found particularly useful include: Carlos Escudé and Andrés Cisneros, *Historia General de Las Relaciones Exteriores de la República Argentina*, Tomo XII, *La Diplomacia de las Malvinas, 1966–1989* (Buenos Aires: CEPE/CARI/Nuevohacer, 2000); Federico Lorenz, *Las Guerras por Malvinas* (Buenos Aires: Edhasa, 2006); Federico Lorenz, *Malvinas: Una Guerra Argentina* (Buenos Aires: Editorial Sudamericana, 2009); Vicente E. Berasategui, *Malvinas: Diplomacia y Conflicto Armado, Comentarios a la Historia Oficial Británica* (Buenos Aires: PROA AMERIAN Editores, 2011); and Atilio Borón y Julio Faúndez, *Malvinas Hoy: Herencia de un Conflicto* (Buenos Aires: Puntosur, 1989). Studies focusing on strategic issues are referred to below in note 90.
82. Freedman, *The Official History*, p. 18.
83. George Boyce, *The Falklands War* (Basingstoke: Palgrave Macmillan, 2005), p. 4. Hastings and Jenkins, p. 7.
84. Duncan Anderson, *The Falklands War 1982* (Oxford: Osprey, 2002); Dale, *Memories*; McManners, *Forgotten Voices*, Michael Parsons, *The Falklands War* (Stroud: Sutton Publishing, 2000).
85. Klaus Dodds, *Pink Ice: Britain and the South Atlantic Empire* (London: IB Tauris, 2002); Martin Middlebrook, *The Falklands War 1982* (London: Penguin, 2001); and Robert Miller, *Liability or Asset? A Policy for the Falkland Islands* (London: Alliance, for Institute for European Defence and Strategic Studies, 1986).
86. Margaret Thatcher, *The Downing Street Years* (London: Harper Collins, 1993), p. 174; 'Record of Telephone Conversation between President Reagan and the Prime Minister on 13 May 1982', TNA: FCO7/4532, 1982.

87. Tony Benn, *The End of an Era, Diaries, 1980–1990* (London: Hutchinson, 1992), p. 202.
88. Barbara Castle, *The Castle Diaries, 1964–1976* (London: Macmillan, 1990), p. 207.
89. Lord Carrington, *Reflect on Things Past* (London: Fontana, 1988), p. 349; Richard Luce, *Ringing the Changes, A Memoir* (Norwich: Michael Russell, 2007), p. 135.
90. Accounts that highlight strategic factors include: Oscar Abudara Bini et al., *Malvinización y Desmentirización: Un Aporte Económico, Político y Cultural en el marco de la Patria Grande* (Buenos Aires: Ediciones Fabro, 2013); Rodolfo Balmaceda, *La Argentina Indefensa: Desmalvinización y desmalvinizadores* (Buenos Aires: Editorial Los Nacionales, 2004); Carlos Alberto Biangardi Delgado, *Cuestón Malvinas, A 30 Años de la Guerra del Atlántico Sur* (Buenos Aires: Editorial Dunken, 2012). Borón and Faúndez, *Malvinas Hoy*; Carlos Chubrétovich, *Las Islas Falkland o Malvinas: Su Historia, La Controversia Argentina-Británica y la Guerra Consiguiente* (Santiago: Editorial La Noria, 1987) [Chilean]; Juan José Cresto, *Historia de las Islas Malvinas: Desde su Descubrimiento hasta Nuestros Días* (Buenos Aires: Editorial Dunken, 2011); Julio Laborde y Rina Beraccini, *Malvinas en el Plan Global del Imperialismo* (Buenos Aires: Editorial Anteo, 1987); Rubén Oscar Moro, *La Trampa de Malvinas: Historia del conflicto de Atlántico Sur* (Buenos Aires: Edivérn, 2005); Adolfo Silenzi de Stagni, *Las Malvinas y El Petróleo* (Buenos Aires: Editora Theoría SRL, 1983); and Otto Vargas et al., *La Trama de Una Argentina Antagónica: Del Cordobazo al fin de la Dictatura* (Buenos Aires: Editorial Agora, 2006).
91. Anglo-Argentine Ministerial Talks on the Falkland Islands: New York, 23/24 February 1981, FCO record, TNA: PREM 19/612.
92. Mónica Pinto, 'Islas Malvinas/Falkland, Georgias y Sandwich del Sur: Algunas Consideraciones Relativas a los Hidrocarburos' in Borón & Faúndez, pp. 125–155.
93. Lowell Gustafson, *The Sovereignty Dispute Over the Falkland (Malvinas) Islands* (Oxford: OUP, 1988).
94. Freedom of Information Request to the FCO, reference 1014–14, 12 June 2015. All the files for 1982 have been kept.

CHAPTER 2

Chile 1973–1982

The overthrow of Salvador Allende aroused strong political passions in Britain. Not since the Spanish Civil War had the labour movement been so inspired by an international cause. Politicians' responses to the coup divided along party lines. While Labour politicians regarded it as a terrible, shocking and seminal moment in post-war history, Conservatives were more equivocal, emphasising the chaos under Allende, which—they maintained—had led to the coup. Some on the right of the Conservative party went on to become admirers of Pinochet, extolling the economic prescriptions of his 'Chicago Boys', the US-trained technocrats who introduced free-market policies to Chile.

British policy towards Chile was therefore highly influenced by party-political ideology and can be divided into three clearly distinct phases. The Conservative government of Edward Heath (1970–1974) did not oppose the Pinochet regime. Ministers were happy to leave policy in the hands of Foreign Office officials, who were sympathetic to the coup and who were exasperated by its opponents. British policy abruptly changed when Labour won the election in 1974. An arms embargo was imposed; economic aid and export credits were cut; refugees were welcomed and, in 1976, the British ambassador was withdrawn from Santiago. These measures reflected the abhorrence that the labour movement felt for the Pinochet regime and are an early example of an 'ethical foreign policy'.

© The Author(s) 2018
G. Livingstone, *Britain and the Dictatorships of Argentina and Chile, 1973–82*, Security, Conflict and Cooperation in the Contemporary World, https://doi.org/10.1007/978-3-319-78292-8_2

Margaret Thatcher, on coming to office in 1979, abandoned this 'ethical' stance. She restored arms sales, export credits and returned an ambassador to Chile. Mrs. Thatcher's relations with Pinochet became even more cordial after Chile gave covert logistical aid to Britain during the Falklands War.

This book focuses on how and why these policies were adopted and does not attempt to assess systematically their impact in Chile. It is a sad fact that, despite worldwide condemnation, the Pinochet dictatorship (1973–1990) outlived all the other military regimes in South America. Some military governments may have lasted longer than Pinochet's seventeen years (Paraguay: 1954–1989, Brazil: 1964–1985, Bolivia: 1968–1980), but by the end of the 1980s, Chile was the only country in the continent that was not a democracy. It was not until March 1990 that an elected president, Patricio Aylwin, was sworn in.

Internal factors are the key to understanding the longevity of the Pinochet regime. Underpinning the Chilean dictatorship was a broad and stable alliance between the military and the civilian elite.[1] Right-wing parties and business organisations backed Pinochet loyally throughout his time in office. It was not until the 1980s that divergences within the corporate class emerged over economic strategy, but these were not translated into political opposition. Among Chile's traditional institutions, only the Church gave a voice and protection to those who criticised human rights abuses. It was a highly-personalised regime; power was concentrated in the hands of Pinochet. Early divisions within the military junta were soon resolved and Pinochet became the undisputed source of authority presiding over this civilian-military elite alliance. The armed forces lacked a political project beyond eliminating 'subversion' from Chile, but they remained loyal to the tenets of hierarchy and military discipline. The policies were provided by a technocratic elite of economists, who implemented a shock programme of neoliberal reforms, including privatisation, slashing import tariffs and opening Chile to the world market, reducing the role of the state and dismantling trade unions. The military and the economic projects were intertwined, because the security forces' persecution, torture and killing of thousands of trade unionists and left-wing activists destroyed the power of the labour movement.[2] These economic policies led to rapid growth in the 1980s, but also to a concentration of wealth, a rise in poverty and unemployment, which further weakened the power of organised labour. With the creation of the secret service, the DINA, in 1974, the state refined its technical ability to apply terror, systematically identifying and targeting opponents. A total of 3,197 people were murdered and at least 200,000 forced into political exile.[3]

The role of foreign powers, and in particular the United States, in undermining the Allende government and strengthening Pinochet has been the subject of much debate. Since 1898, the United States had repeatedly intervened in the countries of Central America and the Caribbean, often supporting authoritarian and dictatorial regimes. During the Cold War, and particularly after Fidel Castro's Cuban revolution of 1959, the US government became increasingly involved in the internal politics of *South* America. Determined to stop the spread of radicalism throughout the Western hemisphere, the US military trained the region's armed forces in counter-insurgency and anti-subversive techniques, while US government agencies including the Pentagon, White House, CIA and State Department funded and worked with anti-democratic, right-wing elites who sought to maintain power through the use of repression and military coups. By 1976, all but two countries in South America were ruled by dictatorships.

A US Senate investigation found that, even before Allende had been sworn in as president, the CIA had tried to precipitate a putsch by making contact with several groups of Chilean military plotters and passing weapons to one group.[4] The inquiry also found that the CIA had given the Chilean opposition millions of dollars during the Allende years, had drawn up 'arrest lists' for the Chilean military and identified key buildings that needed to be secured in the event of a coup. After Pinochet's takeover, Richard Nixon's administration gave generous economic aid and advised the junta on how it could 'gain a more positive image, both at home and abroad'.[5] The declassification of US government documents in the 1990s confirmed the complicity of United States in undermining Allende's government: for example, in 1970, a cable was sent from CIA headquarters to agents in Santiago stating: 'It is firm and continuing policy that Allende be overthrown by a coup'.[6] Given these revelations, many academics and journalists felt it important to document the US's actions.[7] A new generation of scholars, however, has rejected the view that Chile can be understood only through the machinations of the super-powers. Some Chilean academics have even suggested that the 'puppet-on-a-string' analytical approach is a new form of 'imperialism', although this seems an unfair caricature of writers who simply sought to record US complicity in human rights abuses.[8] In most cases, these writers did not say that the United States controlled events in Chile; instead they argued that sections of the US state worked in alliance with Chilean elites. Nevertheless, the recent emphasis on re-examining domestic Chilean politics and widening the focus to look at the role of other countries, such as Chile's Latin American neighbours, has yielded fruitful and insightful new research.[9]

A related debate has been the extent to which foreign countries assisted the transition to democracy in Chile.[10] Assessing the role of the international community is complicated by the fact that the policy of most countries, as we have seen with Britain, changed according to which government was in power. In the case of the United States, which was the largest foreign investor, the most important trading power and the regional hegemon, the policy underwent a series of changes.[11] The pro-Pinochet stance of President Nixon's White House dismayed the US Congress, which as early as 1974, put limits on economic aid to Chile and in 1976, imposed an arms embargo. Opinion hardened in Congress after Orlando Letelier—Chile's ambassador to the United States under Salvador Allende—was murdered in Washington by a car bomb planted by a Chilean secret services agent in 1976. Twenty-five-year-old Ronni Moffitt, a US citizen, was also killed in the attack. When Jimmy Carter came to office in 1977, human rights were placed high on the agenda: export credits were cut, aid slashed, and the president made a high-profile visit to a leader of the Chilean opposition. US policy changed again when Ronald Reagan came to office. The ban on arms sales was lifted—but Congress imposed so many restrictions that deliveries were not, in fact, restored. In the early years, Reagan sought a rapprochement with Pinochet, but as opposition to the junta grew in Chile from 1983, the dictator became an embarrassment to Washington, particularly as Reagan needed the support of Congress for his anti-communist crusade in Central America, which was justified on the grounds of 'promoting democracy'. Thus, the Reagan administration, by the mid-1980s, became more critical of Chile's human rights record. It began to look at a transition to democracy and the need to shore up support for 'moderate', business-friendly elements in the opposition.

After the coup, European governments were more willing than the United States to criticise the regime, although it was less costly for these countries to take a moral stance because they had fewer economic and security interests in the region.[12] In the weeks after the coup, most European countries allowed people fleeing the junta to take refuge in their embassies in Chile. The main exceptions were Britain, Germany and Denmark, whose governments ordered their embassy staff to turn away asylum-seekers.[13] Some went much further; the Swedish Ambassador, Harald Edelstam, gained a Scarlet-Pimpernel reputation for touring Santiago and offering sanctuary to people in danger. In Europe, the Chilean coup evoked powerful memories of the anti-fascist struggle in the 1930s and World War II. Many drew parallels with the contemporary anti-dictatorial cause against General Francisco Franco in Spain and the authoritarian Estado Novo in Portugal. Large solidarity movements were formed across Europe, and European leaders denounced Pinochet's brutality, including Swedish prime minister Olof Palme (1969–1976, 1982–1986); Austrian chancellor Bruno Kreisky (1970–1983); Finnish president Urho Kekkonen (1956–1982); French president François Mitterrand (1981–1995); and Italian prime minister Bettino Craxi (1983–1987). Up to 100,000 Chilean exiles found refuge in Western Europe.[14] However, none of the nine members of the European Economic Community—nor any other Western European country—broke diplomatic relations with the regime and none imposed a trade embargo or restrictions on private investment.[15] The United Nations Human Rights Commission set up an ad hoc working party in 1975 to investigate abuses in Chile, one of the first examples of the UN setting up a mechanism to examine human rights in a particular country.[16] The ad hoc working party was replaced by a UN special rapporteur in 1979. The United Nations General Assembly condemned Chile's human rights record every year from 1974 to 1989. (The US voted against or abstained on 11 of these 16 votes. Britain abstained twice: in 1982 and 1983, to 'repay' Chile for help in the Falklands war).

The lack of a coordinated response by the international community, however, weakened its opposition to the Pinochet regime. In 1973, when the Conservative Heath government was in power, activists criticised the British Embassy in Santiago for taking a less welcoming attitude towards refugees than that of other European countries. But when Labour came to office in 1974, policy changed and Britain went much further than most of its European counterparts. Austria was the only other Western European country to ban arms sales to Chile in the 1970s.[17] It was not until 1976 that the United States also imposed an arms embargo. Although an embargo by Britain and the US, Chile's two largest arms suppliers, caused the Chilean military difficulties—at one stage, the Chilean air force feared its entire fleet of aircraft might be grounded—in the longer run Chile was able to switch to other suppliers, including France and Germany. (When socialist François Mitterrand came to power in 1981, France then imposed a ban on arms sales to Chile, by which time the Thatcher government had lifted the British embargo).

Britain also imposed more stringent controls on export-credit guarantees than most of its major competitors in the 1970s, refusing to provide medium or long-term cover to exporters to Chile. But once again Chile switched to other suppliers; between 1973 and 1977, Britain saw its share in Chilean imports fall from 5.8 to 2.4%, and the UK fell from being Chile's fourth largest trade partner to its tenth.[18] Meanwhile the US reaped the benefits, as its trade more than doubled and its share of the market grew from 16 to 20%. Japan's trade with Chile also grew 400% in this period.[19] Crucially, no country was willing to impose an embargo on all trade to Chile. There is evidence to suggest that a trade embargo would have been effective; when the US union federation AFL-CIO threatened to boycott Chilean trade in 1979, there was an instant reaction from the Pinochet regime, which introduced a new labour law, giving trade unionists limited rights at plant level.[20] Attempts to limit capital flows to Chile faced the same problem. Britain cut all economic aid to Chile and in 1975 refused to reschedule the debts that Chile owed to the British government, but British investment in Chile more than doubled between 1974 and 1978.[21] The Chilean economy never suffered from lack of access to credit because neither Britain, nor any other Western country, was prepared to place restrictions on private lending. International foreign investment in Chile rose from a net outflow of US$143m in 1974, to an inward flow of US$1.1bn in 1979 and US$2.2bn in 1981.[22] It is hard to isolate and assess the impact of measures taken by one country, but it is clear that the lack of coordination by international powers and the unwillingness to interfere in private trade and investment undermined the effectiveness of the sanctions imposed by Britain.

This is not to say that Britain's 'ethical' policies had no impact; telegrams from British diplomats in Santiago make it clear that the Chilean armed forces were incensed by the arms embargo. The withdrawal and restoration of the British ambassador made front-page news in Santiago. The policies had an important humanitarian dimension: the British Labour government gave 3000 refugees sanctuary from persecution and possible death.[23] And who can measure the psychological impact on the political prisoner in a Chilean jail who heard on his transistor radio that trade unionists 8000 miles away in Scotland were showing their solidarity by refusing to work on Chilean warplane engines?[24]

The offering of refuge was one of the most important ways in which the international community helped to undermine the regime in the long run. The experience of exile and the links that Chileans made with governments, NGOs and universities while they lived abroad, played a role in enabling the Chilean opposition to regroup and discuss strategies to bring down Pinochet. This international dimension of Chilean opposition politics was greater, as Alan Angell notes, than in any other South American dictatorship.[25] The British Labour government, working with the charity the World University Service and the group 'Academics for Chile', funded 900 scholarships for Chilean academics and students to study in the United Kingdom—a programme that was ended by Margaret Thatcher's government in 1980.[26] The Joint Working Group for Refugees, a voluntary agency funded by a grant from the Labour government, as well as donations, welcomed and resettled thousands of Chilean exiles.[27] It worked with non-governmental organisations, Labour councils, trade councils and a network of volunteers across the country to find housing for the refugees. With the upsurge in opposition in Chile from 1983, many governments including those of France (now under socialist President François Mitterand), Germany, the US, Canada, the Netherlands and Sweden gave technical and financial support to opposition groups and think tanks.

Rather than trying to pinpoint and assess the impact of Britain's policy on Chile, isolating its effects from those of other countries, this book focuses on why these policies were adopted by British governments. What pressures and influences shaped policy-makers' decisions? The arms embargo on Chile, for example, was a highly unusual unilateral peacetime action. Wilson's government had imposed an arms embargo on South Africa in 1964, but this was in response to the United Nation Security Council's 1963 resolution calling on all member states to voluntarily impose embargos. Britain imposed a near complete trade embargo on Rhodesia in 1965 when Ian Smith unilaterally declared independence for a white minority government. But, similarly, this came after the UN Security Council had urged the UK to take a tough stance. In contrast, the United Nations had never called on member states to stop selling arms to Chile.

From an analysis of the Foreign Office and Cabinet papers of the period, a number of conclusions about policy towards Chile can be drawn. The role of political parties and ideology was crucial in creating policy towards Chile and there was a clear difference between the policies of the Labour and Conservative governments. Domestic pressures were, therefore, crucial to understanding how policy was formed, although all governments tried to keep in step with their European allies and the United States. The ideological outlook of FCO officials was more in tune with the Conservative Party and, when Labour came to office, officials tried to moderate their policies by warning ministers of the dangers of radicalism. Informal social networks between diplomats and private sector representatives reinforced the FCO's pro-business perspective. The Labour leadership was pragmatic and followed some of their advice: for example, not cancelling existing arms contracts. Labour leaders agreed with the Foreign Office that the government should not interfere with private trade and investment or violate international law. Beyond advising caution, the diplomats did not attempt to undermine the Labour government, despite privately disagreeing with its stance. The Labour government was receptive to lobbying from trade unions, party branches and human rights groups, because ministers were already sympathetic to their demands and the campaigners had institutional links to the governing party. The Wilson and Callaghan governments, however, never went as far as social movements and activists would have wished. Conservative governments and the Foreign Office were less susceptible to lobbying from left-wing and liberal organisations, but the scrutiny did make them act more cautiously and think about the presentation of their policies. The Labour government resisted pressure from British exporters and arms manufacturers (to restore export-credit guarantees and end the arms embargo), while Thatcher's Conservative government had an affinity with the outlook of business leaders and rapidly conceded to their demands.

Notes

1. The arguments in this paragraph derive from Carlos Huneeus, *The Pinochet Regime* (London: Lynne Rienner, 2007); Manuel Antonio Garretón, 'Transición Hacia la Democracia en Chile' (Indiana: Kellogg Institute, Working Paper 56, January 1986).
2. Huneeus, p. 4.
3. *Informe sobre Calificación de Víctimas de Violaciones de Derechos Humanos de la Violencia Política* (Santiago: Corporación Nacional de Reparación y Reconciliación, 1996). The 200,000 figure is from Mario Sznajder and Luis Roniger, 'Exile Communities and Their Differential Institutional Dynamics: A Comparative Analysis of the Chilean and Uruguayan Political Diasporas', *Revista de Ciencia Política*, 27 (1) (2007), 43–66.
4. *Covert Action in Chile 1963–1973*, US Senate, Select Committee to Study Governmental Operations with Respect to Intelligence Activities, 18 December 1975, 94th Congress, 1st Session.

5. Ibid.
6. CIA Secret Cable from Headquarters, 16 October 1970 in Peter Kornbluh, *The Pinochet File: A Declassified Dossier on Atrocity and Accountability* (New York: New Press, 2003), p. 64.
7. Samuel Chavkin, *Storm Over Chile, The Junta Under Siege* (New York: Lawrence Hill, 1985); John Dinges, *The Condor Years: How Pinochet and His Allies Brought Terrorism to Three Continents* (New York: New Press, 2005); Christopher Hitchens, *The Trial of Henry Kissinger* (London: Verso, 2001); Kornbluh, *The Pinochet File*; Livingstone, *America's Backyard*; Armando Uribe, *The Black Book of American Intervention in Chile* (Boston: Beacon Press, 1975); and Joan Garcés et al., *La Intervención de Estados Unidos en Chile* (Santiago: Editorial 30 Años, 2003).
8. Joaquín Fermandois, 'La Internacionalización de la Historia Internacional' in Fernando Purcell and Alfredo Riquelme (eds.), *Ampliando Miradas: Chile en un Tiempo Global* (Santiago: RiL Editores/Instituto de Historia, Pontificia Universidad Católica de Chile, 2009), p. 37. See also Olga Ulianova, 'Algunas Reflexiones' in Purcell and Riquelme, *Ampliando Miradas*; and Max Paul Friedman, 'Retiring the Puppets, Bringing Latin America Back in: Recent Scholarship on United States-Latin American Relations', *Diplomatic History*, 27 (2003), 621–636.
9. Tanya Harmer, *Allende's Chile and the InterAmerican Cold War* (Chapel Hill: University of North Carolina Press, 2011). See also Kristian Gustafson, *Hostile Intent: US Covert Operations in Chile* (Washington, D.C.: Potomac Books, 2007); Fermandois, *Mundo*; John R. Bawden, 'Cutting off the Dictator: The United States Arms Embargo of the Pinochet Regime, 1974–1988', *Journal of Latin American Studies*, 45 (2013), 513–543; and Jonathan Haslam, *The Nixon Administration and the Death of Allende's Chile: A Case of Assisted Suicide* (London: Verso, 2005).
10. O'Donnell, Schmitter and Whitehead, *Transitions*, 1986; Laurence Whitehead (ed.), *International Dimensions of Democratization* (Oxford: OUP, 2001). See Bibliography for further titles.
11. Heraldo Muñoz and Carlos Portales, *Elusive Friendship: A Survey of US-Chilean Relations* (Boulder: Lynne Rienner Publishers, 1991); Paul E Sigmund, *The United States and Democracy in Chile* (Baltimore: John Hopkins University Press, 1993).
12. Laurence Whitehead, 'International Aspects of Democratization', in O'Donnell, *Transitions*, 1986, p. 16.
13. Reginald Secondé, Santiago, to FCO, 23 October 1973, The National Archives (TNA): FCO7/2421. The German and Danish governments subsequently took in a small number of asylum seekers.
14. Thomas C. Wright and Rody Oñate Zúñiga, 'Chilean Political Exile', *Latin American Perspectives*, Vol. 34, No. 4, July 2007, pp. 31–49.

15. Italy's ambassador was on leave at the time of the coup and was not sent back. The Belgian ambassador left when his tour of duty ended in 1977 and was not replaced. Both countries maintained consular links and kept their embassies open.
16. Other early examples were South Africa and Israel. Patrick James Flood, *The Effectiveness of UN Human Rights Institutions* (Connecticut: Praeger, 1998), p. 87.
17. The Netherlands put restrictions on arms sales to the Pinochet regime, but did not impose a complete embargo. Nevertheless no arms were sold by the Netherlands to Chile between 1973 and 1980.
18. IMF Direction of Trade statistics in 'Chile: ECGD', TNA: BT 241/2762, 1978–1979.
19. Ibid.
20. Sigmund, p. 206.
21. UK outward direct investment overseas attributable to UK companies, book value of net assets by country at end 1974–1984. *Business Monitor MO4, Census of Overseas Assets* (London: HMSO, 1984).
22. Authorized net foreign investment in Chile. *Inversión Extranjera y Empresas Transnacionales en la Economía de Chile (1974–1989), Estudios e Informes de la Cepal*, 86 (Santiago: ECLAC, 1992), p. 67.
23. This is the total figure from the Latin America refugee scheme introduced in 1973, but most of the refugees were Chileans. G.A. Duggan, FCO, to Mr. Harding, FCO, 6 November 1979, TNA: FCO7/3614.
24. Interview with former prisoner in Andy Beckett, *Pinochet in Piccadilly* (London: Faber, 2002).
25. Alan Angell, 'International Support for the Chilean Opposition, 1973–1989: Political Parties and the Role of Exiles', in Whitehead, *International Dimensions*.
26. *A Study in Exile: A Report on the WUS (UK) Chilean Refugee Scholarship Programme* (London: World University Service, 1986), p. 9.
27. *Refugees and Political Prisoners: Report by the Joint Working Group for Refugees from Latin America* (London: Joint Working Group, October 1979).

CHAPTER 3

Welcoming Pinochet's Coup (1973–1974)

Eric Heffer—a former carpenter and Labour MP for the northern city of Liverpool—'wept unashamedly' when he received news of the coup in Chile on September 11th 1973. The grainy black-and-white television pictures of Pinochet's planes bombing the Chilean presidential palace are images that many on the British Left will never forget. The prominent left-wing Labour MP, Tony Benn, like many others, went straight to the Chilean embassy in London the morning after the coup.

The motion passed at the Labour party conference a few weeks later reflected the anger and shock of delegates:

> The Labour Party recognises the events in Chile for what they are, a savage blow to the aspirations of the working people of Chile and a temporary victory for international capitalism.[1]

In contrast, the Conservatives did not lament Allende's fall. Some openly welcomed the coup; MP Harold Soref told colleagues there was 'great cause for rejoicing since Marxism had been overthrown in Chile'.[2] The more mainstream view, publicly articulated by Conservative ministers, was that the lapse from constitutionalism was unfortunate, but that the social unrest under Allende justified the military's actions. Foreign Office minister Julian Amery, for example, told Parliament: 'We have to remember that they [the coup-leaders] knew that the forces opposed to them were also very well armed and…if they had not struck hard there could well have been civil war.'[3]

Conservative Edward Heath was Prime Minister when the coup took place. Heath's own administration would last just six months more. This was a period in Britain of trade union militancy, political polarization, rising prices and balance of payments crises. Faced with a nationwide miners' strike, Heath called a snap general election in February 1974. Amid high inflation and the electricity rationing of the 'three-day week', the Conservatives won fewer seats than Labour and Heath fell from office.

During the remaining six months that Heath was in power, the archival record shows that Conservatives and British diplomats shared the view that the Pinochet regime would be better for British interests. FCO officials were not neutral, but highly critical of human rights campaigners. There was little disagreement over policy and Conservative ministers saw no need to amend the telegrams and letters drafted by officials in their name. Although the Chile solidarity movement grew rapidly in the months following the coup, campaigners were not able to persuade the Heath administration to take action against the Pinochet regime.

Ignoring calls from the Labour party to withhold recognition and cut off aid, the Conservative government recognised the Pinochet regime eleven days after the coup because, as an FCO cable explained, 'we still have enough at stake in economic relations with Chile to require good relations with the government in power and would expect our European partners to feel the same'.[4] The British were careful, however, not to be the first government to recognise Chile, the FCO noting two days after the coup: 'Our present thinking is that HM Embassy Santiago should [recognise the regime]…after the United States and preferably in respectable European company and after some Latin Americans.'[5] Twenty countries gave official recognition to the regime before Britain, including France, Germany, Denmark, Austria, Belgium, Switzerland and Spain.

Foreign Secretary Alec Douglas-Home sent a telegram to British embassies round the world, explaining why it made economic and strategic sense to recognise the Pinochet regime:

> For British interests…there is no doubt that Chile under the junta is a better prospect than Allende's chaotic road to socialism. Our investments should do better, our loans may be successfully rescheduled and export credits later resumed and the sky-high price of copper (important to us) should fall as Chilean production is restored. The junta have inherited an economy in ruins but…there are prospects for steady recovery: under Allende there were none.[6]

The Conservative government also ignored Labour's calls for Britain to offer asylum to Chileans attempting to flee the regime, even though the British ambassador in Santiago, Reginald Secondé, had warned in a private telegram to the Foreign Office on 14 September that, 'these could receive rough justice at the hands of the military and have grounds for fearing for their lives.'[7] The ambassador continued: 'Passing them on to Latin American or Communist missions is no answer because these missions are now watched by the military.' Nevertheless, Douglas-Home's FCO instructed him the following day to refer all applicants to Latin American embassies and offer temporary asylum only in 'hot pursuit' cases, in which a person seeking asylum 'seemed in danger of life or arrest.'[8] The government received sheaves of letters calling for Britain to provide sanctuary for those fleeing the regime—from the public, from Labour Party branches, from student unions and academics; there was even a telegram from a young Gordon Brown, the future Labour prime minister.[9] But the government also came under pressure from its own backbenchers not to admit immigrants. Conservative members of the Home Affairs and Foreign Affairs Committees wrote to the foreign secretary to express 'strong concern about the Government's intention to give asylum to a number of Marxists from Chile'.[10] Some Tory MPs scribbled disparaging remarks on constituents' letters before passing them on the Foreign Office; Margaret Thatcher, for example, wrote: 'I wish some of these people had also written about Russia and Uganda'.[11] The foreign secretary himself, who took little personal interest in Chile and left policy-making to lower-ranking ministers and officials, noted on one brief: 'I do hope that the Home Secretary is not going to let in any more Chileans.'[12]

The Conservatives also rejected the Labour Party's other main demand: to cut arms sales to the new Chilean regime. This call was backed by trade unions: the general secretary of the confederation of shipbuilding and engineering unions led a delegation to the Foreign Office, suggesting that frigates and submarines currently being built in Britain should not be sent to Chile, but bought instead by the British Navy.[13] His union executive voted to support its members 'if action [were] taken...to prevent the delivery of these warships to the present regime in Chile.'[14] At Liverpool docks, trade union members did take action, 'blacking' crates of Hawker Hunter aircraft destined for Chile in December 1973. A letter from the head of the Scottish TUC to the foreign secretary summed up the feeling of the labour movement over arms sales to Chile: 'I cannot over-estimate the strength of feeling in our trade union movement [which is] completely opposed to any form of succour being given to the junta.'[15] The government's response was to send intelligence agents to shipyards in case workers tried to sabotage vessels destined for Chile.[16]

One of the strengths of the Chile solidarity movement was its breadth of support. Within a few weeks of the coup, activists had established the Chile Solidarity Campaign (CSC). This campaign would go on to attract affiliations from 30 national trade unions, 85 constituency Labour parties, 54 trade councils and 56 student unions.[17] The early meetings of the CSC in the House of Commons brought together Labour and Communist party members, as well as smaller left-wing parties, trade unionists, representatives of the Association for British-Chilean Friendship formed by British artists and intellectuals, and members of Liberation (formerly known as the Movement for Colonial Freedom), an organisation which had strong links to the labour movement. Labour MP Judith Hart was a prominent supporter of the Chile campaign from the start. Her son, Steve Hart, a Communist party member and general secretary of Liberation, played an important organising role in the early stages, writing to dozens of Labour MPs and trade union leaders asking for support.[18] Other key figures included Mike Gatehouse and Wendy Tyndale. Gatehouse had been in Santiago at the time of the coup; he was arrested by the Chilean military and spent a week as a prisoner in the National Stadium. He joined the British Communist party on his return to the UK and went on to become a highly efficient joint-secretary of the CSC throughout the 1970s. Tyndale, a young teacher who had studied in Chile, helped to organise the early meetings of the CSC. Recognising that the CSC was heavily identified with the Left, Tyndale and representatives of non-governmental organisations formed, in early 1974, the Chile Committee for Human Rights to focus more narrowly on legal issues and human rights.[19] This committee brought together religious groups, lawyers, journalists and NGOs, including OXFAM, Amnesty International, CAFOD, Christian Aid and the Catholic Institute for International Relations. They went on to work closely with the Joint Working Group for Refugees, which was formed a few months later. Meanwhile, at a meeting in the London School of Economics, in October 1973, the campaign group Academics for Chile was launched by Oxford lecturer Alan Angell and others. This grew into a network in sixty universities. The different Chile campaigning organisations thus appealed to a wide range of different constituencies and classes.

It is apparent from the Foreign Office files that British diplomats were sympathetic to the Chilean junta and exasperated by its opponents. Hugh Carless, head of the FCO's Latin America Department, complained of 'the systematic campaign being mounted against the Junta abroad'. He added:

> Chileans must be wondering why on earth, in these days of shattering international economic events produced by the oil crisis, so much unfair attention is being paid to their change of government. The answer is that Chile is now being subjected to the full treatment by an international front organisation, the Chile Solidarity Movement. Chile has been chosen by the organised left as a new crusade. The Marxist experiment has not been buried and forgotten: it is being kept alive, and is passing into the mythology of international socialism...[20]

Although the Conservative government did not change its initial policies in response to the CSC's efforts, Carless's next comments suggest that the organisation did have an impact, obliging the Foreign Office to adjust its public behaviour and consider campaigners' responses when thinking about future policies towards Chile:

> It looks as though we shall have to live with the Chile Solidarity Movement for as long as the Junta rules Chile. This means we shall, occasionally, have to adopt a lower profile than we would like. We shall have to be wary over any new arms sales...We shall not be able to rescue them from being pilloried in international meetings.[21]

In some cases, Foreign Office officials adopted rather duplicitous ways of responding to critics. When 'Christians for a Just World' invited Foreign Office representatives to a memorial service for Salvador Allende, in which the sermon was to be given by the pacifist priest, Bruce Kent, and the address by a Labour MP, a Foreign Office official from the Latin America Department wrote in a memo:

> The opposition and the Left are demanding that we should not recognise the Chilean Government and suspend aid. We shall certainly be resuming relations with the new government in a week or so if Ministers see no objection...I think therefore that we must make every effort to disarm opposition criticism as far as possible by expressing sympathy with the old President and his family to the extent compatible with the resumption of relations with the new government.[22]

He recommended that he attend the service on behalf of the Foreign Office and sign any memorial book. On another occasion, Henry Hankey, director of the FCO's Americas section, wrote about the former Chilean ambassador to London, Alvaro Bunster, who had been displaced by the coup:

> Bunster himself has been looked after with embarrassing kindness by particularly Wedgwood Benn in the Labour Party...For our part we have bent over backwards to ensure he was given all suitable courtesies, if only in order to prevent him from representing to his Labour friends that we had failed to do so.[23]

The Foreign Office kept a close eye on media reports and was highly critical of British journalists; one official in the Latin America Department complained of their 'black propaganda against the Chilean armed services' and another about the 'wolfish propaganda lurking in the sheepish guise of journalism which is reaching the British public about Chile.'[24] Where possible, British diplomats tried to influence the tone of the reporting; when a team from the British BBC documentary programme, *Panorama*, visited Chile in November 1973, staff at the British Embassy obtained for them 'maximum co-operation from the Junta'.[25] The Embassy was optimistic about the slant of the documentary, which included interviews with members of the Anglo-Chilean community speaking approvingly about the coup. An official at the British embassy wrote: 'The balance of the programme about which the producer, Bill Cran and Julian Pettifer have been extremely conscientious, should be 60 to 75% favourable to the new regime—so Cran told me yesterday just before he left'.[26] The Embassy was not so pleased with a *World in Action* team that arrived at the same time. The same official wrote: 'I gathered, in confidence, from Cran, that the WIA producer...came to cover torture and shootings...Granada's activities were certainly known to the Junta whose Press Secretary told me that they had been seeing "things they should not see"'.[27] An FCO official back in London scrawled in hand on the letter: 'Ominous news about the World in Action film'. This incident indicates that the media were not simply another outside pressure for the Foreign Office to deal with, but a force that they sought to mould and influence.

The Foreign Office was aware that torture and extrajudicial executions were taking place, and, while not approving of them, sought to justify them. Christopher Crabbie, an official in the FCO's Latin America Department wrote:

> I do not think anyone seriously doubts that torture is going on in Chile. But it is a pity that the [World in Action] programme made no attempt to say why such a situation had come about. It was irresponsible simply to describe the abuses without any discussion of the causes...The Panorama programme was quite different...The evidence for torture and persecution were put but it was well balanced by the case against the excesses of the Allende regime.[28]

Henry Hankey, an assistant undersecretary at the Foreign Office, wrote in a similar vein:

> It is a pity of course from every point of view that the force commanders in Chile have found it necessary to do so much killing. However, in view of the well-stocked arsenals uncovered in factories and elsewhere it may well be that by displaying a ruthless resolution at the outset more lives were saved than lost.[29]

In the immediate aftermath of the coup, the British ambassador in Santiago, Reginald Secondé, shared the same view, writing in one cable:

> I think I should make it clear that, whatever the excesses of the military during the coup, the Allende administration was leading the country into economic ruin, social disorder and political chaos...It was only under extreme provocation and with the greatest reluctance that the armed forces moved.[30]

He added in another telegram a few weeks later:

> The current regime has infinitely more to offer British interests than the one which preceded it. The new leaders are unequivocally on our side and want to do business, in its widest sense, with us. I hope that Her Majesty's Government will respond.[31]

Other British diplomatic staff were even more enthusiastic: journalist Hugh O'Shaughnessy, who took shelter in the embassy on the morning of the coup, saw a British naval officer 'who was beside himself with joy' that Allende was being overthrown. 'He was most vociferous in delight.

He made no secret of it,' recalled O'Shaughnessy.[32] However, as the accounts of mass executions and torture filtered through, the ambassador, who had been criticised by the Labour Party for his perceived pro-military stance, began, in private, to express some disquiet. A good summary of his opinions is contained in this letter to the Foreign Office in London:

> [The junta] already have some impressive achievements to their credit, particularly in the economic field, where there is already evidence of some return of foreign confidence. The lack of political activity is, for the time being, no loss. But the Government's attitude towards Marxism is naïve and will build up intellectual resentment. And the manner in which they are hounding opponents and the methods being used is not only distasteful but politically unsound.[33]

The Anglo-Chilean business community in Chile, who were 'pro-junta virtually to a man', according to one FCO official, had no such qualms.[34] In the weeks after the coup, the British-Chilean Chamber of Commerce published a shrill defence of Pinochet in a booklet which they circulated to MPs.

There was a convergence of views, therefore, between the Conservative Party and Foreign Office officials under the Heath government. Both agreed that protecting British trade and investment was paramount and that the stability brought by Pinochet was welcome, if not the methods he used. They saw no need to impose any sanctions on the regime or withhold recognition. This was an immediate, instinctive pro-business ideological response to the coup, rather than a result of direct lobbying from British companies. The Foreign Office was keen to keep in step with its European allies—as one Foreign Office official noted: 'As a rule of thumb we should keep in line with the Germans, Dutch and French'—but the British were nevertheless prepared to take a harder line on asylum than most of their allies.[35] Human rights groups and trade unions could not persuade an unsympathetic government to change their key policies. With a Conservative majority, the campaigners had no leverage in parliament; nor did they have any institutional links to the governing party through which they could apply pressure. The Conservative government, for example, approved the delivery of eight Hawker Hunter aircraft, as well as arms and explosives, although campaigners did win at least one concession: the foreign secretary cancelled a shipment of 1400 machine guns and rifles to Chile, which the FCO had approved, because of the outcry it might cause. ('I wonder if it would not be best...not to go ahead with this particular order until things settle down. It is chicken feed and what matters is good relations between Chile and Britain,' he remarked.[36]) While unwilling to meet the main demands of pressure groups, it is very clear the Foreign Office paid great attention to what they called the 'Chile lobby'. The scrutiny made officials act more cautiously and certainly caused them to consider the presentation of their policy, if not the substance.

***

During the Heath administration, the Foreign Office and the Conservatives not only shared a similar ideological outlook on Chile; at times they even appeared to be allies against Labour. After one meeting between Foreign Secretary Douglas-Home and a deputation of Labour MPs led by Judith Hart MP, an official from the FCO Latin America Department remarked rather gloatingly:

> Our policies towards Chile are under attack on several fronts. The Secretary of State was reportedly in fighting form during his interview with Mrs Hart and her colleagues, who emerged somewhat chastened from the encounter.[37]

The general election of February 1974 would bring these committed Labour politicians into office and face to face with their behind-the-scenes critics.

***

Notes

1. 'Chile'. Labour Party NEC statement, 30 September 1973, The National Archives (TNA): FCO7/2608.
2. Conservative Parliamentary Foreign and Commonwealth Affairs Committee (Latin American group), minutes, 22 November 1973, CPA CRD 3/10/17.
3. *Hansard*, HC Deb, 28 November1973, Vol. 865, cc462–537.
4. Alec Douglas-Home to Washington, Bonn, Brussels, Copenhagen, the Hague, Madrid, Ottawa, Paris, Rome, 13 September 1973, TNA: FCO7/2411. Drafted by FCO official J.M. Hunter.
5. Ibid.

6. Douglas-Home to Certain Missions and Dependent Territories, 21 September 1973, TNA: FCO57/439.
7. Reginald Secondé to FCO, 14 September 1973, TNA: FCO7/2411.
8. Douglas-Home to British embassy, Santiago, 15 September 1973, TNA: FCO7/2411.
9. Gordon Brown to Douglas-Home, 15 December 1973, TNA: FCO7/2424. Letters also contained in TNA: FCO7/2423.
10. Sir F. Bennett to Douglas-Home, 15 November 1973, TNA: FCO7/2424, 1973.
11. Margaret Thatcher to Julian Amery, 14 November 1973, TNA: FCO7/2423.
12. Note by Douglas-Home on Hugh Carless to Douglas-Home, 17 December 1973, TNA: FCO7/2432, 1973.
13. P.G.P.D. Fullerton to D.R. Spedding, 28 December 1973, TNA: FCO7/2432.
14. J. M. Service to Christopher Chataway, 22 November 1973, TNA: FCO7/2432.
15. James Jack to Douglas-Home, 17 October 1973, TNA: FCO7/2432.
16. Carless to Commander Handover, 22 November 1973, TNA: FCO7/2432, 1973; Letter from Mrs. B.A. Dunphy, SY 2 (PE) to DS13a, 14 December 1973, TNA: FCO7/2432. See also Fullerton to R.A. Lloyd-Jones, Head of DS 11 MOD, 12 November 1973, TNA: FCO7/2433.
17. Manchester People's History Museum, Labour History Archive (MPHM): CSC/13/1/1. Minutes. 1973–1974.
18. MPHM: CSC/13/2 Correspondence, 1973.
19. MPHM: CSC/13/1/1. Minutes. 1973–1974; Author's interview with Wendy Tyndale, 7 January 2015.
20. Carless to Secondé, 28 December 1973, TNA: FCO7/2416.
21. Carless to Secondé, 28 December 1973, TNA: FCO7/2416.
22. J.M. Hunter to Henry Hankey, FCO, 17 September 1973, TNA: FCO7/2016.
23. Hankey to Secondé, 28 September 1973, TNA: FCO7/2413.
24. Fullerton to Spedding, 24 December 1973, TNA: FCO7/2416; Letter from Carless to Secondé, Santiago, 28 December 1973, TNA: FCO7/2416.
25. Antony Walter to A.E. Clarke, 22 November 1973, TNA: FCO7/2416.
26. Ibid.
27. Ibid.
28. C.D. Crabbie to A. McN. Walter, 14 December 1973, TNA: FCO7/2416.
29. Hankey to Secondé, 28 September 1973, TNA: FCO7/2413, 1973.

30. Secondé to FCO, 18 September 1973, TNA: FCO57/439.
31. Secondé to FCO, 1 October 1973, TNA: FCO7/2425.
32. Author's interview with Hugh O'Shaughnessy, 14 January 2014.
33. Secondé to Carless, FCO, 23 November 1973, 'Chile', TNA: FCO7/2416.
34. Crabbie to Mr. Collins and Carless, 19 November 1974, TNA: FCO7/2606, 1974.
35. Speaking notes drafted by Carless, attached to Carless to Private Secretary, FCO, 20 March 1974, TNA: FCO7/2605.
36. Carless to Hankey, 15 November 1973, TNA: FCO7/2433, 1973. See also note from Fullerton to Hankey, 22 October 1973, TNA: FCO7/2433.
37. C.D. Crabbie to Spedding, 20 November 1973, TNA: FCO7/2416, 1973.

CHAPTER 4

Ethical Foreign Policy? Labour Versus the Foreign Office (1974–1979)

Labour's election victory in 1974 makes it possible to examine the power of the elected politician versus the appointed civil servant. Labour was committed to a radical change in British foreign policy towards Chile, but the officials in charge of drawing up and implementing that policy were deeply sceptical of the new government's stance. The suspicion that a left-wing government could be undermined by a conservative civil service had been long held by the left of the Labour party, from Harold Laski and Stafford Cripps in the 1930s, to Tony Benn and Richard Crossman in the 1960s and 1970s.[1] The failure of Harold Wilson's 1964–1970 government to introduce the far-reaching policies demanded by the left had heightened fears that the civil service was the establishment's tool for neutralising radicalism. The government-commissioned Fulton Report of 1968 had attempted to address concerns that the civil and diplomatic service were an upper-class clique, by proposing a fast-stream recruitment system to make it easier for people from humbler backgrounds to reach the top jobs. However, the Foreign Office, in particular, remained the preserve of the upper-class public school-educated Oxbridge graduate. Between 1960 and 1964, 68% of Foreign Office officials had attended public schools, a figure that rose to 80% for senior officials and ambassadors. Even as late as 1993, 66% of fast-track entrants—those destined for top posts—had attended public schools.[2]

© The Author(s) 2018
G. Livingstone, *Britain and the Dictatorships of Argentina and Chile,
1973–82*, Security, Conflict and Cooperation in the Contemporary World,
https://doi.org/10.1007/978-3-319-78292-8_4

The archival record for this period also allows us to consider how 'ethical' foreign policy is constructed and the ways in which campaigners (or social movements) can affect policy. The 1973 party conference and the party's National Executive Committee had committed the Labour government to opposing 'all British aid or trade designed to sustain the [Chilean] military regime in power'.[3] The Labour leadership shared the rank and file's distaste for the Pinochet regime; soon after becoming prime minister, Harold Wilson, told parliament that it was an 'oppressive fascist government', comments that provoked a formal complaint from the Chilean government.[4] But once in office, ministers had to weigh up their commitment to a radical foreign policy with economic and geopolitical considerations. It is noteworthy that while the Conservatives were happy to allow Foreign Office officials to act with a large degree of autonomy, content in the knowledge that officials shared the same values as ministers, during Labour's period in office a flood of memos and deliberative meetings show that officials and politicians spent far more time negotiating policy. There was also more debate among ministers, Labour MPs and party activists. The question of Chile was much more important to the Labour Party than it was for the Conservatives: neither Prime Minister Heath nor Foreign Secretary Douglas-Home, nor any other Conservative politician from the period, mentions Chile in their memoirs, but many of the key Labour players and diarists, including Wilson, Callaghan, Barbara Castle and Tony Benn, devote space to Chile in their autobiographies and journals.[5]

The Labour administrations of 1974–1979 were either minority governments or had a very slim majority of seats in the House of Commons. The February 1974 election had resulted in a hung parliament and Wilson formed a minority government. A second general election in October 1974, gave him a majority of three seats. Wilson unexpectedly resigned in March 1976 and James Callaghan became prime minister. Within a year of taking office, Callaghan's majority in parliament was eliminated by by-election defeats and he was forced to rely on the votes of Liberals, Ulster Unionists and Scottish Nationalists. These fragile administrations were in constant danger of collapse and they relied on every Labour MP's vote; backbenchers, therefore, were in a powerful position to win concessions from government. Both the Chile Solidarity Campaign and the Chile Human Rights Committee had strong support among Labour parliamentarians, who frequently lobbied ministers urging them to take an 'ethical' stance. Trade unions were also in a strong bargaining position because the government sought their approval on wage and spending policies. The breakdown of communication between ministers and unions would eventually lead to a public sector strike in 1978–1979—'the winter of discontent'—that precipitated the government's downfall. During these years, ministers grappled with many other severe problems—violence in Northern Ireland; a referendum on whether to remain in the European Community that split the Labour party (1975); the collapse of the pound and the negotiation of an IMF loan (1976); and a devolution referendum in Scotland whose terms led the Scottish Nationalists to withdraw their support for Callaghan, bringing his government to an end (March 1979). To a certain extent, Chile became part of Labour's domestic political calculations: it was a radical cause that had resonance throughout the labour movement and ministers could appease their supporters by taking action against the Pinochet regime, but they were also aware that in the context of sterling crises and rising unemployment, placing restrictions on trade or cancelling large orders for British-built warships could have a deleterious impact on British economy. Moreover, these potential risks to British trade and investments were repeatedly brought to ministers' attention by civil servants.

Three days after Wilson became prime minister, Judith Hart—now minister for International Development—wrote to him asking to include the words: 'My government will suspend aid to Chile' in the Queen's Speech.[6] On the same day, Hugh Carless, head of the FCO's Latin America Department, sent an internal memo warning that 'if a statement of this kind is made in the Queen's Speech, it could affect our trading interests in Chile.'[7] He warned that the public sector in Chile owned 50% of the economy and Britain could lose contracts. Trying to limit what he regarded as a damaging proposal, he concluded: 'Even if a decision is taken to suspend aid to Chile, we would hope that no reference to it need be made in the Queen's Speech.'[8] The cabinet accepted this advice, deciding at a meeting that evening to include none of Hart's suggestions in the Queen's speech.[9] The tenacious Mrs. Hart then wrote to foreign secretary James Callaghan, saying 'I can well understand that it may not have been appropriate to include this in the Queen's Speech, but I want, if you agree, to announce very quickly that this is my intention.'[10] Once again, Hugh Carless was quick to warn ministers of the dangers of rapid action. In a memo he wrote: 'Problem: How to reply to the attached letter in which the Minister for Overseas Development states her intention…to announce in a speech this week…that aid to Chile will be suspended'.[11] He warned that 'our ambassador says…our prospects of winning public sector contracts would be weakened at a time when Chile is planning a major expansion.' Pointing out that Chile was Britain's fifth-largest market in Latin America, with exports averaging £21m a year, he added: 'The Chilean military…are likely to be very sensitive to any publicly announced changes in our policy towards them.' Carless drafted a letter for Callaghan to write to his Labour colleague, Hart, which was duly sent:

> I know the strong feeling on this subject and I think that you may well be right in suggesting that aid or at any rate some of it should be suspended. My instinct is however that we should not rush to announce decisions on specific subjects like this…[12]

These exchanges show how effectively Foreign Office officials persuaded the minister to act cautiously and refrain from any immediate action, and how they played on the division between pragmatists and idealists within the government.

Foreign Office officials, however, did not simply ignore the will of the new government or the new political realities. The next immediate problem facing Hugh Carless was a planned Royal Navy visit to the Chilean port of Valparaíso. In a memo, he explained that the Royal Navy and Chilean Navy had 'the closest of ties dating back to the founding of the Chilean Navy by Admiral Cochrane' and noted that 'our warship construction programme is worth £50m [and] future orders depend on continuing liaison between the Royal Navy and the Chileans.'[13] He warned that if the trip was cancelled, the Chileans could retaliate by denying port facilities to *HMS Endurance*, an ice patrol ship which was due to disembark a Royal Marine detachment in southern Chile en route to the Falkland Islands. The Ministry of Defence wanted the trip to go ahead, he added. However, recognising that the trip was 'potentially embarrassing for the government in view of the strong feeling in parliament against the Junta in Chile,' he concluded, 'in view of the strength of parliamentary opinion, it would be wise to cancel the visit'. The head of the FCO's Americas department, Henry Hankey, wrote: 'This is most unfortunate since these long-standing relations between the Royal Navy and the Chilean Navy bear constant fruit in naval orders. However, I agree that this is not a suitable moment for such an exercise.'[14] After consultations with the ambassador, in which he was asked to sound out how affronted the Chilean government would be, the trip was cancelled.

Two weeks after coming into office, Jim Callaghan put his name to a memorandum outlining the new government's 'Policy Towards Chile'. The paper, drafted by Hugh Carless, shows the Foreign Office making a genuine attempt to reflect the Labour government's new priorities, while also highlighting the British economic interests at stake in Chile. As Carless's FCO superior noted, 'I think the Draft submitted by Mr. Carless strikes about the right balance. In signifying disapprobation of the Chilean regime, we need to be watchful against positive reprisals'.[15] The paper includes a summary of the Foreign Office's view of British interests in Chile, which are regarded as 'mainly economic'. These comprise:

- trade
- 20% of Britain's copper is supplied by Chile
- £14m investment in Chilean industry and utilities
- 150-year old tradition of supplying the Chilean Navy.[16]

The 'political' interests cited were the fact that Britain and Chile were co-signatories of the Antarctic Treaty of 1959 and British use of the port and airport at Punta Arenas, in southern Chile, as a staging post for Marines going to the Falkland Islands.

The 'Considerations' drafted by Carless illustrate the balance between pragmatism and Labour-pleasing principles that he was trying to achieve: 'Any changes in policy towards Chile', he maintained, 'should be guided by the aims of: (a) persuading the Junta to treat their opponents humanely and to work towards the restoration of democracy; (b) avoiding damage to our material interests.'

It is striking, however, that in the section devoted to 'Recommendations for Decision', all Labour's main objectives were included, which amounted to a radical shift of policy:

- no new export licences for arms should be granted
- aid to Chile should be suspended
- active liaison between the armed British and Chilean armed forces should be kept minimum
- refugee policy should become more flexible
- the ambassador should also be instructed to express concern about political prisoners and Britain should be associated with future representations made by the UN and the Nine [group of European Community nations].[17]

The only way in which the Foreign Office attempted to apply a brake to Labour radicalism was by advocating that outstanding contracts should be honoured and spare parts for existing contracts delivered. In practice, this meant going ahead with a large order to build two frigates and two submarines and to refit two destroyers, which had been agreed in 1969, as well as completing the overhaul of eight engines for Hawker Hunter fighter planes. The Foreign Office also recommended that the government should go ahead with a draft agreement to reschedule Chile's debt.

The Sale of Warships and Aero-Engines

Just as Robin Cook's 'ethical' foreign policy fell into disarray when the New Labour government decided to deliver Hawk jets to Indonesia in the 1990s, the question of honouring existing arms contracts was the most controversial aspect of Wilson's policy towards Chile and brought him into conflict with backbenchers, human rights campaigners and the trade union movement. In one case, trade unionists in Glasgow took matters into their own hands, refusing to touch bomber-plane engines destined for Chile. A total of 170,000 people were employed directly and indirectly in the arms manufacturing sector and some Labour ministers feared that failing to honour contracts would lead to a loss of jobs at a time when British manufacturing, and particularly the shipbuilding industry, was in decline. There has, in fact, only been one case in peacetime when a British government has broken a signed arms contract on human rights grounds; this was in 1978 when Labour cancelled a shipment of armoured cars to El Salvador.[18]

The Labour leadership prevaricated for two years before honouring all of the arms contracts, carefully gauging the level of opposition and changing position numerous times in response to grass-roots pressure. Callaghan initially accepted the FCO recommendation that all the contracts should be respected, but wobbled after 90 backbenchers protested.[19] When he unveiled the new government's policy on Chile in March 1974, instead of announcing, as planned, that the warships would be delivered, he told parliament that the defence contracts were 'under review'.[20] In a discussion in cabinet the next day, Bob Mellish, the chief whip, advised Callaghan to meet with backbenchers before any decision to avoid an 'embarrassingly hostile reaction'.[21] A week later, Callaghan reported back to cabinet: 'There was no doubt that the supply of warships to Chile was widely disliked in the Parliamentary Party', but only 27 members had attended his consultation and many had understood the 'formidable difficulties' of trying to frustrate the contracts.[22] Michael Foot spoke up with a 'defiant desperation' against the contracts, but was backed only by Tony Benn.[23] The prime minister concluded that there was no alternative to delivering the two frigates, two submarines and refitting the two destroyers. It is a striking indication of the importance of Chile to the Labour Party, that so much cabinet time was devoted to it by a newly-elected government, which had just resolved the crisis of the three-day-week caused by a miners' strike and was simultaneously dealing with upheaval in Northern Ireland, Wilson having re-imposed direct rule at the end of March 1974.

The cabinet's decision to deliver the warships caused dissension in the party. The NEC, with 'resolutions from local parties pouring in', passed a motion calling on ministers to reconsider their decision and Stan Newens MP led a deputation of MPs to see Callaghan, one of many such deputations during Labour's period in office.[24] Eric Heffer, now minister of state for industry, wrote to Harold Wilson, arguing:

> Surely we cannot say one thing in opposition and something entirely different in Government…It would be terrible if we now put ourselves in the wrong with the movement at home and abroad. We should tell the Military Junta that the warships will be handed over after full democracy has been restored.[25]

Heffer told Wilson that he intended to make a speech in a Liverpool Labour club condemning the cabinet's decision. The prime minister sent Heffer two formal warnings, explaining that, as a minister, he was breaking the principle of collective responsibility, but Heffer went ahead regardless.[26]

In this instance, the Labour government resisted campaigners' demands and two frigates and a destroyer set sail for Chile by the end of 1974. However, as pressure from activists mounted, the Cabinet wavered on the despatch of the two submarines. Two letters illustrate the depth of feeling in the party. Ron Hayward, general secretary of the Labour Party, wrote to Callaghan asking for a meeting to discuss the contracts.[27] Wilson, meanwhile, received a four-page letter from Jack Jones, the leader of the Transport and General Workers Union (TGWU), the largest union in the country. Jones was a veteran of the international brigades in the Spanish Civil War, a conflict which, for many on the Left, had parallels with Chile. He urged the prime minister to impound the submarines, adding: 'You will, I know, recognise the depth of my feelings about this problem and understand why I have written to you direct.'[28]

The Treasury, Department of Trade, Ministry of Defence and Attorney General's office, all warned of the repercussions of failing to honour contracts and the cabinet agreed in 1975, once again, that that the submarines should be allowed to sail.[29] But twelve months later, as anger mounted following the torture of a British citizen Sheila Cassidy (see below), ministers hardened their position. They decided, in May 1976, that while it was too late to act on one submarine, which had already become Chilean property, they would maintain a lien on the second, refusing to hand it to the Chilean navy, until Chile paid the arrears due on the contract. This decision provoked indignant headlines in the Chilean dailies—an 'unfriendly gesture of a political nature,' opined *El Mercurio*, and a violation of Chile's 'human rights', according to *El Cronista*.[30]

The arrears were eventually paid by the Chilean government in August 1976 and the remaining submarine was handed over to the Chilean Navy. The two years of agonizing over the warship contracts illustrated the Labour government's attempts to balance a commitment to act against the dictatorship with the need to protect British industry and jobs, as well as the country's reputation as a reliable supplier. Repeated requests for legal advice from the attorney general show a desire to abide by the law, while at the same time exploring legal ways to delay or frustrate contracts, in order to satisfy the demands of activists.

Direct Action at Rolls Royce

But the case that caught the imagination of the labour movement most vividly, and that ministers found most difficult to grapple with, was that of the 'blacking' of four aeroplane engines in Scotland. When workers at the Rolls Royce plant in East Kilbride discovered in their works yard in March 1974 four engines for Hawker Hunter planes—the very aircraft that had bombed Allende's presidential palace—they refused to work on them. The action was a considerable threat to the Chilean air force, whose fleet was almost entirely made up of Hawker Hunters, but ministers were concerned about the legal implications of the strike, as well as the damage to Britain's image as a reliable supplier. 'The Chilean air force will be grounded if we don't service them. Good this may be, but profound repercussions', Callaghan scribbled on a note to Wilson in April 1974, after the FCO had produced for him a long briefing warning of the dangers of failing to fulfil the Rolls Royce contracts.[31] After seeking legal advice, the cabinet decided it could not immediately break off the contracts to service Chile's Hawker Hunter engines, as recommended by Industry Secretary Tony Benn, but it would ask Rolls Royce, a state-owned company, to exercise its contractual right to end its contract with the Chilean air force with three months' notice. The workers' action, therefore, had a profound impact on the capability of the Chilean air force: by 1978, 22 of its 34 Hunter aircraft were grounded awaiting spares and engines.[32] However, in 1974, ministers continued to face a problem, because Rolls Royce was still legally obliged to return the overhauled engines to the Chileans before ending the contract. The engines could not be moved from the plant because no trade union members would touch them. Ministers feared a 'Grunwick' situation could develop if the engines were removed by force.[33] A strike by mainly Asian women employees of the Grunwick photo-processing plant in London, in 1976–1978, had led to violent clashes between thousands of activists and police. For four years, the engines lay in crates in the Glasgow works yard, as the Chilean authorities pursued a long legal challenge to try to get them back.

When the Chileans won a court injunction for the return of the engines in 1977 and applied for an export licence, Foreign Secretary David Owen wrote in a confidential memo: 'I fear that we cannot grant a licence without sparking a major row.' If the Chileans tried to remove the engines, he added, the union would probably 'take steps to prevent the engines being removed. This could create a very nasty incident and would also provoke controversy of the 'union versus the law' variety.'[34] Edmund Dell, the Trade Secretary feared that the image of trade unionists clashing with police 'could be deplorable in its international as well as domestic consequences.'[35] Owen spoke to Moss Evans, the new leader of the Transport and General Workers Union (TGWU), but he was not willing to dissuade unionists from blocking the removal of the engines.[36]

The dispute also worried British diplomats, who articulated the concerns of the British business sector. Ambassador Reginald Secondé reported that he had received a formal complaint from the Chilean government and that a group of senior British businessmen had called to tell him 'they were greatly concerned about the effect that this could have on existing British commercial interests'.[37] When the embassy staff reported that the Chilean state oil firm was not buying any more supplies from British companies as an act of retaliation, a Foreign Office official in London wrote: 'The evidence which you have given us of the cold-shouldering of UK firms…is very useful. Our difficulty is to convince some of our Ministers that damage is indeed being done by the measures taken against Chile'.[38] As the case dragged on, a Department of Trade official complained:

I have every sympathy with the [Chilean] solicitors: the delay in this case has reached embarrassing proportions…In the meantime we are left with the job of trying to placate irate customers and, as a consequence the reputation of [the Department of Trade's] Export Licensing Branch suffers in the commercial world.[39]

Some in the Labour Party feared the dispute could be exploited by right-wing organisations, such as the National Association for Freedom (NAFF), a direct action group aimed at combating trade union power. Owen's political advisor David Stephen warned that 'if the Chileans tipped off their right-wing supporters in this country and for example a "midnight recovery operation" were to be depicted in the *Daily Telegraph* as a heroic exploit of anti-leftist buccaneers—this would politicize the whole question.'[40]

A group of Chilean officials did, in fact, travel to London in 1978 to discuss with a small group of British right-wingers how to gain possession of the Rolls Royce engines. Sir Peter Hill-Norton, the strongly anti-communist Admiral of the Fleet, attended a lunch with the Chileans, as did historian and former MI6 spy, Alistair Horne, and journalists Alistair Forbes, Tom Stacey and Chapman Pincher of the *Daily Express*. The director of Rolls Royce, Sir John Russell, turned down an invitation.[41]

In June 1978, the attorney general advised that it would be illegal for the government not to issue an export licence. Callaghan, now prime minister, agreed that the licence should be issued.[42] In the early hours of Saturday 26 August, a bank holiday weekend, lorries with false number plates from an unregistered haulage firm, accompanied by sheriff's officers, arrived at the plant and quietly removed the engines.[43] The FCO suspected the British intelligence services had been involved in their removal, but as one official wrote, 'I did not ask any further questions [of the Chilean attaché] …our position has hitherto been that we know nothing about this: I thought we should keep it that way.'[44]

The East Kilbride action is a clear case of trade unions influencing government policy. Not only did the government ask Rolls Royce to terminate the contract for servicing engines, but for four years the government did not intervene to return the 'blacked' engines to Chile, because they feared a confrontation with the trade unions. They watched as the Chileans went through a drawn out legal process and did not issue an export licence until a year after the Chileans had obtained an injunction.

Debt Campaigns

Pressure from below also persuaded Labour leaders to change their position on rescheduling Chilean government debt. On coming to office in 1974, the Wilson government agreed to reschedule Chile's 1973–1974 debts. A draft agreement had already been signed by the twelve creditor countries of the Paris Club while Heath was in power and the Labour cabinet agreed to ratify it. But backbenchers and Labour party activists believed rescheduling would give the regime a vital cash life-line, particularly since Britain was Chile's second-largest creditor, after the United States. The Labour Party conference of 1974 passed a motion urging the government not to reschedule in 1975, and Ian Mikardo MP led a delegation of MPs to see the chancellor of the exchequer, Dennis Healey.

Most Foreign Office and Treasury officials were firmly in favour of rescheduling and Wilson's advisor, Bernard Donoughue, even alleged that the two departments had been 'in cahoots to misrepresent the alleged advantages of continuing loaning money to Chile and the cost of breaking off'.[45] Reginald Secondé, Britain's ambassador to Chile, however, took a more nuanced position. Conceding that placing conditions on loans might be a way of exerting leverage on the regime, he nevertheless counselled a low-key, cautious approach: 'I would hope that we would not get isolated [from other countries] in this operation or appear to be taking the lead in it…I had in mind flexible and unpublicised action in the corridors.'[46]

But Wilson, Callaghan and Healey took a bolder stance. They decided not to reschedule and to try to persuade the Germans to follow suit. They agreed not to approach the Americans and French because that might 'increase the risk of American pressure on the Germans'.[47] The Labour government went ahead with its decision to boycott the Paris Club meeting even when Germany refused to do likewise. However, Britain's action did prompt France, Belgium and Denmark to withdraw from the Paris Club talks. Far from taking the ambassador's advice to maintain a low-key approach, Britain had, in fact, taken the lead in the international community. The government had acted unilaterally and had acted despite knowing that it would cause 'displeasure' to the Republican administration of Gerald Ford in the US.[48] Within one year, lobbying by Labour supporters had persuaded cabinet ministers to entirely reverse their position and this domestic pressure had outweighed external considerations such as the desire to keep in step with Britain's key international allies.

Limits to Labour's Intervention in the Market

Labour's decision not to reschedule Chile's debts to the British government, however, was undermined by the fact that privately-owned British banks were happy to offer Chile credit and British companies were keen to get a share of the thriving Chilean market. British direct foreign investment in Chile (excluding oil companies, banks and insurance companies) more than doubled from £13m in 1974 to £28m in 1978.[49] Britain was Chile's third largest source of foreign direct investment (FDI) during 1974–1981, after the USA and Canada, although Britain's 2.3% share of Chile's FDI market was dwarfed by the USA's enormous 76% share.[50] British banks also rushed to lend money to Chile. In June 1977, British-owned Lloyds Bank International was the leading partner in a London-based consortium which raised a loan of £75m for Chile. A year later, the same consortium raised £200m for Chile.[51] The Labour government ruled out putting curbs on private investment, nor did it heed calls for an embargo on all trade with Chile. Although the Chile Solidarity Campaign and the National Union of Students had called for a complete trade boycott of Chile since 1974, it had not been a central demand of campaigners, who had focused instead on halting arms deliveries. In early 1979, however, Chilean trade unions began to call for a trade embargo, and the Chile Solidarity Campaign led a delegation to trade minister Michael Meacher to ask the government to act. But, as Meacher pointed out, no other country had imposed a trade boycott and Labour was not willing unilaterally to impose an embargo, which might threaten British jobs and businesses.

The Business Lobby, the FCO and Trade

To the irritation of British exporters, however, Labour refused to restore medium-term and long-term export guarantees. The Heath government had stopped guaranteeing export credit in 1972 during Allende's government, but even when the Chilean economy improved under Pinochet, Labour refused to restore them. This was clearly a political decision, not an economic one, although Labour did not announce this publicly. Labour came under increasing pressure from businesses and officials to restore export credits. Informal and semi-formal encounters between officials and business executives served to consolidate their shared antagonism to Labour's stance and officials repeatedly conveyed the concerns of the private sector to ministers. As early as 1974, when an FCO official attended a seminar on Chile organised by the Confederation of British Industry (CBI), he noted:

> British firms were becoming anxious about the effects on their businesses there as a result of the political situation and of the continued suspension of medium and long term cover.[52]

In the same year, an executive from one of the leading British insurance brokers operating in Chile, Antony Gibbs, met the FCO's Hugh Carless for lunch and gave him a list of firms that had lost business as a result of Labour's policies.[53] Among the companies that complained to the Board of Trade about the lack of export credit for Chile were: Stanton and Staveley iron works; Dave Lowey Ltd. (copper tube manufacturers), International Harvester tractor makers, Lazard Brothers and Co., Balfour Beatty, Simon Engineering (hydraulic platform makers), Bentley Engineering, Hunt and Moscrop tractor manufacturers, GEC and Racal Communications. In an exceptionally strongly-worded letter, a high-ranking official at the Board of Trade wrote to Edmund Dell, the trade secretary, in early 1978, urging him to lift restrictions on export credit:

> Except in times of war or when acting in support of mandatory UN sanctions, British policy has been to encourage the development of civil trade with all overseas countries, irrespective of their political philosophies or internal policies. This has been the clear-cut and politically defensible stance of successive administrations. To abandon it now would represent a fundamental change of policy in a direction contrary to our interest as a major trading nation.[54]

Dell, convinced of the case, recommended that cover be restored.[55] However, Foreign Secretary Owen, having just recommended that an export licence for the 'blacked' Rolls Royce engines be granted, felt the government should make no more concessions on Chile, an argument with which the cabinet agreed.[56] The Labour government did not relent on this decision despite receiving protests from Tory members of both Houses of Parliament and from the Chambers of Commerce of London, Glasgow and Birmingham.

Chile was a small market for Britain—accounting for 0.1% of British exports. If it had been a more important market, the business lobby might have been stronger and Labour might have relented on export credits. Labour had, in fact, accepted much of the business community's argument: ministers accepted that their policy towards Chile should not damage Britain's material interests; they respected contracts and allowed ordinary trade and investment to continue. However, given that that they were under strong counter-pressure from their own supporters and that the amount of lost business was relatively small, Labour resisted the business lobby's demands on export credits.

The Anglo-Chilean Business Lobby

The most vociferous opponent of Labour's policy towards Chile was the Anglo-Chilean business community based in Chile. Among the British companies that operated in Chile were: EMI, Antony Gibbs Holdings, Unilever, BAT, Reckitt & Colman, Shell and British Leyland, the state-owned British car-maker. Just after the coup, the British ambassador reported that British businessmen would be 'overjoyed' by the consolidation of the military regime.[57] British Leyland even decided to give the military junta four cars in September 1973 without realizing the outcry that this would cause at home. The gift was hastily withdrawn after pressure from London.

Just weeks after Wilson took office, the British Chamber of Commerce in Chile sent the prime minister an angry telegram complaining that the Labour government was allowing 'partisan interests' to hamper their members' business interest in Chile.[58] Six weeks later, the Chamber sent another telegram, this time with copies to the *Daily Telegraph*, the *Daily Mail*, the chairman of Rolls Royce and the leader of the opposition:

> We consider it our duty once again to communicate to you our grave apprehension for the future if the unfriendly attitude of certain sectors of your Government and of certain Trade Unions continues to prevail...
>
> We who have a far more intimate and unbiased knowledge of events in this country during the Allende regime and since the military take-over than most people outside Chile...must emphatically and authoritatively declare that many statements made about conditions in Chile are clearly based upon either misinformation or deliberate misrepresentation.[59]

Throughout Labour's time in office, the Anglo-Chilean business community vigorously lobbied the government to change its policy on Chile. Anglo-Chilean businessmen had frequent meetings and drinks at the embassy in Santiago and embassy officials reported their concerns to London.

The British ambassador, Reginald Secondé, echoed their views that there were business opportunities in Pinochet's Chile. In September 1973, he wrote: 'Now is the time to get in. If we delay too long, while we may not miss the bus, we are likely to have difficulty in finding a comfortable seat.'[60] A year later, when the scale of the repression had become apparent, he wrote: 'Politically, the Chilean Government's policies leave very much to be desired, but commercially Chile is worth watching.'[61]

Others in the Embassy held more trenchant views. Denis Amy, the commercial secretary, who became chargé d'affaires in 1978, said in an interview after he left his post:

> [Pinochet] was a much nicer man than anyone would tell you; he is not the wicked, big, bad wolf that they tell you about on television now even. It was clear that he was running a very good economy…The oppression was marginal and most important of all, he was a popular Governor…. the stupidity that is being talked by the media, the left-wing media about Pinochet is totally absurd.[62]

Sheila Cassidy

Even if ministers had been disposed to compromise, the shocking revelation that a British subject had been tortured in Chile hardened public opinion in 1975 and compelled the government to take tougher action on Chile. Sheila Cassidy was a British doctor working in Chile. On the night of 1 November 1975, Cassidy was tending to a sick nun at the house of a religious order in Santiago, when armed men burst in firing guns. Cassidy was blindfolded and bundled into a car. She was taken to an interrogation centre, where she was stripped of her clothes, tied to a metal bed-frame and given electric shocks. Her interrogators also repeatedly slapped her, touched her and subjected her to indecent remarks and innuendos.[63] She had been arrested for treating a wounded member of an outlawed armed opposition group. In the early hours of the morning, she was driven around Santiago, while her captors demanded she show them the house where she had treated him. She was then taken back to the interrogation centre where she was subjected once again to electric shocks. An electrode was placed in her vagina and a roving pincer electrode was used to apply current to other parts of her body.

Foreign Secretary Callaghan and his junior minister Ted Rowlands agreed that no retaliatory measures should be announced while Cassidy was in captivity in order not to jeopardize her release, but they asked the FCO to draw up a list of possible actions to be taken against Chile once she was free.[64] An official noted that '[Callaghan] is concerned that our reaction should be strong enough to justify itself to the mass of public opinion. It should also be swift so our actions do not appear to be dragged out of us in response to the pressures of public opinion.'[65] The FCO's Hugh Carless understood that Labour ministers would want a robust response, and suggested a series of possible actions, including a letter of protest to the Chilean government, the recall of the ambassador from Santiago and action at the UN.[66] Callaghan, pleased with this 'good piece of forward thinking', agreed to these three measures.[67]

At this stage, it was not decided whether the ambassador's recall should be temporary or permanent, or even, as Ted Rowlands proposed, whether diplomatic relations should be cut off altogether. However, a briefing by the FCO strongly opposed withdrawing the ambassador permanently and/or cutting off diplomatic relations. The FCO briefing accepted that this would be a 'dramatic gesture long demanded by the anti-Junta lobby', but argued that 'we should maintain links while there is the slightest chance of influencing these governments'. It noted that it would 'take us out of line with other like-minded states' and 'would imply the complete abandonment of UK material interests in Chile'.[68] Once again, gently steering ministers to take the more moderate path, officials advised them to defer a decision on both a permanent withdrawal and cutting diplomatic relations and instead, 'confine immediate action' to recalling the ambassador for consultations.

On 29 December, after two months of captivity, Sheila Cassidy was finally released. The next day, the British ambassador delivered a strongly worded protest from James Callaghan to the Chilean foreign minister, before he too boarded a flight back to London. For the first time, Callaghan publicly confirmed that Sheila Cassidy has been tortured and announced the withdrawal of the British ambassador.[69]

Callaghan's announcement met with the widespread approval from government supporters and a public horrified at the revelations of torture.[70] But Ambassador Secondé warned against taking any more drastic steps, saying: 'There is a danger of us being caught in a retaliatory spiral and inflicting damage on ourselves'.[71] Meanwhile, the British ambassador's wife, keen that her husband should be able to return to Chile, enlisted the help of Hernán Cubillos, a prominent Chilean businessman who had supported the coup and who had been owner of the right-wing daily *El Mercurio* during the Allende years. Cubillos went to see Pinochet and urged him to make a conciliatory gesture in response to the outcry over Cassidy. Illustrating the social ties between embassy officials and the right-wing Chilean elite, Mrs. Secondé wrote to her husband: 'Hernán adores England and did it for you…He has really done it after my telephone conversation with him as the most effective effort he can think of to get you back.'[72] Two years later, Hernán Cubillos became Pinochet's foreign minister.

But in England, the revelations of torture had caused such public revulsion that it was politically impossible to send the ambassador back to Santiago. After six months, ministers agreed his withdrawal should be made permanent. However, the cabinet, accepting the FCO's advice, decided not to break off diplomatic relations entirely, because 'the work our Embassy in Chile could do for prisoners and refugees was well known and valuable'.[73]

Not everyone, however, had sympathy for Sheila Cassidy. The British chargé affaires described a meeting of Anglo-Chilean businessmen at the British Embassy in Santiago:

> Most of the members of the group are pretty right wing, and enthusiastic supporters of the Junta: you can therefore imagine that we have had some fairly lively discussions of the Cassidy case and HMG's reactions resulting from it…
>
> Tom Peddar, the local representative of Antony Gibbs, said that he had been assured personally by two members of the Junta…[that there was no evidence Cassidy had been tortured]…I said…I and everyone else in the Embassy firmly believed her story.[74]

Among Britain's allies, the US government of Gerald Ford, was one of the few to have shown scepticism of Dr. Cassidy's story.[75]

The Disappearance of William Beausire

The Labour government was also confronted with the disturbing and perplexing disappearance of William Beausire, a case that illustrated the difficulties of dealing with a secretive and mendacious dictatorship. William Beausire was a 26-year-old business studies graduate, born in Chile to a British father and Chilean mother. He left Chile to seek work in Europe on a flight via Argentina on 2 November 1974. In Buenos Aires airport, a tannoy announcement called him to the information desk. He never arrived in Europe. On the same afternoon, his mother and sister were arrested in Chile, though later released. Despite having no involvement in politics, they were under suspicion because another of Beausire's sisters was married to a nephew of Salvador Allende, who was now a leading member of the opposition. Over the next seven months, several witnesses saw Beausire in Chilean prisons, but the Chilean authorities refused to admit he was even in the country. Piecing together the story from witnesses who signed sworn statements, his family discovered that he been detained in Buenos Aires airport by armed men who had beaten him and held him captive for three days. He had then been put on a plane back to Chile. He was held in several Chilean interrogation centres, including the notorious Villa Grimaldi torture house in Santiago. During his detention, he was subjected to torture, including having electric shocks applied to his body, sticks thrust up his rectum and being left hanging from the ceiling for long periods of time. After July 1975, he was never seen again.

After repeated requests for information about William Beausire, the Chilean Embassy in London gave the Foreign Office this response in February 1975: 'William Robert Beausire is not detained and it is presumed that he escaped to the Argentine.'[76]

A Foreign Office official wrote:

> This is somewhat puzzling as there are several well-substantiated reports indicating that he is indeed detained. HM Embassy are pursuing this as a matter of urgency, but it's difficult to insist on information in a case about which the Chileans deny all knowledge.[77]

The family contacted a distant cousin in Liverpool, who was bemused by what he heard. James Beausire sent his MP—who was the Speaker of the House of Commons—a letter written by William's sister, describing its contents as 'rather terrible and frightening.' James Beausire added, 'Although I may not agree with Francisca's politics, it is definitely a question of humanitarianism.'[78] The Speaker sent a telegram to the Foreign Office asking for enquiries to be made. But the British government's repeated requests for information were met with silence.

The ambassador even made a personal appeal to the Chilean foreign minister, but he reported back to London that 'they have made extensive enquiries and the interior ministry have no trace of him in any place of detention'.[79] The Foreign Office asked the family's solicitor to put together a dossier of evidence but when it was presented to the Chileans, it was dismissed. Over the following year, the embassy and FCO desk officer, Susan Binns, in London gathered statements from witnesses from as far afield as Caracas, trying to build a dossier of evidence that the Chileans could not refute.[80] But once again, when they submitted it to the Chilean foreign ministry, it was denounced as a collection of 'false rumours and…accusations which form part of a campaign aimed at denigrating Chile abroad.'[81] The Chileans denied that one of the interrogation centres even existed and described the claim that the Argentine and Chilean security forces had collaborated as 'absurd'. Declassified US government documents have since shown conclusively that the military regimes of Argentina, Chile, Brazil, Bolivia, Paraguay and Uruguay did, in fact, work together to track down and assassinate opponents as part of the so-called 'Operation Condor'.[82]

In June 1976, Foreign Secretary Anthony Crosland sent a letter with a dossier of evidence to the Chilean government. But the British were again disappointed with the Chilean response, which an FCO official described as 'totally negative, not only in content but also in spirit'.[83] The British government then submitted a formal case to the United Nations Human Rights Commission. Between 1975 and 1979, the Foreign Office also pressed the Argentine authorities for information, but the Argentine military regime maintained that the records were no longer available. A British lawyer, Geoffrey Bindman, went to Chile to present a petition of habeas corpus on behalf of the family in March 1979, but the Chilean magistrate simply returned the files on the grounds that there was no new evidence to examine. The case has never been solved.

The Foreign Office and the Chile Solidarity Campaign

Archival sources show that FCO officials were suspicious about the activities of British activists and left-wingers. The Chile Solidarity Campaign was formed in 1973 and by 1977 thirty trade unions had affiliated with it and nine Labour MPs had joined its executive committee. Its magazine, *Chile Lucha* [*Chile Fights*] sold 10,000 copies a year and it could attract high-profile speakers to its events, such as minister Judith Hart, trade union leader Jack Jones and the widow of President Salvador Allende, Hortensia Bussi Allende. A week after Labour had taken office, the FCO commissioned an intelligence service report on the Chile Solidarity Campaign to present to Callaghan. The spies' report highlighted the campaign's links with the Communist Party and 'the interest of the CSC in establishing local committees in port towns—presumably for the purpose of obstructing naval contracts and shipments of materials to Chile'.[84] The Deputy Under-Secretary at the Foreign Office remarked: 'I hope the Secretary of State may have time to glance at this before tomorrow's DOP [Defence and Oversea Policy Committee meeting]'.[85]

Diplomats even carried out their own observations first-hand; Christopher Crabbie, an official in the FCO's Latin America Department, reported in November 1974, how he and a Foreign Office colleague had 'donned our blue jeans and T-shirts' to attend a meeting of the Chile Solidarity Campaign 'as part of our continuing efforts to keep in touch with shades of opinion on Chile'.[86] On another occasion, Crabbie had lunch with the joint secretary of the campaign, Mike Gatehouse, remarking: 'I was surprised to discover he was a fellow Greats man, so he cannot be all bad, even though he does come from Balliol.'

The files of the Foreign Office show that many officials viewed the 'Chile lobby' with irritation and scorn. The head of the chancery in the British embassy complained of the Chile Solidarity Campaign's 'constant hyper-selective criticism', while an FCO official described an appeal on behalf of a political prisoner as 'one of the many ill-documented cases which the Chile Solidarity Campaign passes around to its sympathizers as ammunition with which to pepper our Ministers.'[87] He added: 'Most of these we treat with the reticence they deserve, but occasionally we have to…make enquiries when an MP or other influential person becomes involved.'[88]

However, the CSC did have the support of a large number of trade unions and MPs, making their demands hard for the FCO to ignore. Furthermore, ministers themselves had sympathy with the campaigners' objectives and officials were obliged to take this into account when recommending policies. It is noteworthy that on every FCO briefing and discussion paper on policy towards Chile, the views of the so-called 'Chile lobby' are considered. A fairer summary of the campaign's impact was given by the head of the FCO's South America department, John Ure, when he briefed the incoming Thatcher government on the Chile Solidarity Campaign:

> With Labour Party and trade union support, the campaign effectively organised and canalised much of the pressure on the…[Labour] Government to maintain an uncompromisingly hostile policy towards the Military regime in Chile…the Campaign does represent a significant body of opinion, and the issues they wish to raise are ones of genuine public concern.[89]

LABOUR AND THE MANDARINS

Throughout its time in office, the Foreign Office tried to steer Labour ministers away from the radicalism demanded by campaigners. Labour minister Ted Rowlands, in an interview some years later, described later how officials tried to water down Labour's Latin American human rights policy by continually 'putting up submissions and recommendations…saying "Don't you think we ought perhaps bend a little in this respect or give a little? Don't you think in the interests of trying to influence the events in Chile we might soften our attitude in this respect or that respect?"'[90]

This chapter has tried to illustrate these subtle ways in which officials sought to moderate Labour's policies. Rowlands even argued that British diplomats refused to follow ministers' wishes. 'There were a number of times when I was in the Office…when in fact I said: "No, we don't want to get on with that government,"' but embassy staff ignored those directives, Rowlands suggested, because it was their 'natural instinct' to try to get on with host country governments. As Geoffrey Moorhouse, a journalist who interviewed many FCO officials in the 1970s, noted, British diplomats became 'very impatient with an emphasis on morality purveyed by Labour politicians, and what they regard[ed] as naive notions about the brotherhood of man'.[91]

Rowlands did not think the difference in outlook between himself and officials reflected a 'political' or 'class' bias at the FCO, but was 'more to do with environmental background' and 'cultural perceptions', noting 'generally speaking people from Merthyr Tydfil do not envisage becoming Her Majesty's Ambassador in Paris'.[92] Although Rowlands did not regard this as a class difference, arguably his comments do fit a broader definition of social class and illustrate the gulf in perceptions between a largely southern-based public-school educated elite and a trade-union backed party, many of whose MPs came from the north of England, Wales or Scotland.

But despite this difference in outlook, FCO officials found, perhaps to their surprise, that Labour ministers had a basic pragmatism. Labour's concern that their policies should not harm British industry or commerce gave them common ground with officials that made a working relationship possible. The Labour leadership agreed with the Foreign Office that contracts should be respected and that the government should not interfere with private trade or investment. The head of the FCO's Latin America Department, Hugh Carless, a Sherborne-and-Cambridge-educated former intelligence officer, came to 'immensely admire' Callaghan's 'steadfastness' in standing up to party pressure.[93] Unlike some left-wing ministers, such as Benn and Richard Crossman, who complained of civil service obstruction, Callaghan, a former tax clerk who had been too poor to sit the entrance exam for university, had no criticism of the Foreign Office and its Oxbridge-educated diplomats. He reminisced in his memoirs that he had 'spent two happy years in this Rolls Royce of Departments', and praised FCO officials who in a crisis 'worked tirelessly and with skill'.[94] While respecting Foreign Office advice, Callaghan, did, however, make sure he took soundings from other quarters, including the trade unions and the CBI, arguing in a Fabian pamphlet that such matters should not 'be left as the sole prerogative of a few foreign policy "experts"'.[95] He also insisted on having his own political advisor, Tom McNally. David Owen and Judith Hart also ensured they had independent advisors who could give an alternative perspective to that of the FCO. Owen, at 38, the youngest foreign secretary since Eden, had a tense relationship with Foreign Office staff, clashing with them over Europe and South Africa, where he accused them of trying to water down his human rights policy. But there was less friction over Chile, which was a lower priority for Owen. Wilson also had a prickly relationship with the Foreign Office, but he too always made clear that his policy towards Chile should not damage Britain's material interests.[96]

Ministers, under pressure from campaigners and trade unionists, did, however, frequently go further than officials recommended: for example, by ending the Rolls Royce contract, refusing to reschedule debts, permanently withdrawing the ambassador, and refusing to restore export credits. As the years wore on, officials privately complained that Labour was treating Chile as a special case. As one FCO desk officer wrote:

> Ministers continue to take the firm view that Chile is wholly repugnant and thus merits the scale and intensity of criticism which is otherwise reserved only for a small handful of countries such as Uganda. Whether we shall be able to modify this attitude I do not know.[97]

It was not until the Conservatives returned to office that Foreign Office officials once again had ministers who, by upbringing, education and political inclination, were more in tune with their outlook.

Foreign Office officials, nevertheless, did make a genuine attempt to design and implement policies that reflected Labour's wishes, albeit while repeatedly warning them of the dangers of radicalism. The result was a Labour policy towards Chile that was very different from that of Heath's Conservative government. Labour stopped new arms sales, welcomed refugees, cut economic aid, refused to restore export credits and withdrew the British ambassador, a record of unilateral action that was without precedent in peacetime. The Wilson and Callaghan governments had intended to keep in step with their European allies and the United States, but ended up taking tougher economic and diplomatic sanctions than all the other major Western powers. Domestic pressures are the key to explaining policy-making in this period. Labour ministers had an ideological antipathy to the Pinochet dictatorship and were under constant pressure to take radical action from their own party members, trade unionists and human rights campaigners. The Labour government may not have gone as far as activists wanted, but in retrospect, those activists might well conclude that this was the most 'ethical' foreign policy a Labour government has ever adopted.

Notes

1. See note 7 in the Introduction.
2. Data for 1950–54 and 1960–64, comes from FCO sources, cited in Geoffrey Moorhouse, *The Diplomats: The Foreign Office Today* (London: Jonathan Cape, 1977), p. 59; The 1961 figure comes from Anthony Sampson, *Anatomy of Britain* (London: Hodder and Stoughton, 1962), p. 304; 1993 figure from: Ruth Dudley Edwards, True Brits (London: BBC Books, 1994), p. 91.
3. 'Chile'. Labour Party NEC statement, 30 September 1973, The National Archives (TNA): FCO7/2608.
4. Hugh Carless to Henry Hankey, 10 June 1974, TNA: FCO7/2606.
5. Alec Douglas-Home, *The Way the Wind Blows: An Autobiography* (Glasgow: Fontana, 1978); Edward Heath, *The Course of My Life: My Autobiography* (London: Hodder & Stoughton, 1998); Peter Carrington, *Reflect on Things Past: The Memoirs of Lord Carrington* (London: Collins, 1988); Nicholas Ridley, *My Style of Government: The Thatcher Years* (London: Hutchinson, 1991); James Callaghan, *Time and Chance* (London: Fontana, 1987); Harold Wilson, *Final Term: The Labour Government 1974–76* (London: Weidenfeld and Nicolson, 1979); Barbara Castle, *The Castle Diaries 1974–76* (London: Weidenfeld and Nicolson, 1980); and Tony Benn, *Against the Tide: 1973–76* (London: Hutchinson, 1989).
6. Judith Hart to Harold Wilson, 7 March 1974, TNA: FCO7/2605.
7. Hugh Carless to Mr. Elliot, 7 March 1974, TNA: FCO7/2605.
8. Ibid.
9. M.O'D.B. Alexander to PS/PUS, 8 March 1974, TNA: FCO7/2605.
10. Hart to James Callaghan, 8 March 1974, TNA: FCO7/2605.
11. Carless to Hankey and Duncan Watson, 11 March 1974, TNA: FCO7/2605.
12. Callaghan to Hart, 12 March 1974, TNA: FCO7/2605.
13. Carless to Hankey, 11 March 1974, TNA: FCO7/2605.
14. Note by Hankey, 11 March 1974, on Carless to Hankey, 11 March 1974, TNA: FCO7/2605.
15. Memo by Watson, 15 March 1974, TNA: FCO7/2605.
16. 'Policy Towards Chile', memorandum by the foreign secretary, DOP Committee, 19 March 1974, TNA: FCO7/2605. That this final draft is little changed from Carless's original is shown by the handwritten note on the memo by Duncan Watson, 15 March 1974, 'Policy Towards Chile', TNA: FCO7/2605, which reads: 'The Secretary of State agrees with this draft, subject to minor amendments he has noted on it'.
17. Ibid.

18. Mark Phythian, *The Politics of British Arms Sales Since 1964* (Manchester: Manchester University Press, 2000), p. 139.
19. DOP Committee, minutes, 21 March 1974, TNA: CAB 148/145.
20. Conclusions, Cabinet meeting, 28 March 1974, TNA: CAB 128/54/7.
21. Conclusions, Cabinet meeting, 9 April 1974, TNA: CAB 128/54/9.
22. Ibid.
23. Castle, p. 77.
24. 'Pouring in' quote from Castle, p. 64. 'Record of Conversation Between the Foreign Secretary and a Delegation from the Chile Solidarity Campaign', 30 April 1974, TNA: FCO7/2608.
25. Eric Heffer to Harold Wilson, 25 March 1974, TNA: PREM 16/202.
26. Wilson to Heffer, 2 May 1974, TNA: PREM 16/202.
27. R.G. Hayward to Callaghan, 27 June 1975, in TNA: PREM16/758.
28. Jack Jones to Wilson, 16 July 1975, TNA: PREM 16/758.
29. DOP Committee, minutes, 19 September 1975, TNA: CAB 148/154.
30. 'Chile's Debts to Great Britain', *El Cronista*, 20 October 1975, TNA: T383/11, 1975; 'Great Britain Demands Total Payment', *El Mercurio*, 21 October 1975, TNA: T383/11, 1975.
31. Note by Callaghan, 10 April 1974, Cabinet (CC (74) 10th), TNA: PREM 16/13.
32. D.S. Mitchell, Rolls Royce Ltd., to R.P. Maynard, 30 May 1978, TNA: FCO7/3490.
33. Note by David Stephen, 25 April 1978, TNA: FCO7/3490.
34. David Owen to Secretary of State for Industry, 11 May 1978, TNA: FCO7/3490.
35. Edmund Dell to Owen, 22 May 1978, TNA: FCO7/3490.
36. Owen to Callaghan, 14 June 1978, TNA: FCO7/3490.
37. Reginald Secondé to FCO, 3 June 1974, TNA: FCO7/2605; Secondé, to FCO, 11 June 1974, TNA: FCO7/2606.
38. P.G.P.D. Fullerton to W.R. McQuillan, 27 June 1974, TNA: FCO7/2614.
39. D.F. Smedley to G. Davies, 15 May 1978, TNA: FCO7/3490.
40. Note by David Stephen, 25 April 1978, TNA: FCO7/3490.
41. J.B. Ure to Mr. Hall, 28 June 1978, TNA: FCO7/3490.
42. DOP Committee, minutes, 10 July 1978, TNA: CAB 148/147.
43. Bob Sommerville and John Keenan, East Kilbride shop stewards, said they were taken by surprise during the bank holiday weekend and had no time to organise a protest: interview with the author, 9 April 2014. See also Beckett, *Pinochet*, p. 154.
44. Ure to Mr. Hall, 2 October 1978, TNA: FCO7/3490.
45. Bernard Donoughue, *Downing Street Diary with Harold Wilson in No. 10* (London: Jonathan Cape, 2005), pp. 315–316.

46. Secondé to Mr. Edmonds, FCO, 21 November 1974, TNA: FCO7/2619.
47. Wilson, Callaghan and Healey met to take this decision on 24 February 1975. It was later ratified by cabinet. Memo from P. Wright, 10 Downing Street, to A. Acland, FCO, 24 February 1975, TNA: PREM 16/758.
48. The prime minister had opposed attending an informal meeting of Chilean creditors in April 1975 because: 'Our representative would be bound to speak strongly on the human rights issue and we would risk renewed American displeasure at our activity...' Private Secretary, Kingston, to FCO, 28 April 1975, TNA: PREM 16/758.
49. UK outward direct investment overseas attributable to UK companies, book value of net assets by country 1974–84 (figures for 1971–81 exclude oil companies, banks and insurance companies). *Business Monitor MO4, Census of Overseas Assets* (London: HMSO, 1984).
50. Authorised foreign direct investment (%). *Inversión Extranjera y Empresas Transnacionales en la Economía de Chile (1974–1989), Estudios e Informes de la Cepal, 86* (Santiago: ECLAC, 1992), p. 67.
51. Michael D. Wilkinson, 'The Chile Solidarity Campaign and British Government Policy towards Chile, 1973–1990' in *European Review of Latin American and Caribbean Studies*, 52 (1992), 57–74.
52. Fullerton to Carless, 15 July 1974, TNA: FCO7/2614.
53. G.B. Worne, Antony Gibbs Holdings, to Carless, 20 November 1974, TNA: FCO7/2614.
54. K. Taylor to Secretary of State, DoT, 27 January 1978, TNA: BT 241/2762.
55. Dell to Callaghan, 30 May 1978, TNA: BT 241/2762.
56. Owen to Callaghan, 14 June 1978, TNA: FCO7/3490.
57. Secondé to Hankey, 19 September 1973, TNA: FCO7/2412.
58. Chairman, Council and Members of the British Chamber of Commerce in Chile to Wilson, 30 March 1974, TNA: PREM 16/13.
59. Text of telegram sent on 5 June to the Prime Minister by the British Chamber of Commerce in Chile in Secondé to FCO, 16 June 1974, TNA: FCO7/2606.
60. Secondé to Hankey, 19 September 1973, TNA: FCO7/2412.
61. 'Britain's Commercial Interest in Chile', report by Secondé, 11 April 1974, TNA: FCO7/2614.
62. Interview with Denis Amy, 1998, British Diplomatic Oral History Programme (BDOHP), Churchill College, Cambridge, p. 25.
63. Secondé to FCO, 18 December 1975, TNA: FCO7/2793.
64. J.R. Young to Mr. Collins, 10 December 1975, TNA: FCO7/2792.
65. Dales to Young, 16 December 1975, TNA: FCO7/2792.
66. Carless to Mr. McNally, 12 December 1975, TNA: FCO7/2793.
67. Dales to Rowlands, 15 December 1975, TNA: FCO7/2793.

68. Briefing by Latin America Department, FCO, 17 December 1975, TNA: FCO7/2793.
69. 'Statement to be made by the Secretary of State following the release of Dr. Sheila Cassidy', TNA: FCO7/2792.
70. Cabinet, minutes, 17 June 1976, TNA: CAB 128/59/10.
71. Secondé to Carless, 8 January 1976, TNA: FCO7/3802.
72. Extract from a letter from Mrs. Secondé dated 5 February 1976, TNA: FCO7/3082.
73. Cabinet, minutes, 17 June 1976, TNA: CAB 128/58/10, 1976.
74. D.K. Haskell to FCO, 13 April 1976, TNA: FCO7/3078.
75. A.J. Collins to Mr. Tilling, 26 January 1976, TNA: FCO7/3028.
76. Aide Memoire, Chilean Embassy, London, 14 February 1975, TNA: FCO7/2786.
77. Crabbie to Mr. Guest, 21 February 1975, FCO7/2786.
78. H.J. Beausire, Liverpool to Selwyn Lloyd MP, 10 January 1975, FCO7/2786.
79. Telegram no. 92, Secondé to FCO, 3 March 1975, FCO7/2786.
80. Note by Collins on Binns to Collins, 15 July 1975, TNA: FCO7/2786.
81. Statement by MFA to HM Embassy, 29 August 1975, TNA: FCO7/2787.
82. Grace Livingstone, *America's Backyard* (London: Zed Books, 2009), p. 64.
83. Collins to PS/Mr. Rowlands, 12 November 1976, TNA: FCO7/3079.
84. Carless to Hankey and Watson, 19 March 1974, TNA: FCO7/2608.
85. Note by Watson on Carless to Hankey and Watson, 19 March 1974, TNA: FCO7/2608.
86. Summerscale from Crabbie, 28 November 1974, TNA: FCO7/2608.
87. Haskell to A.J. Sindall, 14 February 1978, TNA: FCO7/3482. The comment also refers to the attitude of the UN Ad Hoc Working Group.
88. Crabbie to Summerscale, 1 April 1975, TNA: FCO7/2786.
89. Ure to Hall, FCO, 13 August 1979, TNA: FCO7/3611.
90. Ted Rowlands interview in Simon Jenkins and Anne Sloeman, *With Respect, Ambassador: An Inquiry into the Foreign Office* (London: BBC Books, 1985), p. 105.
91. Moorhouse, *The Diplomats*, p. 157.
92. Rowlands interview in Jenkins and Sloeman, p. 105.
93. Interview with Hugh Carless, 2002, BDOHP, Churchill College, Cambridge, p. 32.
94. Callaghan, *Time and Chance*, pp. 294, 336.
95. James Callaghan, *Challenges and Opportunities for British Foreign Policy* (London: Fabian Society, 1975), p. 1. See also Theakston, *British Foreign Secretaries*.
96. See Wilson to the Lord Bridges, 18 May 1974, TNA: PREM 16/13.
97. Sindall to Haskell, 10 February 1978, TNA: FCO7/3482.

CHAPTER 5

Tea with a Dictator: Mrs. Thatcher and the General (1979–1982)

The Conservative government of Margaret Thatcher dramatically changed policy towards Chile. An ambassador was reinstated, the arms embargo was lifted and export credit guarantees were restored. The special programme for welcoming Chilean refugees was closed and funding for Chilean exiles to study in the UK was stopped—although the government did later fund a programme for exiles to return to Chile. The policy of ostracizing the regime was abandoned; four months after coming to office, Foreign Secretary Lord Carrington met the Chilean foreign minister in London, the first time a member of the cabinet had received a Chilean minister since the coup. Trade minister Cecil Parkinson visited Santiago a year later. A British defence attaché to Chile was appointed in 1981 to encourage arms sales. After Chile helped Britain in the Falklands war, Britain further loosened restrictions on weapons sales and helped to undermine United Nations' efforts to investigate human rights in Chile.

Margaret Thatcher herself did not meet Pinochet until 1994, after she had stepped down as prime minister. They met at a drinks reception in the British embassy in Santiago, where they became friends. Pinochet had tea at Baroness Thatcher's house in London, ten days before he was arrested in October 1998.[1] A Spanish judge was seeking Pinochet's extradition on 95 counts of torture, one count of conspiracy to torture, and one count of murder, and he was held under house arrest in Britain for a year and a half while the British Law Lords examined whether he could be extradited. The Lords ruled that he could be extradited to

Spain, but the Labour Home Secretary, Jack Straw, eventually decided that Pinochet could return to Chile on the grounds of ill-health. Thatcher became his most high-profile defender, speaking in his favour in the House of Lords, writing a letter to *The Times* and visiting him in the Surrey mansion where he lived while he was under house arrest. Her visit was televised live on the BBC and she thanked him for helping Britain in the Falklands and 'bringing democracy to Chile'.[2] Writing some years later in her book *Statecraft*, Thatcher made clear that she thought any abuses Pinochet may have committed were justifiable:

> I do not know how I would have felt if I had thought he was guilty of great crimes. I would still have considered his arrest wrong...But I never had to wrestle with that problem because although I could not be sure about every detail of every accusation, I was and am convinced that General Pinochet by his actions turned Chile into the free and prosperous country we see today.[3]

Margaret Thatcher had shown an interest in Pinochet's Chile since attending the seminars of the new-right think tank, the Institute of Economic Affairs (IEA), while she was leader of the opposition in the 1970s. At the IEA, she met Alan Walters, an economist working for the World Bank, who became her chief economic advisor in 1981–1983. Walters had met Pinochet in Chile in the 1970s and continued to visit the country throughout the 1980s. Walters helped convert Thatcher to monetarist policies and explained to her that monetarism was being successfully applied in Pinochet's Chile. He said in an interview later:

> Everyone hated Chile—except Margaret. I'd probably talked to her about it for the first time in the 1970s. She knew I'd been there, and she asked me about it...She admired Pinochet for putting Allende out of office.[4]

Thatcher was also a supporter of the anti-trade union lobby group, the National Association for Freedom (NAFF), attending the organisation's inaugural subscription dinner in 1977. At NAFF, she met Robert Moss, editor of the *Economist*'s *Foreign Report*. Moss had written a book called *Collapse of Democracy* in 1975, which warned that the power of the unions in Britain was leading to socialist totalitarianism, and argued that 'authoritarian' government was preferable to totalitarianism. He painted a grim picture of Britain's future, where a 'Working People's Government' had replaced Buckingham Palace with a 'Ministry for Equality' and the Royal

Family had fled to New Zealand. In a chapter on 'Lessons from Chile', he argued that the Chilean middle class were justified in overthrowing Allende because they had a 'right to resist tyranny'.[5] In March 1973, six months before the military takeover, Moss had written an article for *SEPA*, a CIA-funded journal aimed at the Chilean armed forces, entitled: 'An English Recipe for Chile—military control'. After Allende's overthrow, he wrote a book justifying the coup, *Chile's Marxist Experiment*. The Chilean government bought 10,000 copies of it and distributed it through its embassies in Washington and London.[6] Thatcher hired Moss as a speech writer and he wrote her famous anti-Soviet 'Iron Lady' speech, which she gave in Kensington Town Hall in 1976. She warmly praised Moss in her autobiography.[7] Thatcher also met Brian Crozier at NAFF and he became her unofficial adviser on security and intelligence between 1976 and 1979, frequently visiting her at her flat in Chelsea.[8] Crozier was the director of the Institute for the Study of Conflict, which specialized in studying trade union 'subversion' in Britain. Crozier had written a book warning against 'the bombardment of our minds with subversive poisons' in 1970 and, in a speech to military officers in Harrogate in the late 1970s, had called for an army takeover in Britain.[9] Crozier became a confidant of Pinochet, helping him draft a constitution.

Margaret Thatcher devotes two separate paragraphs to praising Pinochet's economic policies in the first volume of her autobiography. Perhaps this is not surprising because most of her memoir was ghost-written by her longstanding special advisor, Robin Harris. During her premiership, Harris had been the Director of the Conservative Research Department and a member of the prime minister's Policy Unit. Harris went on to pen a pamphlet, *A Tale of Two Chileans: Pinochet and Allende*, published by Chilean Supporters Abroad when Pinochet was arrested in London. Harris claimed that Pinochet was the victim of a 'politically motivated kidnapping'.[10] His pamphlet is a staunch defence of Pinochet's coup against 'Marxist terrorism' and claims Pinochet brought 'order, stability, legality and prosperity' to Chile. Harris wrote: 'democracy had…first been saved and then later fully restored—thanks to the vilified "dictator" against whom the vituperation still continues unabated.' Writing of the human cost of the coup, he added: 'You can't make an omelette without breaking eggs… Some eggs—too many, probably—were also broken under Pinochet, but surely Latin America never saw a larger omelette.' Thatcher declared Harris's pamphlet 'excellent'.[11]

A number of Thatcher's other associates were admirers of Pinochet. Paul Johnson was a former editor of the centre-left magazine, *New Statesman*, who in 1977 became a convert to the new-right cause and went on to become a *Daily Mail* columnist and a speech-writer for Thatcher. In 1998, Johnson chaired a news conference for Chilean Supporters Abroad, in which he declared that 'the demonization of General Pinochet is the most successful, mendacious propaganda exercise ever carried out in the twentieth century.'[12] There was 'not a single scrap of evidence' linking Pinochet to human rights atrocities, he claimed.[13] It was at this news conference that Norman Lamont, a Thatcher protégé who had gone on to become chancellor of the exchequer, described the former dictator as a 'good, brave and honourable soldier'.[14] Conrad Black, the owner of the *Telegraph* and a friend of Thatcher's, also came to Pinochet's defence, visiting him for lunch while he was under house arrest.[15] Tim Bell, the advertising executive behind Thatcher's three successful election campaigns, including the famous 'Labour isn't working' slogan in 1979, was knighted by Thatcher and later became her official spokesman. Bell masterminded a £200,000 public relations campaign to rehabilitate Pinochet's image while he was in Britain. 'Our strategy has been to communicate with opinion makers in order to counter 23 years of Marxist propaganda,' said Bell.[16]

But in 1979, when Margaret Thatcher came to office, Chile was not an important issue for mainstream Conservative politicians, even those on the right. The right-wing MP, Nicholas Ridley, for example, hated being sent to deal with such a backwater:

> I confess to being bitterly disappointed at finding myself dealing with the problems of Latin America and the Caribbean from the Foreign Office, where she sent me in 1979, while the Cabinet was packed with supporters of the old consensus, Heathite policies.[17]

Whereas the Labour cabinet had discussed Chile many times, it was never raised in Thatcher's cabinet meetings. Before the Falklands war, the Oversea and Defence Committee, a sub-committee of the cabinet, discussed Chile only once—to approve the reinstatement of the ambassador. While this reflects the fact that there was less dissension within the party and less disagreement between officials and ministers on Chile during the Thatcher years, it is also an indication that other matters were regarded as more important. Finding a settlement in Rhodesia was by far the most pressing matter for Foreign Secretary Lord Carrington in the early years of the administration. The British colony was wracked by civil war, as black opposition movements sought to overthrow the white minority regime of Ian Smith, which had unilaterally declared independence. Britain brokered talks that led to the Lancaster House Agreement of December 1979 in which all sides agreed to establish a new constitution and participate in elections. The white minority was guaranteed 20% of the seats in parliament and land reform was postponed for ten years. Rhodesia raised strong emotions in the Conservative party—right-wing backbenchers who thought the foreign secretary had sold out the white minority held up 'Hang Carrington' banners after the Lancaster House agreement was signed.[18] Negotiating a rebate from the European Economic Community was another key issue that took ministers' time and animated Tory MPs.

But the issue that most gripped politicians and the country in 1979–1981 was the impact of the Thatcher government's free-market, monetarist policies. These marked a sharp break from the consensus-seeking, state-led approach of all post-war governments. In the early years of Thatcher's administration, these monetarist policies provoked a sharp recession, business bankruptcies, high unemployment and inner-city riots. Certainly, domestic politics dominated most of the prime minister's time, although she also grappled with the republican hunger strikes in Northern Ireland, the EEC rebate debate and the invasion of Afghanistan. Chile was far lower down the agenda and while she approved the main changes in Chile policy, the prime minister was not involved in the detail.

The Foreign Office had for some time wanted a change in policy towards Chile. In the latter years of the Labour government, officials increasingly complained in internal memos that Labour was unfairly singling out Chile, when other countries' human rights records were equally bad. It was an anomaly that Chile lacked an ambassador, they fretted. Meanwhile, British exporters had been lobbying hard for a renewal of export credits and the lifting of the arms embargo. While there was a broad consensus within the civil and diplomatic services on the need to soften policy towards the Pinochet regime, the government departments with the closest links to the private sector advocated the most rapid change. The Department of Trade and the defence sales department of the Ministry of Defence, therefore, lobbied most vigorously for trade restrictions to be lifted. The Foreign Office, while favouring change, advocated a more gradual approach, one that would not alienate Britain's overseas allies. It was aware that the United States, under President Jimmy Carter (1977–1981) was putting greater emphasis on human rights in Latin America. It was also concerned that if Britain weakened sanctions on the Pinochet regime, at the same time as seeking a compromise in Rhodesia, the UK's relations with Commonwealth countries could be soured. As Anthony Parsons, Deputy Under Secretary at the FCO, put it: 'We would be foolish to present the Third World and others with a gratuitous stick with which to beat us if we are already being heavily clobbered over Southern Africa.'[19]

Within the Conservative party there was a spectrum of views; while many on the right were admirers of Pinochet, others thought that the human rights abuses perpetrated by the regime were distasteful, but not sufficient to justify jeopardizing British commercial interests by maintaining sanctions. Most Conservatives thought Allende was responsible for provoking the coup and admired Pinochet's economic success. There was no disagreement within the party on what measures should be adopted, but there were differences between right-wing radicals and the more moderate 'wets' on the timing and presentation of the policy. Nicolas Ridley, a junior foreign minister in the Foreign Office and a Thatcherite, wanted a rapid reversal of Labour's policy, while the foreign secretary, Lord Carrington, and his second-in-command, the Lord Privy Seal, Ian Gilmour, who were both 'wets', favoured the more gradual approach advocated by the Foreign Office.

The Conservatives were sympathetic to lobbying from British exporters and manufacturers because they had a similar ideological outlook. Moreover, social ties between Conservatives, business leaders, diplomats and members of the Chilean elite gave those opposed to sanctions informal access to policy makers. The Thatcher government was less receptive to campaigning by trade unions and human rights groups and these organisations now had far less influence because they had no institutional links to the governing party. Their allies in the Labour party could do little because the Thatcher administration had a comfortable majority of 43 seats in the House of Commons. Nevertheless, officials did carefully monitor the activities of the Chile Solidarity Campaign and human rights groups, and attempt to gauge how much support they had. Campaigners were not able to prevent the government from softening its policy towards Pinochet, but they did slow the pace of change, because ministers and the Foreign Office were anxious to avoid a public outcry.

Restoring the Ambassador

Five days after the Conservatives won the 1979 election, the FCO's South America Department wrote a briefing paper on Chile for the new government. It pointed out that the previous Government had taken 'exceptionally strong action' to demonstrate disapproval of the Pinochet regime.[20] It recommended that export credit guarantees be restored to Chile and included an annex of potential business put at risk in Chile by lack of Export Credit Guarantee Department (ECGD) support, with a list of British companies that had lost deals in Chile. The FCO briefing also asked ministers to consider whether an ambassador should be restored and whether 'in due course' the arms embargo should be lifted. Nicholas Ridley, the minister with responsibility for Latin America in the FCO, responded by saying:

> My feelings are that economic and diplomatic sanctions are not a good weapon for securing political changes: they have been used as a means of expressing political dislike (in which case I could make up a very different list to our predecessors!). I'd rather drop the lot.[21]

Ridley asked officials to prepare a note about human rights under Allende and to compare Pinochet's Chile with the USSR, Vietnam and Tanzania. 'I think we would find Chile far from bottom of the league,' he wrote.[22]

Meanwhile, Trade Secretary John Nott wrote to the foreign secretary, Lord Carrington, saying that the Export Guarantee Advisory Council, a body of bankers and industrialists which advised the government on trade, had, 'because of growing pressure from…UK exporters', recommended that export trade credits be restored.[23] Ridley, keen to see all restrictions on the Pinochet regime dropped as soon as possible, recommended to Carrington that both ECGD cover and an ambassador be restored at the same time. No one in government was opposed to lifting restrictions on trade with Chile and medium-term export credit guarantees were restored on 8 June 1979, a month after the Tories came to office.

The 'wets' were more cautious, however, about restoring an ambassador; Sir Ian Gilmour, Ridley's superior at the Foreign Office, thought 'the question should be played long given the need not to ruffle feathers on Rhodesia.'[24] In a briefing for ministers, the head of the Foreign Office's South America department, John Ure, recognised that there would be 'vocal criticism' if an ambassador was restored, but suggested that if the Chilean government were prepared to give an apology for the torture of Sheila Cassidy and agree to make genuine enquires about the disappearance of William Beausire, this would 'take the wind out of the sails of critics'.[25] Ridley met the Chilean chargé d'affaires in London in June 1979—the first time a British minister had met the chargé since the coup. He told him that the government wanted to have full relations with Chile, but 'there were domestic political reasons for taking things slowly'.[26] The Chilean government 'could help in defusing the situation', he added, by taking action on the Beausire and Cassidy cases. The chargé asked if these demands would be followed by others, but Ridley said they would not. 'It was simply that, in view of the climate of opinion, it would be easier for us if there were something to put forward as a reason for improving relations.'[27]

But when Carrington wrote to the Chilean foreign minister in July 1979, expressing willingness 'in principle' to normalise relations but asking for a 'proper explanation' of Sheila Cassidy's treatment and an 'adequate account' of William Beausire's fate, the reply from the Chilean government was uncompromising; they refused to accept Cassidy had been tortured or that Beausire had ever been detained in Chile.[28] There then began months of semantic wrangling over a statement on the Beausire and Cassidy cases. The Chileans eventually agreed to state that they regretted any improper treatment Cassidy 'may have' received and that they would re-open the Beausire investigation in the light of new evidence. The Foreign Office realised they would never get genuine cooperation in resolving these cases from the Pinochet regime and their aim in getting a statement, was, as the FCO's John Ure said, to 'disarm criticism' at home over the re-instatement of ambassadors.[29] A telegram from the FCO to the British embassy in Santiago makes this clear:

> Whereas the Chileans seem to think an agreement to the exchange of ambassadors is contingent on their giving us public satisfaction on these two cases [Cassidy and Beasuire]... our real concern is to be able to use these apologies in our presentation ex post facto of an announcement that we have agreed to the exchange of ambassadors.[30]

Or, as Nicholas Ridley told the Chilean chargé d'affaires:

When the exchange of ambassadors was announced, left-wing opinion in the UK would immediately ask what concessions the Chileans had made in the cases of Cassidy and Beausire. This made it essential for him to have a new piece of paper.[31]

The Pinochet government never accepted that Sheila Cassidy was tortured, nor did it accept that Beausire had been detained in Chile. The regime's judicial investigation into Beausire's fate was shelved a few months after ambassadors were exchanged.

Lord Carrington wrote to the prime minister in September 1979, recommending, in principle, that ambassadors be exchanged but noting that 'the problem as I see it, is one of presentation and timing'.[32] Presentation was important because the reinstatement of ambassadors would 'attract criticism in Parliament, from trade unions, from the churches and from organisations like Amnesty International'. Or, as the *Daily Mail* put it a few days later: 'It is clearly on the cards that the Government will shortly restore our embassy in Chile…and rent-a-mob is already on the rampage with protests and boycotts.'[33] The main issues affecting the timing, apart from the Cassidy-Beausire cases, were, said Carrington, the Rhodesia conference and US-Chilean tensions resulting from the assassination in Washington of Orlando Letelier, a former minister in Allende's government, and his assistant Ronni Moffitt, a US citizen. The US temporarily withdrew their ambassador to Santiago in October 1979, in protest at Chile's refusal to extradite the secret service officers suspected of the murder. The cabinet's Defence and Oversea Policy Committee agreed to reinstate ambassadors but to 'proceed cautiously in timing and presentation'.[34]

But the Conservatives were also under pressure from the private sector and their own right wing, as one FCO official noted: 'The City, exporters and Conservative opinion think we should send back an ambassador before our trading position deteriorates further.'[35] Trade minister Cecil Parkinson wrote to the prime minister saying the sooner diplomatic relations and the arms sales were restored, the better this would be for British exporters.[36] Dennis Amy, the British chargé d'affaires in Santiago, said that he had been guest of honour at a lunch given by 'a club of the 20 most influential businessmen' in Chile, who regarded the lack of a British ambassador as a 'slight'.[37] Nicholas Ridley encouraged Conservative backbenchers to put pressure on the government to hurry events along. When Sir Frederic Bennett, a right-wing MP, offered to raise the matter in Parliament, Ridley told him 'such pressure would help: at the moment the lobbying was all coming from the left-wing.'[38]

Meanwhile, Conservative ministers also ensured they sent positive signals to the Pinochet regime. Carrington met the Chilean foreign minister, Hernán Cubillos, in September 1979. Nicholas Ridley attended a drinks reception in honour of the Chilean finance minister, Sergio de Castro, who had been invited to visit London in November. Cecil Parkinson also met de Castro and 'congratulated the Chileans on their economic success'.[39] De Castro's meeting with Industry Secretary Keith Joseph was even more cordial; according to the Chilean chargé d'affaires, it ran overtime and Joseph accompanied the Chilean in his car to the House of Commons so that they could continue talking.[40]

Once the Lancaster House talks were over, Carrington recommended to the prime minister, in December 1979, that ambassadors be exchanged. Margaret Thatcher agreed and the decision was announced in Parliament in January 1980, prompting 300 letters of protest from trade union branches, Amnesty International supporters and 50 MPs.[41] The leader of the Transport and General Workers Union, Moss Evans, and Dame Judith Hart led a delegation to the Foreign Office in protest. The Conservatives had expected a political outcry and had already discounted it.[42] In February 1980, John Heath was sent as the new ambassador to Chile. The Pinochet-supporting media in Chile were delighted and his arrival was given 'lavish front page treatment'.[43]

Lifting the Arms Embargo on Chile

The Conservatives and the Foreign Office also agreed on the desirability of lifting the arms embargo, but the Chile solidarity movement was sufficiently strong to force them once again to consider the question of timing and presentation. The most enthusiastic support for lifting the embargo came from the defence sales department of the Ministry of Defence, which was being lobbied heavily by arms manufacturers. An FCO official wrote in July 1979: 'The MOD have told us that an increasing number of companies with good defence sales prospects in Chile are now seeking an indication of the Government's position.'[44] Trade minister Parkinson also wrote to the prime minister saying that, 'from the strict trade point of view the sooner the embargo on arms can be relaxed the better,' although he recognised that it was a controversial issue and the timing needed to be considered carefully.[45] Nicholas Ridley had no objection to lifting the arms embargo in principle, writing: 'Restoring ambassadors is not condoning the regime…Arms sales are a very different matter. They *do* imply condonation… but subject to our usual criteria, and actions in comparable cases, they could be resumed after ambassadors are exchanged.'[46]

But the FCO and moderate Tories such as Carrington and Gilmour, while agreeing in principle about the need to begin selling arms again, were more cautious about the timing. 'We shall need…perhaps to restrain the enthusiasm of our colleagues in Defence Sales Department,' wrote one official.[47] 'Arms sales to Chile would cause a major outcry not only from Labour Party supporters but from Liberals and others for whom this may be a touchstone of the Government's attitude to human rights. We shall also have to bear in mind possible reactions of the Argentines, Peruvians and the US Government.'[48]

A large part of the FCO's concern was the question of presentation. When the new ambassador, John Heath, arrived in Santiago, he made a point of raising human rights questions with the president, the foreign minister, the minister of interior and a host of other officials. In a telegram to the FCO in London he wrote:

> Having raised these issues on so many occasions at Ministerial level should, I imagine, be enough to satisfy the human rights lobby for a while. But they are bound to be asking sooner or later what the results of my enquiries have been. If I am then supposed to go through the exercise all over again I may well receive a less tolerant hearing [from the Chileans]…It may be that at this point you should take the firm line that we have done what we can but there is genuinely no more mileage to be gained e.g. from the Cassidy/Beausire cases. If so, it will be a relief to me, though I can well understand if the decision is to continue.[49]

He added:

> Frankly I doubt whether any of these cases are likely to be resolved to our satisfaction and certainly not so long as Pinochet is still in the saddle. And we do of course have the wider consideration of the future of Anglo Chilean relations to take into account which suggest to me at least that the bilateral struggle on human rights cases should not in our own interests be continued indefinitely.

In London, FCO official Robin Fearn, wrote on the ambassador's telegram: 'Mr Heath has done well: but need not over-egg henceforth. We are through the immediate problem on ambassadors.'[50] Another FCO official then noted: 'But when the arms embargo is lifted we shall want to show some recent HMA [Her Majesty's Ambassador] effort—i.e. perhaps a follow up in late June/July.'[51]

A month later Fearn wrote to the ambassador:

> We have much admired the persistence and skill with which you have, since your arrival, pursued human rights matters at a high level...This has enabled us to cope very adequately with the lobby's reactions to the fact of the exchange of ambassadors...
>
> We have no illusions that this will produce results but we must clearly put Ministers in the best position possible to defend the embargo decision...
>
> When the hurdle of the arms embargo is cleared, however, it should not be necessary for you to devote so much of your time to human rights. I agree that it should not become an incubus, detracting from your pursuit of our other more positive interests in Chile. We have no wish to dwell negatively on Chile's past.[52]

Another example of the FCO viewing human rights representations in a purely presentational way, to smooth the passage for lifting the arms embargo, came in July 1980, when the ambassador, after a long conversation with the Chilean foreign minister about promoting British business in Chile, mentioned the Beausire and Cassidy cases. An FCO official wrote on the ambassador's despatch. 'Good work by Mr Heath. The discussion with Rojas on human rights, Cassidy/Beausire etc. will be most timely for use in the post-arms embargo flurry'.[53] Another official agreed. 'Excellently timed,' he wrote.[54]

Like the defence ministry in London, the embassy staff in Santiago were lobbied by arms manufacturers and sometimes socialised with them. As soon as the new British ambassador arrived in post in Chile, the radar manufacturer Plessey asked to host a reception in the British embassy. The new ambassador felt this was inappropriate but told them he would be happy to attend a Plessey drinks reception held elsewhere. The British chargé d'affaires, Dennis Amy, showed less restraint, inviting the sales director of the warship manufacturer, Vosper International, to a 'pleasant party' at his house in March 1980.⁵⁵ The Vosper executive was in Santiago to offer design consultancy services to the Chilean armed forces, hoping for a spin-off arms contract that would be 'significant enough to bring to HMG's attention the commercial disadvantage of the embargo'.⁵⁶ Amy had no doubts about the need to lift the embargo. In a despatch to London, he reported a conversation with three Chilean admirals: 'All of them were of course talking arms and I find it very difficult to completely turn them down for ever and I do not think that is entirely in our interests...I am painfully conscious of the money we are losing and of the fact the longer we go on with our present attitude, the more difficult it is ever to get back again.'⁵⁷

Five months after John Heath had been posted to Santiago, the head of the FCO's South America Department, Robin Fearn, judged that 'the controversy over ambassadors has...abated', and recommended it was now time to act. With the approval of the whole cabinet, Carrington announced the lifting of the arms embargo on 22 July 1980. Two days later, two British arms salesmen from the Ministry of Defence touched down in Santiago.⁵⁸

When the Thatcher government came to office, both the FCO and the Conservatives thought it was right to lift the arms embargo on both commercial and ideological grounds (i.e. that the Pinochet dictatorship was no worse than other regimes to which Britain sold arms). Only the timing and presentation of the decision was a matter of debate. Human rights campaigners did not prevent a change in policy, but did slow the pace of change because officials and politicians were sensitive to how their measures were perceived and tried to time announcements for when they were least likely to provoke anger.

Promoting Arms Sales to the Pinochet Regime

Less than a month after the arms embargo had been lifted, trade minister Cecil Parkinson visited Chile, the first visit by a British minister since the coup. Parkinson met General Pinochet and extolled the economic success of the Chilean regime. The British ambassador reported:

> Mr Parkinson said that he had also been impressed by the skill and intelligence of the economic team which was directing the Chilean economy

and by the high growth rate; he commented that some of the businessmen in his party had begun to have feelings that they would like to operate within the Chilean system of free enterprise, despite what Mrs Thatcher was doing in Britain.[59]

Pinochet said he admired Mrs. Thatcher, commenting that 'she was both soft and hard, with perhaps the emphasis on the hard part.' 'In passing', the ambassador added, 'Mr Parkinson…referred momentarily to human rights'.[60]

Parkinson's visit was the start of a sustained effort by the Conservatives to increase trade with the Pinochet dictatorship. An important component of this was arms sales. As soon as the arms embargo had been lifted, the Ministry of Defence began to press for a British defence attaché to be restored in Santiago:

> It is imperative that we improve our links with the Chilean Services if our defence industry is to be seriously considered for new contracts. In a military society such as exists in Chile we strongly believe that our contacts and general acceptance will be greatly improved by the involvement that only a serving officer can bring…[61]

The MOD's sales department took every opportunity to improve relations with the Chilean military, on one occasion presenting a pair of prize binoculars to Chile's naval school, which the ambassador noted was a good way to 'rebuild the good will that should now exist between the MOD and the Chilean armed services.'[62] Nicholas Ridley was keen to promote sales; when the FCO recommended that Britain take over a German contract to supply submarines to Chile, Ridley wrote: 'Strongly agree. We have more friends now that Reagan has normalized relations with Chile.'[63] Ridley's department approved licences for aircraft cannons, equipment for the manufacture of spares for small arms, a light cruiser, 200 revolvers, an ammunition factory, Gazelle helicopters, bullet-proof vests for the army and submarines in January 1981. Later that year, Ridley loosened the restrictions on the sale of arms, now assessing applications on the 'likelihood' rather than the 'capability' of equipment to be used for internal repression.[64] Margaret Thatcher was fully behind the drive to sell arms to Chile, telling cabinet colleagues that 'the present regime in Chile had been a particular target for left-wing propaganda in this country and it was unfortunate that the hollowness of much of the left-wing case had not been exposed, as Chile represented a good potential market for British military and civil goods'.[65]

Ministers decided in February 1981 to reappoint a defence attaché in principle but to think carefully about the timing. The FCO, however, decided to keep this decision confidential 'as long as possible in order to reduce the number of opportunities for the Chile lobby to attack us.'[66] Recommending that the appointment of the defence attaché be held off for three months until October, an FCO official noted: 'We need to bear in mind that the Chile Solidarity Campaign will be holding a rally on 20 September and we would not want to offer them an easy target which the announcement of a DA post would provide', a clear example of campaigning groups affecting the timing, if not the substance, of government policy.[67] A defence attaché was eventually appointed in December 1981.

In the meantime, the government did its best to promote trade with the dictatorship. In the spring of 1981, the British ambassador hosted a 'Britain in Chile' festival to encourage Chileans to buy British goods. As well as an exhibition of darts in a traditional British-style pub, a display of Scottish dancing and a film of the *Taming of the Shrew*, there was a seminar on invisible exports and a stall promoting British foodstuffs. Local British businesses provided £50,000 sponsorship money, among them Shell, British Caledonian Airways, Lloyds Bank, Beefeater Gin, John Players Special, Morgan Grenfell and Gibbs and Company. Kenneth Clarke, the parliamentary under-secretary of state for transport, led a delegation of UK-based businessmen and officials to Santiago to bang the drum for Britain. According to the ambassador, 'most of the irritants' to Anglo-Chilean relations no longer existed but there was a need 'to improve and update Britain's image after so many years of low profile.'[68]

In an effort to promote arms sales, the chief of the general staff of the Chilean navy, Vice-Admiral Maurice Poisson, and the chief of the Chilean air force, General Carlos Degroux were invited to London to meet Ministry of Defence officials and prospective arms suppliers in May 1981. The British Overseas Trade Board (BOTB) offered to sponsor ten British companies, including British Aerospace, Ferranti, Racal and Rolls Royce, to take part in an international air fair in Santiago, organised by the Chilean air force in July 1981.[69]

Informal Social Networks

Informal contacts between Conservative politicians, business leaders and FCO officials gave company executives channels through which they could influence policy-makers. A director of Rothschild, for example, phoned the Foreign Office after a personal meeting with Pinochet. He said the senior partner in Rothschild wanted Lord Carrington to know how anxious the Chilean ambassador was to meet him.[70] The head of the FCO South America department duly recommended that Carrington meet the ambassador. On another occasion, Tory MP Eldon Griffiths wrote to Nicholas Ridley telling him he had 'struck up a friendship' with the Chilean ambassador, who was going to spend a week in his Suffolk home. The ambassador had asked if a government minister would be prepared to receive 'one or more senior members of the Pinochet regime', suggesting the mines minister, José Piñera. The mines minister was consequently invited later that year and met trade minister Peter Rees, as well as the editor of *The Economist*, senior representatives of BP, Consolidated Goldfields, RTZ and other mining companies.[71] He lunched with directors of Rothschild, Lloyds of London, Standard Chartered Bank and Baring Brothers and was a guest speaker at the London Metal Exchange. He also met the head of two Thatcherite think tanks, the Centre for Policy Studies and the Institute of Economic Affairs. Piñera was delighted at his reception; he told the British ambassador that 'he really valued his discussions with the public and the private sectors' and he predicted 'some envy when he wears his Adam Smith tie at the next meeting of the Chilean cabinet!'[72] A month later, Miguel Kast, the Chilean labour minister responsible for anti-trade union legislation, was invited to London, where he met foreign office minister Richard Luce and trade minister Peter Rees. He had a private meal with Margaret Thatcher's advisor Alan Walters, and was guest at a dinner hosted by the heads of leading banks, including Lloyds, Morgan Grenfell, Samuel Montague and Charter Consolidated.[73] The wining and dining paid off: British foreign direct investment in Chile rose sharply after Margaret Thatcher came to power: from £28m in 1978, to £94m in 1981, and £114m in 1984; a 300% increase between 1978 and 1984. British exports to Chile rose 80% from US$72m in 1978 to US$130m in 1980.

The Human Rights Lobby

Relations between the Thatcher government and human rights activists were far less convivial. Helen Bamber, a life-long campaigner against torture, recalls the atmosphere when she was part of a delegation to discuss Chile with Nicholas Ridley at the Foreign Office in 1980 in a 'palatial room lined with crimson studded-leather sofas…and ten-foot long mirrors reflecting heavy chandeliers':

> There were polite words and officials looking at their watches, and total confidence in what they were doing and saying; they assumed that they held knowledge that we did not. It was a dialogue of the deaf. Ridley didn't say much; he was indifferent to the case, and he looked utterly contemptuous of us. The officials had made up their minds, and patronized us.[74]

Frank Dobson, a Labour MP who was part of another delegation to Nicholas Ridley, also remembers the minister having a 'disdainful' attitude to the visitors.[75] The Thatcherite members of the cabinet certainly had little sympathy for the campaigners' cause, Ridley frequently compared Chile favourably to Eastern Bloc countries, commenting, for example, when he met the widow of Salvador Allende: 'Left-wing governments seemed not to condemn abuses of human rights in left-wing countries'.[76] Right-wing MP Norman Tebbit had the same attitude; in a letter to Ridley he wrote:

> I have been receiving a few letters from supporters of Amnesty International who have worked themselves up into a state of indignation about the fate of political prisoners not in Liberia, Mozambique, Angola, Afghanistan, Russia, or anywhere like that, but in Chile.
>
> I would be glad of a few copies of your standard letter on the subject so that I need not waste the time of your officials by forwarding the letters concerned.[77]

Foreign Office officials were not sympathetic to the campaigners, but at times recognised that they represented an important body of opinion. Soon after the Conservatives came to office in 1979, the head of the FCO's South America department advised Ridley to accept a delegation from the Chile Solidarity Campaign, saying: 'The issues they wish to raise are ones of genuine public concern. I do not think it would be good tactics to give them and their supporters gratuitous offence by rebuffing them completely...even though such discussion is unlikely to be very productive.'[78] On another occasion, an official recommended that Ridley meet Mrs. Allende to 'outflank' criticism of the government's Chile policy: 'Mr Ridley would need to do no more than listen politely to what Sra Allende had to say,' he added.[79] Similarly, just after the British ambassador had been restored to Chile in February 1980, an FCO official recommended that ministers receive a high-level trade union and Labour party delegation, noting that 'over 300 letters of protest have been received' and that to refuse would 'give offence to the Opposition and give the Chile Lobby a further excuse to continue its campaign of protest'.[80] His superior wrote: 'I agree it's an unavoidable chore'.[81] Later in the year, however, the Foreign Office recommended turning down a request for another trade union deputation arguing that 'the Chile lobby have been given ample opportunity to make their views known to HMG in recent months.'[82]

Foreign Office officials regularly counted up the letters they received and the number of requests for delegations (even if they were denied). In 1980, the FCO received 336 protest letters from MPs and this rose to 343 in 1981. Hundreds more letters were sent by members of the public and trade union branches.[83] The FCO continued to take great interest in the activities of the solidarity activists and at times attended their events; one FCO official reported back from a picket of the Chilean embassy in London in September 1981 and another attended a rally in Trafalgar Square where the speakers included miners' leader, Arthur Scargill and left-wing Labour MP, Ken Livingstone. 'Mr Knight Smith is to be commended for having sacrificed his Sunday to this worthy cause!' joked another FCO official.[84] Meanwhile, the British ambassador and the FCO took out a subscription to *Chile Fights*, the magazine of the Chile Solidarity Campaign.[85] Despite having little sympathy for the campaigners, the FCO was not prepared to intervene in the protests at the behest of the Chilean government. When asked by the Chilean foreign ministry to prevent a Cuban embassy official speaking at a Chile protest in Dundee, the FCO refused, saying that 'such activity stretches the limits of permitted diplomatic behaviour'.[86]

British embassy staff, Foreign Office diplomats and Conservative politicians were all critical of Amnesty International's human rights material, the ambassador calling it 'blatantly partial'.[87] Nicholas Ridley suggested it would not be wise to 'fight Amnesty International in public now' but that the ambassador's material might be useful for that purpose in the future.[88] He added:

> However I remain unhappy that Amnesty's biased accounts should go without the other side of the argument even being stated. We will never convert Amnesty International—but the middle ground must be converted.[89]

His successor, Richard Luce, also wondered whether Amnesty's claims should be challenged publicly, but a Foreign Office official warned this would be 'dangerous ground', saying 'Few people are going to believe HMG's [Her Majesty's Government's] word against AI's, especially on Chile'.[90]

COVERING UP INACTION ON WILLIAM BEAUSIRE

The Foreign Office's focus on the presentation rather than the substance of policy is very clear in their handling of the William Beausire case during the Thatcher years. Foreign Office officials during the 1970s had genuinely tried to solve the case of the Anglo-Chilean who had disappeared from Buenos Aires airport in 1975 and was subsequently seen by several witnesses in Chilean torture centres. The FCO had built up a dossier of evidence and pressed the Chilean government to investigate. But British efforts failed because the Chileans refused to accept that Beausire had ever been detained in Chile. The Beausire case came to public attention again in 1981 when a shocking TV documentary, containing graphic reconstructed torture scenes and interviews with the missing man's family, was broadcast by the BBC. An FCO official, anticipating that the programme would provoke a public response, wrote to the British embassy asking them to make inquiries about two of Beausire's alleged torturers, because 'we may now start to get a renewed surge of letters and PQs on the Beausire case and it would be good to be able to quote a recent approach to the Chileans in order to demonstrate our continuing concern.'[91] He added: 'PS. We have just received the first letter on the TV programme. Copy enclosed for your amusement.'

But the news from Santiago was discomfiting for the FCO: the Chilean authorities had 'temporarily shelved' investigations into the Beausire case a year earlier. FCO official Knight Smith complained that the news 'knocks away the first prop of our public position'.[92] Suggestions by the Chilean ambassador that the FCO follow up the Argentine angle or investigate, at first hand, Beausire's alleged places of detention, were 'impractical', he wrote, adding that such investigations 'would be too slow for our immediate presentational needs and it would also make us look very silly'.[93]

After the TV documentary was aired, letters began to pour into the Foreign Office; by the end of the year, 128 MPs and 185 members of the public had written about the Beausire case. Although most of the letters from Members of Parliament were from Labour MPs, there were a good number from Conservative MPs too, appalled that a holder of a British passport could be subjected to such horrors. 'This is surely an argument for some plain speaking,' wrote one Tory MP.[94] But the FCO was dismissive of the correspondence: 'Of course we are under no illusions that these letters represent a spontaneous outburst of popular concern' wrote one official.[95] He added: 'Their origin is rather in Amnesty International's circular...However, it all goes to show that for the time being at least we cannot afford to let the matter drop.' Although the FCO was well aware that the Chilean authorities had 'shelved' the Beausire case, they decided to omit this fact when replying to MPs and members of the public. As one official wrote: 'there is no advantage to us in publicising it too widely at this stage.'[96]

Assistant Under-Secretary of State John Ure queried why facts were being withheld from MP Timothy Renton. He was satisfied with the response from the FCO's South America Department, concluding:

> Mr Renton...is writing on behalf of a constituent and our reply (which will be the model for other answers) will inevitably be passed back to the Chile lobby. It seems unnecessary to give them further fuel for agitation at this juncture.[97]

Only David Owen, as a former foreign secretary, was told that the Chilean investigation had been closed, but this information was withheld from all the other MPs who wrote asking ministers about the Beausire case. The Foreign Office maintained that the British government still regarded the case as open, but this was just a form of words to appease the public. As Robin Fearn stated:

> It is almost certainly unrealistic to expect that the circumstances of Mr Beausire's disappearance and probable death will ever be clarified… However, particularly in the aftermath of the television programme, it would only invite controversy if we were to abandon our public line that we do not regard the case as closed.[98]

The Foreign Office took little further action on the Beausire case, apart from making an occasional routine inquiry. No sanctions were applied to Chile. On the contrary, the relationship between the Conservative government and the Pinochet regime became ever closer, particularly after during and after the Falklands war.

CHILE AND THE FALKLANDS WAR

Chile's role in helping Britain during the Falklands war has, for many years, been shrouded in secrecy. Thirty years after the war, when the British government opened its archives on the Falklands conflict, the parts relating to Chile were heavily censored. Margaret Thatcher, of course, based her support for the dictator after his arrest on the 'vital assistance' he had given during the war, but she gave very few details.[99] In 2002, the former commander of the Chilean air force, General Fernando Matthei, gave an interview in which he revealed key ways in which Chile had helped British forces.[100] The account that follows is based primarily on the account of Matthei and that of Britain's official historian of the Falklands war, Lawrence Freedman, who was given access to a wide range of official sources.[101]

Chile remained officially neutral during the Falklands conflict, but was willing to help Britain covertly because she feared Argentine expansionism. Chile had come close to war with Argentina in 1978 in a dispute over the strategic Beagle channel and three small islands located beneath Tierra del Fuego at the southern tip of South America. Throughout the Falklands war, Chile stationed forces along the border with Argentina, fearing that Argentine troops, after victory in the Malvinas, would go on to launch an offensive against Chile. This forced Argentina to station some of its best infantry brigades on the mainland, instead of sending them to fight in the Falklands, a deployment that indirectly helped Britain.

The Pinochet regime also saw the conflict as an opportunity to procure arms, which had become increasingly difficult in the wake of the US arms embargo on Chile and the election of the socialist François Mitterrand as president of France. In a secret deal, Britain offered to sell Hunter Hawker bomber planes to Chile, in exchange for support. At least six Hunters were delivered to Chile during the war, with the promise of many more.[102] More importantly for Britain's war effort, Britain agreed to sell Chile three ex-RAF Canberra photographic reconnaissance aircraft. The Canberras and two Hercules transport aircraft were painted with Chilean air-force markings and transported to an airbase in southern Chile, but for the duration of the war, the Canberras were manned by British RAF pilots, who used them for reconnaissance flights.[103] Britain and Chile tried to hide this cooperation by white-washing the windows of Punta Arenas commercial airport so that visitors could not see the military runway.[104] The British also sold the Chileans Blowpipe anti-aircraft missiles and a sophisticated radar system. All of the British arms sales to Chile during the Falklands war were heavily discounted and some may not have been paid for at all.[105]

But the most important way in which Chile helped was by giving Britain intelligence. A state-of-the art British-made radar system was set up in the southern Chilean city of Balmaceda, enabling the Chileans to provide Britain with intelligence from Comodoro Rivadavia, the Argentine city that was the 'military nerve centre' of Argentina's Falklands campaign.[106] The British also benefitted from Chile's French-made long-range radar based further south in Punta Arenas. An underground intelligence bunker was set up in Punta Arenas that sent information on Argentine air-force movements directly back to Britain's Northwood base via satellite.[107] The Chileans also allowed Britain to base Nimrod reconnaissance aircraft on the Pacific island of San Félix. British air-crews were given permission to fly over Chilean airspace to the South Atlantic and refuel at the Chilean airbase at Concepción, enabling them to collect information from outside the cover of Argentine radar and transmit it back to the taskforce.[108] The Chileans also agreed to delay the handover of a British tanker, *HMS Tidepool*, which they had bought from Britain before the war, enabling the tanker to join the British task force.

But unanswered questions remain about Chile's role in the Falkland War. We do not yet know the full role played by the Chilean navy or army.[109] Journalistic reports, for example, suggest that Chilean navy sources gave the British the coordinates of the Belgrano just hours before it was sunk.[110] Nor is it known what role the Chileans played in an aborted SAS mission to cripple Argentine aircraft.[111]

Whatever the full extent of Chilean cooperation during the Falklands war, it certainly cemented the already cordial relationship between the Thatcher government and the Pinochet regime. A month after the British victory, Robin Fearn, the head of the FCO's South America Department, wrote that Britain needed to review its relations with Chile and 'decide what price we are prepared to pay for long-term Chilean cooperation over the Falklands'. He suggested:

a) Assisting with the modernisation of the Chilean armed forces (while continuing to prevent supply of equipment which is in our view likely to be used for internal repression)…
b) Expanding contacts and exchanges at both Ministerial and official level
c) Putting lesser emphasis in our bilateral relations on human rights issues (while continuing to take the minimum action necessary to deflect criticism from the domestic lobby)
d) Associating ourselves more positively with those of our EC partners who wish to end Chile's selective treatment in international fora.[112]

Fearn's superior, Sir John Ure, was more cautious, saying: 'I think we need to think through rather more carefully the proposals about putting "lesser emphasis…on human rights issues" if we are not to be accused with—with some justification—of adopting a cynical policy.' He agreed, however, that it was an anomaly that Chile should be treated 'as more of an international leper' than Argentina and proposed 'drawing a line under past events on which there is no reasonable prospect of progress being made e.g. Beausire', but continuing to make representations about any new or current infringements.[113]

The policy approved by government ministers, however, showed very little of this caution. An FCO official wrote in August 1982:

> The idea of pursuing a steady improvement in our relations with Chile has been approved and the importance of securing a better long-term relationship with Chile in the context of achieving our policy objectives in the South Atlantic has been recognised…

> We are also prepared to play a major role in supplying arms to assist Chile in the modernising of her Armed Forces to counterbalance those of Argentina...
>
> On the question of human rights we have been exploring with our EC partners what can be done to mitigate the selective treatment at the UN.[114]

The main changes in policy towards Chile after the Falklands war were, therefore, an increase in arms sales and a far softer line on Chilean human rights abuses by Britain at the United Nations. By the end of 1982, the Thatcher government had sold the Pinochet dictatorship over £20m worth of arms including: 10 Hawker Hunter fighter planes; a warship (*HMS Norfolk*); a tanker (*RFA Tidepool*); 8 Blowpipe missile launchers with 60 missiles, naval pyrotechnics, aircraft gun sights, communications equipment, revolvers and assorted naval spares. After the Falklands conflict, the British government was willing to approve the sale of a far greater range of weaponry, even if it could be used for civilian repression. For example, in May 1982, a consignment of machine guns and machine-gun pods for the Chilean naval fleet's aircraft, which had previously been turned down, was approved for clearance because, wrote the private secretary to Francis Pym, 'We are...very conscious of the helpful attitude which the Chileans have adopted during the Falklands crisis and the various military facilities which have been offered by them'.[115] He added: 'Because of the human rights situation in Chile, there must remain a risk that this sale would attract criticism... both within Parliament and the country if it were to become known'. Among the other weaponry and hardware that the Thatcher government approved for sale to the Pinochet regime between 1980 and 1982 were: Jaguar aircraft, Sea Harrier aircraft, Sea King and Lynx helicopters and Canberra bomber planes, body armour, bullet-proof vests and helmets, armoured Land Rovers, machinery to manufacturer small arms and ammunition, night-sights for use with small arms, gun-turrets and cannons for armoured vehicles and cluster bombs.[116] Clearly, much of this equipment could be used for internal repression, so violated the government's own guidelines. The government also approved a deal for Britain to provide Chile with enriched uranium for a nuclear power plant.[117]

Britain and the United Nations

The Thatcher government had already weakened Britain's stand on Chile in the United Nations before the Falklands war. In February 1981, for the first time since the coup, Britain failed to condemn Chile's human rights record in a UN forum, abstaining on a motion submitted to the UN Commission for Human Rights. In December 1981, Britain voted in favour of a UN General Assembly motion criticising Chile's human rights, but attached a note to their vote expressing reservations. After the war, Britain not only softened its line, but also tried to persuade other countries to weaken their stance on Chile.[118] The head of the UK mission to the UN noted: 'In the wake of the Falklands crisis…the Chileans here clearly expect us to be as helpful as we can.'[119] General Pinochet met trade minister Peter Rees in September 1982 and made a 'specific request' that Britain soften its stance at the UN.[120] Britain then worked behind the scenes to try to end the mandate of the UN special rapporteur on human rights in Chile by lobbying other governments and placing amendments to UN resolutions. Although these machinations failed to end the special rapporteur's mandate they did succeed in watering down the final resolution passed by the UN General Assembly, for which the commander in chief of the Chilean air force expressed his gratitude: 'Matthei went out of his way to say that he and other members of the junta were very grateful to us for the way in which we had introduced, and managed to steer through, our amendment,' a British official wrote.[121] In December 1982, Britain, for the first time since the coup, did not vote in favour of the United Nation General Assembly's annual resolution condemning human rights in Chile. Britain and Germany were the only European countries to abstain.

Notes

1. 'Thatcher always honoured Britain's debt to Pinochet', *Daily Telegraph*, 13 December 2006.
2. 'Thatcher Stands by Pinochet', BBC News Website, 26 March 1999.
3. Margaret Thatcher, *Statecraft* (Harper Collins: London, 2002), p. 268.
4. Walters cited in Beckett, *Pinochet*, pp. 177–178.
5. Robert Moss, *The Collapse of Democracy* (London: Abacus, 1977), pp. 23, 160, 222.

6. Robert Moss, *Chile's Marxist Experiment* (Newton Abbot: David & Charles, 1973); 'Only the views we want you to read', *The Guardian*, 20 December 1976.
7. Margaret Thatcher, *The Path to Power* (London: Harper Collins, 1995), p. 361.
8. Richard Cockett, *Thinking the Unthinkable: Think-Tanks and the Economic Counter-Revolution, 1931–1983* (London: Harper Collins, 1995), p. 225; Beckett, p. 191.
9. Brian Crozier, '*We Will Bury You*', p. vii; Harrogate speech: Beckett, p. 192.
10. 'Pinochet victim of political kidnap', BBC News Online, 19 January 1999. http://news.bbc.co.uk/1/hi/uk_politics/258031.stm.
11. 'Britain's only "political prisoner"', *The Times*, 20 January 1999.
12. 'Right-Wing Fan Club Tinkers with Chile History', *The Guardian*, 20 January 1999.
13. Ibid.
14. Ibid.
15. Conrad Black, *A Matter of Principle* (New York: Encounter Books, 2012), p. 57.
16. 'The powerful regiment lined up behind the general', *The Financial Times*, 11 February 1999.
17. Ridley, *My Style of Government*, p. 25.
18. Harry Bennett, 'Lord Carrington' in Theakston, *British Foreign Secretaries*, p. 127.
19. M.A. Wickstead to Ure, 2 August 1979 enclosing 'Confidential Note' by Sir Antony Parsons, 1 August 1979, The National Archives (TNA): FCO7/3613.
20. 'Policy Towards Chile', FCO briefing, 9 May 1979 [no date on draft, date on covering letter] in TNA: FCO7/3612.
21. K.D. Temple to J.B. Ure, FCO, 11 May 1979, TNA: FCO7/3612.
22. Ibid.
23. John Nott to Lord Carrington, 18 May 1979, TNA: FCO7/3612.
24. R.M. White, 'Chile: ECGD Cover and Ambassadors', 23 May 1979, TNA: FCO7/3612.
25. 'Chile: ECGD Cover and Ambassadors', briefing by Ure, 18 May 1979, TNA: FCO7/3613.
26. FCO to British Embassy, Santiago, 22 June 1979, TNA: FCO7/3612.
27. Ibid.
28. Carrington to Hernán Cubillos, 19 July 1979, TNA: FCO7/3613.
29. Ure to Hall and Parsons, 9 July 1979, TNA: FCO7/3613.
30. FCO to British Embassy, Santiago, 10 December 1979, TNA: FCO7/3614.

31. Record of a Call by the Chilean Chargé d'Affaires, 11 December 1979, TNA: FCO7/3614, 1979.
32. Carrington to Margaret Thatcher, 17 September 1979, TNA: FCO7/3613.
33. 'Recognising Chile', *Daily Mail*, 19 September 1979.
34. DOP Committee, minutes, 19 September 1979, TNA: CAB 148/183.
35. Ure to Harding, 18 September 1979, TNA: FCO7/3613.
36. Cecil Parkinson to Thatcher, 18 September 1979, TNA: FCO7/3613.
37. Amy to FCO, 13 August 1979, TNA: FCO7/3613.
38. Temple to Private Secretary, FCO, 2 November 1979, TNA: FCO7/3614.
39. Minister for Trade's Office Minute, 28 November 1979, TNA: FCO7/3615.
40. 'Call by the Chilean Chargé d'Affaires', 5 December 1979, TNA: FCO7/3614.
41. G.A. Duggan to D. Maitland, 4 March 1980, in TNA: FCO7/3751.
42. Carrington to Thatcher, 20 December 1979, TNA: FCO7/3614.
43. R.A.E. Gordon to B.J. Baxter, FCO, 11 March 1980, TNA: FCO7/3759.
44. Duggan to Hall, 2 July 1979, TNA: FCO7/3612, 1979.
45. Parkinson to Thatcher, 18 September 1979, TNA: FCO7/3613.
46. Note by Ridley on Ure to Hall and Parsons, 9 July 1979, TNA: FCO7/3613.
47. Note by Hall, 11 July 1979 on Ure to Hall and Parsons, 9 July 1979, TNA: FCO7/3613.
48. Ibid.
49. J.M. Heath to P.R. Fearn, FCO, 16 May 1980, TNA: FCO7/3757.
50. Notes by officials on Heath to Fearn, 16 May 1980, TNA: FCO7/3757 [signatures of officials illegible].
51. Ibid.
52. Fearn to Heath, 13 June 1980, TNA: FCO7/3757.
53. Note by FCO official on Heath to Gordon, 3 July 1980, TNA: FCO7/3751.
54. Note by Duggan on Heath to Gordon, 3 July 1980, TNA: FCO7/3751.
55. Barry Bawtree, Vosper International, to Amy, 26 March 1980, TNA: FCO7/3753, 1980.
56. B.J. Baxter to Mr. Cheesman, FCO, 1 April 1980, TNA: FCO7/3753.
57. Amy to Duggan, 8 February 1980, TNA: FCO7/3759.
58. Heath to FCO, 24 July 1980, TNA: FCO7/3754.
59. 'Visit of Mr Cecil Parkinson MP', note by Heath, 19 August 1980, TNA: FCO7/3898.
60. Ibid.

61. Brigadier M.C.M. Steele to Joint Secretary OCSSA Sub Committee, 15 January 1981, TNA: FCO7/3916.
62. Heath to Brigadier P.C.S. Heidenstam, 6 January 1981, TNA: FCO7/3916.
63. Note by Ridley on R.H. Smith to PS/Mr. Ridley, 20 January 1981, TNA/3906.
64. T.J. Rayson, to I. Knight Smith, 3 June 1981, TNA: FCO7/3906.
65. DOP Committee, minutes, 24 July 1981, TNA: CAB 148/197.
66. I. McCrory to Fearn, 10 February 1981, TNA: FC07/3916.
67. Knight Smith to Colonel Whiter, 20 July 1981, TNA: FCO7/3916.
68. 'The Presence of Britain in Chile Promotion' briefing by Heath, 9 June 1981, TNA: FCO7/3909.
69. T.I. Quinn Hall to R. Priestly, BOTB, 3 July 1981, TNA: FCO7/3909.
70. Ure to Fearn, 21 May 1981, TNA: FCO7/3903.
71. Gordon to Knight Smith, 29 October 1981, TNA: FCO7/3914.
72. Ibid.
73. Fearn to PS/Mr. Luce, 9 November 1981, TNA: FCO7/3980.
74. Belton, *The Good Listener*, p. 274.
75. Frank Dobson interview with the author, 9 October 2013.
76. Record of Call by Sra Allende at the FCO, 18 September 1979, TNA: FCO7/3611.
77. Norman Tebbit to Ridley, 30 December 1980, TNA: FCO7/3895.
78. Ure to PS/Mr. Ridley, 13 August 1979, TNA: FCO7/3611.
79. Duggan to Mr. Harding, APS/Mr. Ridley, 14 September, TNA: FCO7/3611.
80. Duggan to Maitland, 4 March 1980, TNA: FCO7/3751.
81. Note by Maitland on Duggan to Maitland, 4 March 1980, TNA: FCO7/3751.
82. Fearn to Harding, 24 April 1980, TNA: FCO7/3751.
83. Fearn to Ure, 22 December 1981, TNA: FCO7/3903.
84. Note by official on a cutting from *The Morning Star*, 12 September 1981, TNA: FCO7/3904.
85. Knight Smith to Library and Records Department, FCO, 1 July 1981, TNA: FCO7/3904.
86. FCO to British Embassy, Santiago, 14 September 1981, TNA: FCO7/3904.
87. Heath to FCO, 12 September 1980, TNA: FCO7/3757.
88. Temple to PS/Lord Privy Seal, 18 September 1980 in FCO7/3757.
89. Ibid.
90. PS/Mr. Luce to Fearn, 25 November 1981, TNA: FCO7/3898; R.H. Smith to Fearn, 27 November 1981, TNA: FCO7/3898.
91. Knight Smith to Gordon, 30 September 1981, TNA: FCO7/3898.
92. Knight Smith to R.H. Smith, 8 October 1981, TNA: FCO7/3898.
93. Ibid.

94. Maurice Macmillan to Carrington, 18 November 1981, TNA: FCO7/3902.
95. Knight Smith to Gordon, 25 November 1981, TNA: FCO7/3898.
96. Fearn to Ure, 19 October 1981, TNA: FCO7/3899.
97. Note by Ure, 19 October 1981, on Fearn to Ure, 19 October 1981, TNA: FCO7/3899.
98. Fearn to Ure, 12 October 1981, TNA: FCO7/3899.
99. Thatcher, *Statecraft*, p. 267.
100. 'Matthei rompe el silencio sobre el pacto secreto Chileno-Gran Bretaña', *La Tercera*, 24 March 2002. See also Patricia Arancibia Clavel and Isabel de la Maza Cave, *Matthei: Mi Testimonio* (Santiago: La Tercera-Mondadori, 2003).
101. Lawrence Freedman, *The Official History of the Falklands Campaign*, Vol. II (London: Routledge, 2005).
102. Freedman, p. 397; Arancibia Clavel and de la Maza Cave, p. 351.
103. Freedman, pp. 394, 397; Arancibia Clavel and de la Maza Cave, p. 352.
104. Nigel West, *The Secret War for the Falklands: The SAS, MI6 and the War Whitehall Nearly Lost* (London: Little, Brown & Company, 1997), p. 128.
105. Paolo Tripodi, 'General Matthei's Revelation and Chile's Role During the Falklands War', *The Journal of Strategic Studies*, 26 (2003), 208–123, p. 116.
106. Ibid., p. 118.
107. Arancibia Clavel and de la Maza Cave, p. 354.
108. Freedman, p. 397.
109. Tripodi, pp. 119–120.
110. Michael Vestey, 'Did I help sink the Belgrano?', *The Spectator*, 31 October 1998. See also Robert Fox, *Eyewitness Falklands: A Personal Account of the Falklands Campaign* (London: Mandarin, 1992), p. 326.
111. Tripodi, p. 114; West, p. 144; Freedman, p. 433.
112. Fearn to Ure, 12 July 1982, TNA: FCO 7/4184.
113. Note by Ure on Fearn to Ure, 12 July 1982, TNA: FCO 7/4184.
114. R.J. Chase to J.K. Hickman, 31 August 1982, TNA: FCO7/4184.
115. J.E. Holmes to A.J. Coles, 25 May 1982, TNA: FCO7/4196.
116. List (DSR 11C) appended to letter from Knight Smith to S. Waddingham, 14 January 1982, TNA: FCO7/4195, 1982. This list contains items approved for sale to Chile, but the sales may not necessarily have gone ahead. The Chilean armed forces' company, FAMAE, did go on to sign a deal with Britain's Royal Ordnance in 1989 to jointly produce the RAYO cluster-bomb rocket launching system.
117. Deal agreed July 1982, TNA: AB48/1233, Supply of Fuel for 'Herald Reactor', 1979–1982.

118. FCO Briefing: 'Chile Human Rights at the UN (not to be raised), Background' [Date received in FCO registry: 4 October 1982], TNA: FCO7/4210.
119. R.C. Fursland to T. Millson, 7 July 1982, TNA: FCO7/4210.
120. 'Chile Human Rights at the UN (not to be raised)', FCO briefing [Date received in FCO registry: 4 October 1982], TNA: FCO7/4210.
121. J.K. Hickman to head of chancellery, 16 December 1982, TNA: FCO7/4195.

CHAPTER 6

Chile Conclusion

Domestic considerations were central to the formulation of policy towards Chile. The role of political parties and ideology, in particular, was crucial. The Labour and Conservative Parties had very different views on the Pinochet regime and these resulted in clearly distinct policies when in government. Despite facing a diplomatic service with a sympathetic attitude towards the junta, Wilson's Labour government introduced a package of measures—an arms embargo, cuts in aid, the suspension of export credits, the withdrawal of the British ambassador and welcoming refugees—that amounted to a radically different policy from that of Heath's Conservative government. The dead weight of Whitehall was never so paralysing as to prevent a change in policy, although officials did persuade Labour ministers against taking the most radical measures advocated by activists.

A government committed to a clear set of policies, and under pressure from its base to act, can overcome a recalcitrant bureaucracy. The extent to which ministers are willing to act against officials' advice depends on the political and economic costs involved, as well as the type of political pressure they face. FCO officials were adept at tailoring their advice to appeal to the pragmatism of Harold Wilson and James Callaghan, who recognised that the Labour Party demanded significant change, but wanted to avoid irreparable damage to Britain's commercial interests.

© The Author(s) 2018
G. Livingstone, *Britain and the Dictatorships of Argentina and Chile, 1973–82*, Security, Conflict and Cooperation in the Contemporary World, https://doi.org/10.1007/978-3-319-78292-8_6

These ministers, therefore, accepted it would set a dangerous precedent to break existing arms contracts, but in one case, when trade unionists took direct action in Glasgow, they were forced to go further and found a contractual loophole that enabled the government to end the contract early.

There was far less negotiation of policy between politicians and officials during the administrations of Heath and Thatcher because the Conservatives had a very similar ideological outlook to the Foreign Office officials. Whereas Labour politicians had spent a great deal of time examining the detail of policy, Conservatives were happy to grant officials more autonomy, content in the knowledge that they shared the same values. Neither the Heath nor the Thatcher government took action against the Pinochet regime and the only disagreements which occurred between politicians and between departments during the Thatcher years were about the pace at which sanctions should be lifted.

The Foreign Office, like the Conservatives, elevated the interests of business above other concerns. While deploring the abuses committed by the Pinochet regime, the Foreign Office nevertheless thought that a stable military regime was better for British businesses than the left-wing Allende administration. During the years of Labour government, the Foreign Office repeatedly voiced the concerns of British businesses, for example, that the restriction of export credits hampered exporters, and that Labour's 'selective' targeting of Chile was damaging Britain's commercial interests. Foreign Office officials also shared the Conservatives' Cold War-influenced suspicion that Chile activists were motivated by 'political' (i.e. socialist), rather than humanitarian, concerns.

The convergence of views between the FCO and Conservative politicians reflected a common class perception of 'the national interest'. The Foreign Office was imbued with the ethos of the 'gentlemanly capitalist' class. Pro-business, anti-egalitarian attitudes were reinforced by the informal social networks in which officials operated. High-ranking officials not only shared a similar privileged background and education with business leaders and Conservative politicians, but they mixed with them in seminars and drinks parties, or as members of the same private London clubs. Business leaders had informal channels of access and influence; a director of Rothschild, for example, after meeting General Pinochet, had simply to pick up the phone to the FCO to persuade officials that Carrington, the foreign secretary, should meet the Chilean ambassador. And while diplomats and bankers socialised effortlessly in the high-ceilinged rooms of Canning House in Belgravia, officials had to abandon their sartorial codes and don 'blue jeans and T-shirts' to enter the alien environment of a Chile Solidarity meeting. Many officials were critical and even suspicious of Labour and trade union activists. Although there was a range of views among FCO officials, this was on a narrow spectrum. The head of the Latin America Department Hugh Carless, for example, disparaged campaigners more stridently than his successor John Ure, who recognised that they represented a segment of public opinion, but both agreed that the Labour party was too 'selective' in targeting Chile and that its policies were damaging to Britain's commercial interests.

After the Duncan Report of 1969, it was, of course, part of a diplomat's job to promote British companies abroad. The Foreign Office was also under constant pressure from the Department of Trade and the defence sales department of the Ministry of Defence—both of which had close relationships with private corporations—to remove restrictions on trade with the Pinochet regime. While Labour ministers and trade union leaders often shared the view of British companies and the Foreign Office that promoting British business abroad was good for British workers, in the case of Chile, many trade union leaders and shop-stewards lobbied strongly against the sale of arms to the Pinochet regime, even though this could jeopardise their material interests. In this period of heightened trade union militancy and class consciousness among workers, then, there was a clear difference between the position of the Foreign Office and the labour movement, which could be attributed to a difference in class outlook. Class may not be the only factor which influenced the views of Foreign Office officials, but it is one that should not be ignored.

This study has also examined the circumstances in which social movements can best achieve their aims. The broad nature of the Chile solidarity movement was one reason for its effectiveness: the Chile Solidarity Campaign had strong links with the Labour Party, the Communist Party and the trade unions. Meanwhile, the Chile Human Rights Committee focused more narrowly on legal and human rights issues, working with lawyers, church groups, academics and journalists. An array of other NGOs, including Amnesty International, CAFOD and Oxfam, also worked on Chile. The movement therefore extended from the traditional left to moderate liberals and it won—as Nicholas Ridley lamented—the 'middle ground'. The abuses of the Pinochet regime were reported in the media and the liberal press portrayed the campaigners sympathetically. It is hard to measure public opinion, but the Foreign Office certainly judged that the campaigners 'represent a significant body of opinion, and the issues they wish to raise are ones of genuine public concern.'[1] It was, in large part, due to the efforts of national and international activists, and the media coverage they generated, that for many people in Britain, General Pinochet came to epitomise the image of a brutal dictator, one of the few tyrants in the world whom the average member of the public could name. The Conservatives' counter-attack when Pinochet was arrested in 1998—that he was a 'friend of Britain' during the Falklands conflict—had only limited salience even in the right-wing press. Building a broad coalition and winning the centre ground, therefore, were the keys to creating an effective campaign group, which forced policy-makers to consider, if not necessarily concede to, its demands.

But looking at the characteristics and activities of social movements themselves is not sufficient when determining how government policy is made. It is also necessary to examine what makes policy-makers willing to adopt campaigners' proposals. Despite being a well-organised and broad movement, the Chile solidarity movement did not succeed in changing the key policies of either the Heath or the Thatcher government, although they did make policy-makers act cautiously, think carefully about presentation and timing, slow down the pace of change and grant small concessions on occasion (for example, not approving export licences for particular types of arms). As many analysts have pointed out, movements are more likely to achieve success if their demands are consistent with what the government wanted to do anyway.[2] Labour politicians were already sympathetic to the campaigners' views before they came to office (as Conservatives were sympathetic to the business lobby).

But, crucially, the Labour government also had institutional links with the campaigners. There was pressure from the Parliamentary Labour Party—nine MPs sat on the Chile Solidarity Campaign's executive board—and pressure from local party branches, which filtered up to the National Executive Committee and to the annual conference. Labour ministers therefore had to take the issue of Chile into account when making all sorts of political calculations, such as how to maintain their support base, how to maintain the balance of forces in the party, whether 'radical' action on Chile could compensate for more cautious action on another issue. Backbench parliamentarians were in a particularly strong position because the Labour governments in this period had either a minority or a very small majority of seats in the House of Commons. The Labour Party also had an institutional link with the trade unions; they funded the party and sponsored numerous MPs, and some ministers, including Foreign Secretary Callaghan, came from a trade union background. The government was also engaged in a series of sensitive negotiations with the unions over issues such as income policies that would affect the national economy and ultimately the survival of the government. The trade unions also had the weapon of strike action, which the Rolls Royce workers used, for example, to force the government to act. The campaigners therefore had leverage over the key 'gate-keepers' of policy-making during the Labour years. In contrast, the campaigners had far less leverage over key policy makers during the Conservative period in office—neither Foreign Office officials nor Conservative ministers were sympathetic to their cause and campaigners had no institutional or social links with Conservative politicians.

Some have suggested that policy-makers sometimes act against their own material self-interest when an issue fits with their moral values and how they want to present themselves either nationally or internationally.[3] Labour ministers took a moral choice because they believed in the anti-Pinochet cause, but there was self-interested political calculation involved too—the need to satisfy their party and trade union base. Torn between morality and economic pragmatism, it was the pressure of protestors that pushed the government to go as far as it could within the law. It is also important to note that the decision to accede to campaigners' demands was made easier because Chile was a very small market for Britain, accounting for just 0.1% of British exports and less than 1% of Britain's total foreign direct investment.[4] Although there was a material cost involved in adopting an 'ethical' foreign policy—particularly the loss of large arms contracts and the reputational damage to Britain as a reliable supplier—it was comparatively small, and the moral, political and material calculations made by Labour ministers might have been different if they had been considering relations with a country that had a larger economy or was a more important market for Britain.

Notes

1. John Ure to Mr. Hall, PS/Mr. Ridley, 13 August 1979, The National Archives (TNA): FCO7/3611.
2. Joshua Busby, *Moral Movements and Foreign Policy* (Cambridge: CUP, 2010), p. 8; Jack Goldsmith and Eric Posner, 'International Agreements: A Rational Choice Approach', *Virginia Journal of International Law*, 44 (2003), pp. 113–143.
3. Busby, p. 255.
4. IMF Direction of Trade Statistics 1978 and 1979. Investment figure refers to 1975–1979 and excludes oil. *Overseas Transactions, Business Monitor* (London: HMSO, 1982).

CHAPTER 7

Argentina 1976–2 April 1982

Most Labour politicians of a certain age remember hearing the shattering news of the Chilean coup; yet the Argentine coup in 1976 was barely noticed. Neither Tony Benn nor any other Labour diarist recorded it. Unlike Chile, Argentina was not a clear-cut case of 'fascism versus democracy'. While left-wingers had been inspired by Allende's peaceful road to socialism, no Labour politician mourned the fall of the Peronist government; in fact, many in the Labour Party regarded the populist, semi-authoritarian Peronist movement as dangerously close to fascism. Labour politicians and trade unionists had longstanding links with political parties and unions in Chile, whereas the corporatist unions and populist parties of Argentina were alien to them. Furthermore, coups were common in Argentine history and it took some time for the outside world to realise that the atrocities being committed by the new Argentine junta were on a scale that surpassed those of any previous regime. Another key difference was that the Argentine Communist Party did not oppose the coup; this disorientated the British Communist Party, which had been a powerful force in the Chile Solidarity Campaign. The Soviet Union remained an important trade partner of the Argentine military junta and so attitudes towards the regime did not fall so clearly along Cold War lines. Certainly, in Britain, there was far less ideological conflict between the Conservatives and Labour party over Argentina.

© The Author(s) 2018
G. Livingstone, *Britain and the Dictatorships of Argentina and Chile, 1973–82*, Security, Conflict and Cooperation in the Contemporary World, https://doi.org/10.1007/978-3-319-78292-8_7

Consequently, the policies of the Labour and the Conservative governments towards the Argentine junta in this period (1976–1982) were not markedly different. Neither the Labour governments nor their Conservative successor imposed an arms embargo or any type of economic sanction against Argentina—until the invasion of the Falkland Islands on 2 April 1982. Margaret Thatcher's government promoted trade with Argentina more vigorously than Labour had, sending two ministers to visit the military regime, which led to an increase in trade and arms sales to Argentina under the Conservatives. Her government also restored a British ambassador to Buenos Aires in 1979, but Labour had not withdrawn the ambassador on human rights grounds. He had been recalled months before the coup at the behest of the Argentine government during a time of tension over the Falklands. Very few Argentine refugees were admitted, but towards the end of Labour's period of office a small number were allowed entry under the Latin American Refugee Programme—a programme that was ended by Thatcher. Conservative ministers praised the neoliberal economic policies of the junta—Margaret Thatcher met the regime's finance minister Martínez de Hoz in London in 1980—but just as Argentina never became a *cause célèbre* for the labour movement, neither did the Conservative right become involved with, or promote, the Argentine regime as they had Pinochet's Chile.

There was also less ideological tension between Labour politicians and Foreign Office officials on the question of Argentina because Labour was not trying to push through a radical policy. The Cold War strongly coloured Foreign Office perceptions in the case of Chile; they always suspected human rights activists of having a 'political' agenda. But Argentina never became a totemic cause of the British labour movement, so FCO officials were less suspicious of activists and did not feel the need to defend the Argentine regime so stridently against critics. Nevertheless, the Foreign Office abhorred the chaos of Isabel Perón's regime and felt the military had had little choice but to intervene. They praised the new government's economic policies and sought to encourage British trade and investment in Argentina. Days after the coup, the British chargé d'affaires in Buenos Aires noted that 'the new regime should offer opportunities for British businessmen'.[1] In the absence of strong pressure from social movements or politicians, the de facto policy of the Foreign Office towards the South American dictatorships was to maintain relations, impose no sanctions and to encourage trade.

The sales department of the Ministry of Defence and the British military attachés in Buenos Aires were the most vigorous advocates of arms sales within the government. With close links to British arms manufacturers, they constantly lobbied for sales of warships, armoured vehicles, aircraft and ammunition regardless of their possible impact on human rights or potential threat to the Falklands. Just three days before the Argentine invasion, the British military attaché in Buenos Aires made an appointment to meet the secretary general of the Argentine air force to try to sell him bomber planes. After 1979, when the Labour government introduced new arms sales guidelines, the Foreign Office was supposed to assess whether weapons could be used for internal repression or represented a threat to the Falkland Islands, but while some export licences were refused, most potentially large orders were approved because the Foreign Office wanted to promote British exports, as did both Labour and Conservative ministers. Some of this military equipment was later deployed against British forces in the Falklands war, including two Type 42 destroyers, Lynx helicopters and Sea Dart surface-to-air missiles.

The Falklands dispute dominated policy towards Argentina in this period. Argentina had challenged Britain's sovereignty rights since 1833, but the need to resolve the conflict had intensified after 1965 when the United Nations called on both sides to negotiate a peaceful settlement. Both Labour and Conservative governments held negotiations with Argentina in the years 1976–1982 and both governments approved a policy of seeking a 'leaseback' agreement, the transfer of sovereignty to Argentina followed by the leasing of the Islands back to Britain for a long period of time. Some historians and politicians have suggested that the leaseback policy was pursued by the Foreign Office in an underhand manner against the wishes of their political masters. This is untrue. Both Labour and Conservative cabinets approved the policy. James Callaghan and Margaret Thatcher were both sceptical of reaching agreement with Argentina, but both reluctantly agreed to explore the leaseback option. Margaret Thatcher's government went as far as holding secret talks with the Argentines about leaseback.

The central problem, as the war's official historian Laurence Freedman has noted, was that politicians were not prepared to spend the money required to defend the Falkland Islands, but neither were they prepared to spend political capital on pushing a deal with Argentina through Parliament. Despite approving the leaseback policy in principle, both governments drew back from a deal when faced with opposition from MPs, the Islanders and their supporters. The standard British interpretation that domestic political factors—public and parliamentary concern for the fate of the Islanders—were crucial to understanding the British government's actions is correct.[2] Minutes of cabinet meetings, the internal correspondence of politicians and officials, as well as politicians' diaries, show that it was the prospect of a parliamentary storm and the accusation of abandoning the Islanders that caused ministers to draw back at key moments. Most British accounts, therefore, downplay the importance of strategic geopolitical and economic factors. British policy-makers, both politicians and officials, however, spent a considerable amount of time considering questions such as potential oil reserves and fish stocks around the Islands and British rights to Antarctica. Conversely, some Argentine accounts overestimate the importance of these strategic factors, particularly oil, and misinterpret their role in British calculations.

British oil companies and British governments *were* keen to explore and exploit the potential oil reserves in the South Atlantic; but both the government and the corporations felt that this could only be done in cooperation with Argentina, and thus the desire to exploit the oil reinforced the case for reaching a deal with Argentina. During the Thatcher years, however, the Department of Energy grew increasingly concerned that the proposed leaseback deal might not give Britain sufficient access to potential oil deposits and began to urge caution in the talks with Argentina. The Falkland Islands Company, owned by fuel manufacturer Coalite, funded the pro-Islander lobby, but most large British companies that took a view—either because they had investments in Latin America or were interested in oil or fishing in the South Atlantic—favoured a resolution with Argentina. The business lobby did not succeed because British investment in Latin America was relatively small and because Argentina was not a major economic power. If the Argentine economy had been the size of China, for example, the business lobby in favour of rapprochement would have been far stronger—in a clear contrast with the Falklands case, Mrs. Thatcher signed an agreement in 1984 to cede the sovereignty and British administration of Hong Kong to China. One strategic issue that did cause concern for British officials was how the dispute over its territories in the South West Atlantic would affect its sovereignty rights to Antarctica and its access to potential hydrocarbon deposits there. This is still regarded as a sensitive issue and many of the official papers on this subject at the National Archives remain censored or withdrawn entirely from public view. Britain also had concerns about the growing Soviet influence in the South Atlantic, as did the United States, but both countries agreed that the best way to protect their interests was by forming an anti-communist alliance with Argentina and the Southern Cone dictatorships. There was also the intangible strategic factor of Britain's standing in the world and its reputation as a great power, a sentiment that led many Conservative MPs to take an interest in the Falklands question. This was neither fully articulated by politicians nor formally considered by officials in the years before the war, but ironically became a key factor in Margaret Thatcher's decision to send a task force once Argentina had invaded.[3] Britain's political and economic elites, therefore, held a variety of shifting, overlapping or conflicting positions on the Falklands issue in the years before 1982, and these are explored in the following chapters.

The question which has underpinned many accounts of the Falklands dispute is whether the war could have been avoided. The official inquiry into the war concluded that both Labour and Conservative governments may have inadvertently given the impression that they would not defend the Falkland Islands; Labour by failing to respond to an Argentine landing on the South Atlantic island of Southern Thule in 1976 and the Conservatives by announcing the withdrawal of the only British naval presence in the area, *HMS Endurance*.[4] The Conservatives' British Nationality Act (1981), which stripped many Islanders of British citizenship, also signalled that the Falkland Islands were a low priority for the government. Labour politicians, however, claim that they kept a closer eye on the security of the Islands than the Conservatives, highlighting that during a period of tension in 1977, the Labour government sent a nuclear-powered submarine to the South Atlantic and put a task force on standby. In Callaghan's words: 'The Labour Government kept the peace and the Conservative Government won the war.'[5] There is considerable evidence to support this interpretation of events: James Callaghan was the son of a Royal Navy petty officer and took a close interest in defence matters. His official correspondence shows several handwritten notes to officials querying defence arrangements for the islands.[6] He even asked for a weekly map of Britain's naval deployments to understand how quickly forces could reach the South Atlantic.[7] (He received the maps, which showed Britain's ships drawn in pencil and marked with a ruler.) As a former foreign secretary, he understood well the Falklands question. Foreign Secretary David Owen, a former navy minister representing the naval town of Plymouth and a self-confessed 'nuclear submarine aficionado', also recalls watching the Falklands 'like a hawk'.[8] As well as sending a task force in 1977, Labour put British naval forces on standby on two other occasions in 1976–1977 during periods of tension with Argentina, and Owen also proposed sending another nuclear submarine to the area in 1978.[9] The 1977 deployment cannot have deterred an invasion because Argentina did not know about it, but it showed that the Labour government was ready to respond. In contrast, Margaret Thatcher, who instinctively took a pro-Islander stance and scrawled messages in their support on memos presented to her about the Falklands in 1979–1981, failed to watch the issue closely and ignored the warnings about *HMS Endurance* given to her by the foreign secretary, Lord Carrington, and others. However, Carrington can be blamed for failing to impress on his colleagues the urgency of the matter; the cabinet did not discuss the Falklands for more than a year before the invasion.[10] Thatcher and others were later critical of the Foreign Office, but officials had been urging ministers to act on the Falklands; it was the politicians who failed to heed their advice.

Notes

1. 'Argentina's Flight from Freedom', report by John Shakespeare, 1 April 1976, The National Archives (TNA): FCO7/3027.
2. Lawrence Freedman, *The Official History of the Falklands Campaign*, Vol. I (London: Routledge, 2005); Aaron Donaghy, *The British Government and the Falkland Islands* (Basingstoke: Palgrave Macmillan, 2014); and Max Hastings and Simon Jenkins, *The Battle for the Falklands* (London: Pan Books, 2010).
3. Margaret Thatcher, *The Downing Street Years* (London: Harper Collins, 1993), p. 173.
4. *Falkland Islands Review*, The Lord Franks (London: HMO, 1983).
5. James Callaghan, *Time and Chance* (Glasgow: Collins/Fontana, 1988), p. 370. See also Donaghy, *The British Government*.
6. See A.J. Collins to Mr. Edmonds, 9 March 1976, TNA: FCO7/3199; D.G.F. Hall to Neville French, 26 March 1976, TNA: FCO7/3199; and Bryan Cartledge to Martin Vile, 24 October 1977, TNA: PREM 16/1504.
7. Cartledge to Roger Facer, MOD, 11 November 1977, TNA: PREM 16/1504; Nigel Brind to Cartledge, 14 November 1977, TNA: PREM 16/1504.

8. David Owen interview with the author, 3 November 2014.
9. *HMS Eskimo* was sent to the South Atlantic in March 1976; and a task force was put on standby in Gibraltar in 1977. David Owen proposed sending a nuclear submarine in February 1978 and a frigate in October 1978, but his cabinet colleagues did not think it necessary. Freedman, pp. 86, 95 and 98.
10. The Franks report implicitly criticised Carrington for failing to bring the matter up in cabinet. Instead he sent a series of minutes to ministerial colleagues. *Falkland Islands Review*, p. 79.

CHAPTER 8

Business as Usual: Arming the Junta (1976–1979)

Three weeks before the military coup in Argentina, a prominent Anglo-Argentine businessman called at the British embassy in Buenos Aires to make what he described as 'a discreet approach' on behalf of the Argentine military leadership. He said that Argentina's military leaders were anxious to obtain international recognition for their regime once they had 'thrown out' President Isabel Perón and were particularly concerned that the British Government 'in view of its attitude towards the military government in Chile, might withhold such recognition'.[1] The British chargé d'affaires assured him that Britain's attitude was 'by tradition, purely pragmatic' and was extended when a new government was seen to be in control of the greater part of the country and enjoyed a reasonable prospect of permanence. 'This information would be well received by the military,' said the intermediary, Willie Anderson, chairman of the *Review of the River Plate*. Even before the conspirators had taken power, they had an indication that Britain would not take a hard line against the military regime.

Few were surprised when Isabel Perón, the widowed third wife of Juan Perón, was finally overthrown on 24 March 1976. She had presided over economic crisis, institutional deadlock and rising political violence. Peronism, a corporatist alliance between the military, industrialists and organised labour, had begun to unravel. The government had become increasingly authoritarian, clamping down on workers' organisations. An ultra-right-wing death squad, the Argentine Anti-Communist Alliance

(AAA), which had links to the security forces, had emerged and was murdering 'subversives' with impunity. Meanwhile the left-wing Peronist guerrilla organisation, the Montoneros, had become disillusioned with the government and began a campaign of bombings and kidnappings. British diplomats believed a coup was inevitable and some even thought it necessary. 'Despite the reluctance of the military leaders to take this step, the consequences of the Peronist regime's three years in office were so dire that some such action became essential,' wrote John Shakespeare, the British chargé d'affaires, a few days after the coup.[2] 'No one could possibly run Argentina worse than the Peronist regime,' was the early judgement of another high-ranking FCO official in London.[3]

The military closed congress, banned political parties, dissolved the supreme court and arrested dozens of 'left-wingers', including former ministers, in pre-dawn raids, while hundreds of others simply disappeared. A month after the coup, Shakespeare—who was the top official in the British embassy—observed: 'The crushing of subversion is now the government's top priority. Unfortunately, the methods being used both by the subversive groups and the authorities are virtually the same. In spite of the takeover by the military of all matters relating to internal security, the bestial activities of the counter-terrorist gangs continue unabated.' He, nevertheless, concluded that: 'The new government has made a most promising start and hardly put a foot wrong during its first month in power.'[4] He described the junta's style as 'refreshingly modest'.[5]

In London, it took some time for Foreign Office officials to recognise that the disappearances were not simply the work of independent death squads, but were organised by the state.

As early as April 1976, the British military attaché in Buenos Aires reported: 'These casualties are said to be the victims of right-wing terrorism, but such activities can only be carried out by, or with the complete support of, the security forces.'[6] However, Foreign Office briefings throughout the following year continued to attribute the violence to non-state groups, to describe the coup as 'almost bloodless' and to emphasise the 'difficult security situation'.[7] Nine months after the coup, for example the FCO prepared an answer for parliamentary questions in the Commons which stated:

> The present Argentine Government came to power peacefully and enjoys the support of the majority of the people. They inherited a difficult and violent internal security situation. But the Argentine authorities are publicly pledged to respect human rights and dignities.[8]

Shakespeare came close to justifying the violence in a despatch to London in which he wrote:

> Many things have happened and are still happening here which cannot be condoned [nevertheless]...At the risk of stating the obvious, I should like to recommend that in any condemnation of Argentine policy which we make, we also express understanding of the enormously difficult problems the regime faces and condemn at least equally the left-wing terrorist activities which are the root cause.[9]

Within eighteen months, the Foreign Office was receiving evidence that the scale of the atrocities committed by the state in Argentina were greater than those of any South American dictatorship in history.[10] A truth commission later laid bare the industrial nature of the repression. Thousands were tortured in secret detention centres, their bodies dumped in mass graves or thrown from military helicopters into the Rio de la Plata or the Atlantic Ocean. Hundreds of babies were taken from prisoners and given to military couples to adopt. The commission documented 8960 cases of disappeared persons; Argentine human rights groups believe the number could be as high as 30,000.[11]

Recognising the Regime

On the day of the coup, the Labour party was in the midst of a leadership election. Harold Wilson had unexpectedly resigned and within a few weeks, on 5 April 1976, James Callaghan became Prime Minister. Faced with a depreciating currency and imminent financial crisis, which culminated in Callaghan appealing to the IMF for a loan and imposing drastic spending cuts later that year, most Labour ministers' minds were on domestic issues. While the cause of Chile had so inspired the labour movement that it captured ministers' attention despite these domestic problems, they were under far less pressure from campaigners to act on Argentina. Ministers were more willing to accept the FCO's line and there was little debate about policy. The absence of strong social movement and political pressure therefore resulted in a policy that prioritised British business interests and geo-strategic considerations, above 'ethical' concerns. No sanctions were imposed: there was no arms embargo, export credit was not cut, and trade and investment were encouraged.

Although the Foreign Office had been expecting a coup, it did not know the exact date. The day before the military took power, the British government had given a message to the Argentine foreign minister offering secret talks on the Falklands. The Foreign Office's top priority, therefore, on hearing of Isabel Perón's overthrow, was to recognise the regime 'as soon as practicable' in order to ensure that Argentina's new military leaders did not make Britain's secret communication public.[12] The FCO's recommendation was approved without question by Labour minister of state Ted Rowlands, and in contrast to the case of Chile, there were barely any protests from Labour MPs calling on the government not to recognise the junta.[13] Just two days after the military took power, the British government gave formal recognition to the regime and informed the Argentine foreign minister that Britain hoped 'to maintain close and friendly relations' with the new administration.[14]

This was the first of many occasions in which officials and politicians used the Falklands as a justification for maintaining good relations with the regime, although it should be noted that the policy towards the Argentine dictatorship was not exceptional; Britain maintained good relations with all of the other Southern Cone dictatorships—Uruguay, Paraguay and Brazil—except Chile. The common argument in all these cases was that relations with these military regimes, however unpleasant, would be in Britain's commercial and business interests.

Doing Business with the Junta

Just days after the coup in Argentina, Chargé d'Affaires John Shakespeare opined that 'the new regime should offer opportunities for British businessmen.'[15] In London, Hugh Carless drew up a policy paper on relations with the new regime. The ideal policy objective was to 'establish an across-the-board dialogue with Argentina…with the aim of reducing the Falkland Islands dispute to more reasonable proportions'.[16] The content of the dialogue was dominated by economic and commercial considerations and comprised:

- Frigate construction programme
- Security of the South Atlantic
- Argentine credit requirements
- Argentine approaches to oil majors[17]

British manufacturer Vosper Thorneycroft was discussing a multimillion pound contract to build six warships for the Argentine navy and trying to secure this order became one of the main objectives of British policy over the next two years. Britain also envisaged working with Argentina to reduce the 'Soviet threat' in the South Atlantic and to prevent other nations illegally fishing there, while British oil companies were interested in exploring for oil off the coast of Argentina.

But the immediate priority was to ensure that the new Argentine regime had enough credit to stabilise its economy. The junta's finance minister, José Martínez de Hoz, was invited to London by the British government in July 1976—one stop on his tour of Europe and North America aimed at persuading foreign creditors to reschedule Argentina's debts. Martínez de Hoz, who came from one of Argentina's oldest land-owning families and wore tweeds in the style of an English gentleman, was a staunch conservative with longstanding links to the military. He became the most important civilian in the government and masterminded the junta's free-market economic strategy. As in Chile, there was a complementary relationship between the junta's economic policies and its violent repression, since the arrest and murder of trade unionists destroyed their collective bargaining power and ability to resist.[18] FCO officials were impressed with Martínez de Hoz's neoliberal policies, which included cutting public spending, reducing the role of the state and holding down wages. Shakespeare met the minister in Buenos Aires and reported: 'Speaking in impeccable English, Dr Martínez de Hoz….gave a most persuasive account of the new Argentine economic programme.'[19] Whilst in the UK, the minister 'would prefer not to be forced to hold a full press conference at which he might get asked a lot of wider questions outside his sphere (e.g. on human rights),' Shakespeare added.[20] Another British embassy official noted: 'He is a cultured person with a good knowledge of Britain and things British and had an English nanny.'[21]

On arrival in London, Martínez de Hoz was given a lunch at 11 Downing Street hosted by the chancellor of the exchequer, Dennis Healey, Labour's trade secretary, Edmund Dell, and the governor of the Bank of England.[22] Only junior minister Ted Rowlands raised the issue of human rights.

It was, however, the British business community that gave Martínez de Hoz the warmest welcome. The Director General of the CBI hosted a drinks party with selected guests before Martínez de Hoz gave a speech to 150 British industrialists.[23] His presentation was 'considered excellent', wrote a Department of Trade official, 'It was both frank and open and was well received.'[24] In the evening, the Chairman and directors of Lloyds Bank International and Baring Brothers dined with him at Brooks's, a gentlemen's club in St James's Street, and the following day, he met British bankers at the headquarters of Lloyds Bank.[25] Guy Huntrods, the Latin America Director of Lloyds International, produced a confidential briefing for British investors, in which he wrote:

> The [Argentine] Government must thus walk a tightrope between the need for firmness and the danger of being branded by international opinion as repressive—a charge all too lightly bandied around these days and very much *à la mode* in certain quarters only too ready to pass superficial and prejudiced judgements on Latin American countries where forms of government do not fit into the grey mould of social democracy and mediocrity which is their idea.[26]

His report concluded: 'We are relieved by the change of government, pleased with the calibre of the economic team and with its general philosophy and objectives and encouraged by its performance so far.'[27]

British banks, including Lloyds, Barclays, Midland and Natwest, showed their confidence in the new regime by offering US$60m of new loans to the Argentina junta and Martínez de Hoz declared his visit to London to be 'a highlight in his tour of European capitals'.[28] Argentina secured pledges totalling US$340m from European banks, but even this large sum was dwarfed by the US$500m offered by US banks, plus a further US$159m from the IMF.[29]

There followed more visits by Argentine ministers to the UK later that year. Esso and Shell invited the junta's energy secretary, Guillermo Zubarán, to visit their operations in the North Sea, in the hope of securing business in Argentina's offshore industry.[30] Zubarán also met Sir Jack Rampton, the top civil servant at the Department of Energy.[31] Another visitor was the minister for marine resources, Captain Noe Guevara, who was interested in purchasing British ships and discussing fishing ventures in Argentine waters. Staying as a guest of the British government in September 1976, the Argentine navy captain was given lunches by Unilever and BP, and a dinner at the Hyde Park Hotel hosted by Evan Luard MP, parliamentary under-secretary of state at the FCO.[32] He visited British shipyards in Lowestoft and met shipbuilding companies including Brooke Marine and A & P Appledore. Captain Guevara was even invited to dine at the Cambridge home of FCO official John Heap, where he met the director of the British Antarctic Survey. When preparing the evening, Heap, the head of the FCO's Polar Regions section, wrote: 'I envisage, while avoiding rudeness to our lady guests, a sort of mini-teach-in...in which we should touch lightly on the opportunities for Anglo-Argentine co-operation.'[33]

Civil servants and diplomats shared the British business community's view that the military regime provided an opportunity for increased trade and investment. When the head of the Argentine business federation, Guillermo Loncán, visited London a few months after the military takeover, a British embassy official recommended listening to his views 'if we are to take full advantage of the change in direction in the Argentine economy following the coup.'[34] British companies rarely needed to lobby government directly; officials and company representatives held frequent informal conversations. BP, for example, gave officials appraisals of the oil potential of the waters around the Falklands and Unilever shared its thoughts on the fishing prospects. Officials and private sector executives often attended the same seminars and drinks receptions, which provided opportunities for casual exchanges.

In Argentina, there was an even more closely-knit informal social network between British diplomats, the Anglo-Argentine community and Argentine business, military and government circles. When the junta's trade secretary, Guillermo Bravo, visited London shortly after the coup, for example, a British embassy official received a report-back through the informal channel of the Argentine minister's spouse: 'My wife is a personal friend of Sra de Bravo and the latter has said that he thoroughly enjoyed his visit and found it most useful.'[35] Most Anglo-Argentines were—like Anglo-Chileans in Chile—virulently pro-coup. At a lunch organised by the British chambers of commerce in Buenos Aires two months after the military takeover, an embassy official reported that 'there was sincere concern that the army would not have sufficient staying power to cope with any social unrest...and would "give in"'.[36] During the lunch, the chairman of the British chambers of commerce, Mr. Foster of GEC, asked whether 'Amnesty International would spoil the atmosphere...and prejudice Argentina's chances of obtaining money'.[37] On this occasion, the embassy official, Eric Anglin, told the meeting that 'the simplest way to undermine Amnesty International views... would be to name publicly all the persons in detention and to see that they were properly charged (or set free)'.[38]

Embassy staff sometimes, however, appeared to be influenced by the conservative social milieu in which they moved and expressed views which were to the right of those of the Foreign Office in London. On one occasion, a British refugee support group that visited Argentina, complained to the Foreign Office about the 'unsympathetic and unhelpful attitude' of some of the consular staff in the British embassy towards Latin American refugees seeking to flee the Argentine dictatorship.[39] The campaigners alleged that locally-engaged embassy staff had made comments such as: 'lower classes of refugees presented problems', that the refugees were all 'Communists' and 'why did the UK wish to accept these types of people?'[40] Officials in London suspected that there was truth in the allegations and asked the chargé d'affaires to investigate, but he staunchly defended his staff.[41]

DIPLOMATS AND THE MEDIA

The influence of the right-wing Anglo-Argentine community on embassy officials was illustrated once again during a spat between London and Buenos Aires over a 1978 BBC Panorama programme about human rights in Argentina. When the television documentary was shown to the English Club in Buenos Aires, there were 'guffaws' as victims described their experience of torture and applause when an Anglo-Argentine woman interviewed in the film said of the disappeared: 'If I were the government, I'd do ten times more'.[42] Robert Cox, editor of *The Buenos Aires Herald*, was shocked by the audience's response: 'To chortle over human suffering while grasping a glass of gin and tonic is to show such an unawareness of Argentine reality.'[43] Despite disapproving of the attitudes of the more conservative 'gin-swillers of the English Club'—as one British diplomat described them—embassy officials nevertheless agreed that the Panorama programme gave a distorted picture of Argentina.[44] Hugh Carless, now chargé d'affaires in Buenos Aires, wrote to London asking the Foreign Office to make a complaint to the director general of the BBC. The documentary, he said, 'concentrated on torture and murder' and 'distorted the Argentine reality...to resemble the picture put out by the urban guerrilla movement.'[45] But London disagreed; an FCO official wrote: 'Any presentation by the BBC of Argentina which did not meet with the disapproval of the Argentine authorities would hardly have been worth making. No one would expect, surely, the BBC to do a whitewash job.'[46] This was not simply a question of differing personal political opinions, since other embassy officials in Buenos Aires agreed with Carless that the BBC had been influenced by Montoneros propaganda.[47]

While the embassy may have been more sensitive to what it regarded as guerrilla groups' manipulation of the press, the FCO in London was also concerned about critical coverage of Argentina and discussed how to persuade newspapers to soften their line. One particular concern was the reporting of *The Times*. John Shakespeare had written to London in March 1977 when he was chargé d'affaires, saying: 'I am growing increasingly concerned about the anti-Argentine trend of *The Times*'.[48] He was unhappy that a recent article had described the Argentine regime as 'even by South American standards, an exceptionally nasty one', and he suggested that *The Times* stringer was an 'angry young man with some trendily leftist views'.[49] A few months later, Shakespeare reported a conversation with the Argentine finance minister Martínez de Hoz who had said he would be grateful for anything Shakespeare could do 'to persuade *The Times* to take a more objective view of the Argentine situation'.[50] The British chargé d'affaires replied that he would 'be happy to do so in a purely personal capacity if the opportunity arose.'[51] In London, the head of the FCO's South America Department, John Ure, offered to meet *The Times*' Latin America leader writer 'to give him a better perspective' on Argentina and to reactivate a friendship with *The Times* diplomatic correspondent to 'talk to him along similar lines'.[52] However, the FCO's news department thought it would be better to talk to *The Times* staff 'on the basis of a casual encounter, rather than to seek a meeting deliberately for the purpose,' adding that, 'there is everything to be said for trying to get *The Times* to adopt a more objective approach to Argentina, but there is obviously a limit beyond which we should not go in defending Argentina's cause'.[53] A few days later Shakespeare met a *Times* correspondent at a reception in the Argentine embassy in London and complained to him about the paper's 'disgracefully tendentious' reporting on Argentina. The chargé d'affaires concluded: 'Perhaps if we speak to enough members of the staff of *The Times* on these lines occasionally, they will eventually get the message.'[54]

The Difficulties of Solidarity with Argentina

The Foreign Office, then, had the same pragmatic attitude towards the Argentine junta as it had towards the Pinochet dictatorship; however distasteful the regime, trade and business opportunities should be pursued. The difference in the case of Chile was that political pressure forced the government to impose a number of sanctions. Although awareness gradually grew on the left of the human rights violations being perpetrated in Argentina, the anti-junta campaign never achieved the same widespread support in the labour movement as the Chile Solidarity Campaign (CSC). The Argentina campaigners, therefore, never had the political leverage over key policy-makers or 'gate-keepers' that the Chile campaign had had; Labour ministers did not need to fear a back-bench revolt or a protest from leading trade unions, let alone a strike, if they sold arms to Argentina or rescheduled the junta's debts. Whereas the Labour cabinet had discussed the Pinochet regime numerous times, it never considered its human rights policy towards the Argentine junta; all cabinet discussion on Argentina was confined to the Falklands question.

For the left, Chile had been a clear cut case of a democratically-elected socialist versus fascism; Argentina was far more complex. The Labour party had no sympathy for Peronism , which it regarded as authoritarian. Meanwhile, the violent campaigns of the Montoneros and the other guerrilla group, the Trotskyist-turned-Maoist *Ejército Revolucionario del Pueblo* (ERP), held little appeal for most activists in the British labour movement. 'It was hard to know who the good guys were in Argentina,' one campaigner recalled.[55] When the military overthrew Isabel Perón, it was not immediately clear how much more violent the new regime would be. *The Guardian* reported an 'almost bloodless coup' and for the first two months, the only deaths reported were those of guerrilla fighters.[56] It would take many months, even years, before the left around the world began to realise how systematic and widespread the violence was.

The Labour Party and British trade unions had links with organisations in Chile and had organised deputations to the country during Allende's administration. After the Chilean coup, therefore, Labour MPs and trade unionists had a direct source of information and, in some cases, knew the political prisoners on whose behalf they were campaigning. Chilean left-wing political parties (socialists, communists, radicals) and the main

Chilean trade union confederation were of a similar ideology and structure to those in Britain, whereas the populist Peronist party and the corporatist Argentine unions were alien to the British labour movement and they had little personal contact with them.

Another difference was the position of the Communist Party. In Britain, the Communist Party had played a crucial role winning support for the CSC in the trade unions and labour movement and many of the key figures in the CSC belonged to the party. But in Argentina, the Communist party had an ambiguous position towards the military takeover. Extremely hostile towards the Peronist regime, in the months before the coup, they had called for a civic-military union to defend democracy and social justice.[57] When the military ousted Perón in Argentina, the Communist party believed that Jorge Rafael Videla, the junta leader, represented a moderate faction within the armed forces, which deserved support against a more hard-line '*Pinochetista*' faction.[58] Although Communist Party members in Britain received no clear party line, the party's daily newspaper, *The Morning Star*, reported Argentine events in a very different tone from that of its campaigning-style articles on Chile. The coup was reported in a small paragraph under the headline 'A New President for Argentina?'[59] Adding to the ambiguous position of the British Communist Party was the fact that the Soviet Union became an important trade partner of the Argentine military regime. Argentina supplied the Soviet Union with thousands of tonnes of grain a year, a supply line that became vital after the United States imposed a ban on exporting grain to the Soviets in 1980 after the invasion of Afghanistan. Cuba also quietly maintained relations with the Argentina junta. Positions on Argentina, then, never clearly divided along Cold War lines.

The groups working on Argentina were initially confined to people with a close personal interest in Argentina, such as journalists or exiles and refugee support groups. An informal Committee for Solidarity with Argentine Political Prisoners was established in 1974 by Christopher Roper, a former Reuters correspondent in Argentina who had gone on to work for the *Latin American Newsletter* in London. This group tried to help Argentine activists who had been arrested or 'disappeared' under the government of Isabel Perón.[60] In March 1976, Roper and others at the *Latin American Newsletter* launched the Argentina Support Movement (ASM) at a meeting at the London School of Economics (LSE).[61]

Although this inaugural event attracted about 60 people, the group remained small with between five and 15 people attending its weekly meetings in London. Exhausted by the scale of the task and the paucity of the response in Britain, many of the original members of the ASM had withdrawn from political activity by 1977. Those who remained in the ASM helped to found the British Argentina Campaign in 1978, which sought to develop links with British political groups and unions, and focus less on internal Argentine politics.[62] It worked closely with the student organisation Third World First and drew activists from the International Marxist Group (IMG), the Labour Party, and the feminist organisation Big Flame.[63] The peak of its activity was the 1978 World Cup campaign, where it worked with other organizations to raise the profile of human rights abuses in Argentina (see below).

A separate Committee for Human Rights in Argentina (CHRA) was set up in June 1977. The founding members were Father Patrick Rice, an Irish priest who had been kidnapped in Argentina in 1976, and Richard and Cristina Whitecross, a British couple who had been imprisoned in 1975 but later released by the Argentine authorities.[64] This group focused more narrowly on human rights and placed emphasis on directly lobbying the British government, leading several deputations to the FCO and sending letters to ministers and MPs. Later, Amnesty International, CAFOD and other NGOs, as well as the international sections of the TUC and Labour party lobbied on Argentina, but these specialist campaigns did not reach a broad audience.

The Moderating Role of the Foreign Office

Argentina was not a priority for the Labour government and there was far less friction between ministers and officials than in the case of Chile, but if Labour Party members did query Argentina policy, the FCO tended to advocate caution. When Tom McNally, adviser to Prime Minister James Callaghan, asked the FCO for a briefing on human rights in Argentina in preparation for the Labour Party conference of September 1976, Hugh Carless, the head of the Latin America Department of the FCO, gave him an account that downplayed the role of the Argentine state and attributed the violence to 'extremists on the left and right'.[65]

When the prime minister's advisor wondered what line the Labour government should take, Carless advised against Britain taking any unilateral measures. He was nevertheless, aware that Labour politicians might want the government to be *seen* to be taking action. The UK had taken a very soft position when it discussed Argentina with other EEC members in July 1976; according to an FCO memo, the UK government had agreed that 'nothing would be achieved by open criticism of the Argentine Government's handling of the internal situation.'[66] Moreover, during a debate in the European Parliament, Britain was 'among those who resisted attempts to express condemnation of Argentina.'[67] Ahead of the Labour Party conference, Carless suggested raising Argentina at a meeting of the ECC political directors. When an FCO colleague queried whether this meant Britain was hardening its position on Argentina, she was assured this was not the case. An FCO official wrote:

> It is possible that it will be raised in Foreign Affairs debate at the Labour Party Conference this month. If it were, it could be helpful to the Government to be able to let it be known that we had...expressed our concern...The objective would not be to draw parallels with Chile or to inflame passions.[68]

But even this mild proposal was too much for FCO official David Keeling, who warned 'our action in taking the initiative might well get back to the Argentines' and suggested that instead of making a formal statement at the EEC meeting, it might be better to 'to raise the question informally' during the delegates' evening dinner.[69]

The British government took a similarly timid position at the United Nations the following year. Jenny Little, the International Secretary of the Labour Party, asked the government to put Argentina's human rights abuses on the agenda of the UN Commission for Human Rights' annual meeting in Geneva, but the Argentine Government had already asked Britain and 'other friendly governments' to 'do their best to ensure that the subject of Argentina's alleged ill-treatment of refugees is not discussed'.[70] An FCO official wrote:

> For Her Majesty's Government (HMG) to take the lead...would be regarded by the Argentines as an unfriendly act, and thus have unfavourable repercussions on ...forthcoming talks with the Argentineans over the Falklands.[71]

He added, however, that 'it would be entirely wrong for HMG to block discussions of human rights in Argentina over which there is justifiable concern'. The FCO concluded that Britain should 'not seek to initiate debate on Argentina', but neither should it seek to prevent discussion.[72]

This non-committal position was maintained even after Sir Keith Unwin, the British delegate to the UN Commission on Human Rights wrote to the Foreign Office, after reading about abuses in Argentina, saying: 'I am horrified; it is worse than Chile in some ways.'[73] He was particularly shocked by 'the claim that the forces of law and order use buzz-saws on their prisoners'.[74] He asked for FCO guidance on the forthcoming UN meeting and was told:

> We had in mind general statement to the effect that HMG deplore violations of human rights wherever they occur rather than a statement specifically relating to the situation in Argentina. As you know, our relations with Argentina are especially sensitive in view of the Falkland Islands dispute.[75]

Since Labour ministers were not under great political pressure to take radical action, they did not argue against the FCO's cautious line. They also accepted the argument that Britain needed to maintain good relations with Argentina because of the Falklands dispute. Ted Rowlands, the Foreign Office minister who dealt with Argentina and the Falklands, got an early insight into the regime's methods when given a British embassy telegram describing the death of a Radical Party congressman in the custody of the armed forces in October 1976. The congressman, who suffered from a bronchial complaint, had been doused in cold water and left naked in his cell overnight. Rowlands wrote on the telegram: 'Absolutely shameful. I don't want a lot of personal contact with this lot—except where I have to e.g. Falklands'.[76] Rowlands received a number of deputations—for example, one from the Labour Party's International Committee in 1978 and another from the Cambridge Argentina Human Rights Committee in 1979—but on each occasion, he told them that the Falklands dispute tied his hands.[77] The argument could, of course, be turned on its head, that the government should not discuss transferring sovereignty of the Islands to a regime that abused human rights. This was, in fact, the official position adopted by the Labour Party in 1977 but, as the next chapter shows, ministers took little notice of it.[78]

The 1978 World Cup

Human rights activists had most success in broadening their audience during the football World Cup of 1978, which was held in Argentina. Initially, campaigners in Europe and the UK had planned to call for a boycott of the tournament, but that demand was not supported by opponents of the regime in Argentina—neither was it likely to have had much success in Scotland, where excitement at the national team's qualification (and *Schadenfreude* at England's failure to qualify) had caused great excitement. Campaigners therefore concentrated on raising public awareness of human rights abuses in Argentina. Critical articles were published in the press, the National Union of Journalists circulated a letter to members giving them directions on how to behave in Argentina with useful Spanish phrases such as '*dejen de torturarme, por favor*' [Stop torturing me, please]. Vigils or meetings were held in Edinburgh, Dundee, Glasgow, Stirling, Liverpool, Oxford, Newcastle, Leeds, Manchester and London, and members of the public were encouraged to write to the Foreign Office.[79] The FCO received hundreds of letters in 1978—filling seven FCO folders—among them appeals from the historian Eric Hobsbawm; Trent Polytechnic Students Union; the Sheffield Trades Council and an Oxford Quaker group.[80]

The campaign, however, did not mobilise large numbers of MPs or trade union leaders and it was not strong enough to dissuade Scottish Secretary Bruce Millan and sports minister Denis Howell from travelling to Argentina to support the Scottish team. No other European countries sent ministers; among the very few other foreign dignitaries attending was US Secretary of State Henry Kissinger. Sports minister Denis Howell was given a briefing by the Foreign Office which highlighted the junta's 'notable progress' in its 'war against armed subversion' and the revitalisation of the economy.[81] Howell and Millan released a statement which made no mention of human rights, and simply stated that they were 'proud to be representing the Government at Scotland's matches in Argentina'.[82]

Argentina won the Cup. The resulting national euphoria gave a political fillip to the governing junta and, despite the efforts of campaigners, a great propaganda boost.

Chargé d'affaires Hugh Carless wrote:

> Some of the worldwide audience of as many as 1.5 billion…will perhaps have a more human impression of the many-tiered Argentine reality. As well as being a land of physical violence, last month this was a country of meticulous organisation, beautiful stadia and happy and peaceful crowds.[83]

Action on Refugees

The campaign around the World Cup, nevertheless, contributed to a growing awareness in the Labour Party of the human rights crisis in Argentina. The party's International Department issued a report written by Liz Nash entitled, 'Argentina two years after the coup—a terrorist state', which detailed the numbers of killings, political prisoners and disappearances.[84] Shortly after, in June 1978, the party's national executive committee called on the government to suspend arm sales, vote against IMF and World Bank loans to Argentina, and establish a refugee programme for Argentine exiles.[85]

The Labour government made some response, but its measures were limited. In spring 1978, it extended its refugee scheme for Chileans to all Latin Americans, allowing entry to Argentines who could prove they had links to Britain and posed no security risk. But while almost 3000 Chileans were given sanctuary, by January 1979 only 50 visa applications for other Latin Americans had been approved.[86] The Joint Working Group for Refugees estimates that no more than 20 Argentines were admitted under the scheme.[87] The refugee programme was extended partly because the Joint Working Group was an effective pressure group that had built up strong institutional links with Labour ministers and civil servants, but just as important was the fact that, given the small numbers of refugees involved, the cost for the government—politically and financially—was low. (It was nevertheless regarded as too expensive by the Conservatives, who ended the scheme on coming to office.) On issues that had greater financial implications, such as trade sanctions, the Labour government was unwilling to act.

Divisions Within the British Embassy

A limited working relationship also developed between campaigners and the British embassy in Buenos Aires. Embassy staff helped a representative of the Joint Working Group for Refugees by allowing him to send names of political prisoners via diplomatic bag on two occasions, while he was travelling to Argentina, so as not to endanger the detainees. They also allowed Amnesty International to send information to Argentina through embassy channels.[88] A tactic of human rights campaigners was to 'adopt' a political prisoner and the names of detainees were sent to the British embassy in Buenos Aires, where officials tried to find out their whereabouts by making contacts with their relatives. By 1979, the British consular section of the embassy was spending a considerable amount of time tracking down relatives of detainees.[89] That only a small number eventually made it to Britain reflects the grim reality that many of the detainees had been executed and joined the ranks of the 'disappeared'. This cooperation perhaps stemmed from a growing distaste that some in the embassy felt for the regime. The political section of the embassy had been sending regular reports on human rights abuses to the FCO in London, which catalogued the numbers of victims. One despatch sent in 1979 reported that up to 13,000 people might have disappeared, the embassy officer commenting that even if the figures were over-estimated, the numbers were still 'chilling'.[90] According to one official in the embassy, there was a division among officials between those who thought that the priority should be seeking good relations with the regime in order to promote British trade and investment, and those who regarded the junta as 'despicable thugs'.[91] On one occasion, the embassy's commercial section complained, during an internal meeting, that the embassy's reporting on human rights was 'unhelpful' and deterring British investors from doing business. It was particularly unhappy about the briefings given to visiting British trade delegations. The officer responsible for human rights reporting responded by saying: 'I thought that kind of thing went out after Munich.'[92] Despite the differences, it is possible to see from the archived correspondence that those in charge of the British embassy during the Argentine military regime—the two successive chargés d'affaires, John Shakespeare and Hugh Carless, and later the British ambassador, Anthony Williams—took the view, as did the FCO in London, that promoting British trade and investment was the priority, regardless of the nature of the regime.

Britain's Business Lobby

Despite the growing awareness of the human rights abuses, attempts to promote British business links with Argentina accelerated in the later years of the Callaghan government, and an increasing number of British trade missions visited the country. Chargé d'Affaires John Shakespeare wrote of visits by British business leaders: 'We did our best to ensure that they left Buenos Aires in a mood of cautious optimism about Argentina's future prospects.'[93] Lord Nelson, the chairman of GEC, led a London Chamber of Commerce mission in 1978. Accompanied by Sir Anthony

Griffin of British Shipbuilders, Nelson met junta leader General Videla, as well as the Argentine foreign minister and defence minister.[94] A few months later, the Committee on Invisible Exports, an organisation set up by the Bank of England to promote British financial services, held a seminar in Buenos Aires led by Sir Jasper Hollom, the Deputy Governor of the Bank of England, and Sir Francis Sandilands, chairman of Commercial Union Assurance. Other visitors to Buenos Aires in 1978 and early 1979 included Sir Frederick Catherwood, chairman of the British Overseas Trade Board, representatives of the Birmingham Chamber of Commerce and the Birmingham Engineering and Building Centre, and a delegation of Hereford cattle breeders.[95] British investment and trade rose during Labour's period of office; UK net investment in Argentina tripled from £14m in 1975 to £46m in 1979, while British exports jumped from US$146m in 1977 to US$278m in 1979, although officials still continued to lament Britain's failure to win large state contracts.[96] But the clearest example of the British officials' prioritising business over human rights concerns—or threats to the Falklands—was its attitude to arms sales.

Arms Sales to Argentina 1976–1979

Britain had long been a supplier to the Argentine navy and was keen to fend off competition from other European countries. Vickers had signed a contract with the Argentine navy in 1970 to build two Type 42 guided missile destroyers. The first was built in Vickers Barrow shipyard and delivered to the junta in 1977 during the Callaghan government. The second was constructed in Argentina and completed in 1980 during the Thatcher administration. Both were used against Britain in the Falklands War. But a much larger contract for warships was under negotiation during the mid-1970s: shipbuilders Vosper Thorneycroft were in talks to construct six Type 21 frigates for the Argentine navy in a deal that was valued at between £300m and £600m. Trying to secure this contract became one of the key aims for officials between 1976 and 1978 and figured in any official discussion of policy towards Argentina. As the Cabinet prepared to launch a fresh initiative to discuss the sovereignty of the Falkland Islands with Argentina in March 1976, the FCO's speaking notes for Foreign Secretary James Callaghan warned that if Britain did not start serious negotiations, Argentina might attack the Islands or 'a lesser but still harmful option open to the Argentines would be to terminate... valuable contracts for the equipment of their navy and merchant marine'.[97] The rather strange logic was that the Argentine military posed a threat to the Falkland Islands; therefore talks should be pursued which would then enable Britain to sell more military equipment to Argentina.

The most energetic proponent of arms sales was the defence sales department of the Ministry of Defence (MOD). The defence sales officials were virtual lobbyists for weapons manufacturers and their eagerness to promote sales, regardless of the wider strategic consequences, sometimes brought them into conflict with other sections of the MOD. The Department of Trade, which also had close relationships with British companies, was another enthusiastic advocate for arms sales. The Departments of Industry and of Employment were also keen to win contracts in order to defend British jobs. An example of this was their support for the extraordinary proposal to lend or sell one of the Royal Navy's own warships to Argentina, weakening Britain's own defences, in order to clinch the Vosper deal. Sir Anthony Griffin, chairman of the nationalised company British Shipbuilders, wrote to the Industry Secretary Eric Varley in February 1978, suggesting the diversion of a Royal Navy ship to Argentina, noting that delays in negotiating the deal meant that the Argentine navy 'now find themselves in a position where...they will lack operational warships'.[98] Varley supported the idea, as did Labour's employment secretary, Albert Booth, Scottish secretary Bruce Millan and trade secretary Edmund Dell.[99]

Defence sales officials lobbied for the move and when an MOD official from another department warned that 'increasing the Argentine maritime capability in the near future by diverting a ship presents significant implications, both politically and militarily, given the not so remote possibility of the RN finding itself in confrontation with the Argentine navy,' Roger Harding, a senior defence sales official, remarked: 'I would have thought that "damaging consequences both military and political" is a rather extravagant claim.'[100]

But the commanders of the armed forces were strongly against diverting a ship to Argentina and convinced the defence secretary, Fred Mulley and foreign secretary David Owen to oppose the move.[101] It is important to note, however, that both Mulley and Owen were in favour of Vosper selling the six warships to Argentina; they just did not want to divert a Royal Navy ship to Argentina in order to win the contract.[102] The fact that four Labour ministers and senior MOD defence sales officials had contemplated strengthening the capability of the Argentine navy at the expense of the Royal Navy, despite the possibility of a conflict in the Falklands—and despite the regime's poor human rights records—is an indication of how politicians and officials, particularly those in departments with close links to private companies, could become tunnel-visioned when large business contracts were at stake.

The frigate contract was eventually awarded to the German manufacturer Blohm and Voss, which had offered a better price and a shorter delivery time. The Falkland dispute and Argentine concerns about the inefficiency of nationalised British shipbuilding companies were also factors. But British officials and senior business figures also blamed Foreign Secretary David Owen for 'snubbing' the head of the Argentine navy, Admiral Emilio Massera when he visited London in July 1978. Admiral Massera was one of the architects of the dirty war, responsible for the notorious *Escuela de Suboficiales de Mecánica de la Armada* (ESMA), the naval mechanical schoolwhere thousands of detainees were tortured and murdered. After the fall of the dictatorship Massera was convicted in Argentina of crimes against humanity and the naval school was turned into a museum testifying to the horrors perpetrated by the regime. While the extent of his crimes might not have been apparent in 1978, he was well known as one of the most hard-line leaders of the coup. Massera came on a 'private' visit to London on 3 July 1978 to look at the prospects for arms purchases. He met the British Chief of the Naval Staff, Sir Terence Lewin, at a function at the Argentine embassy, as well as officials from the MOD.[103] It is extraordinary that the commander of the Argentine navy met the commander of the British navy four years before the Falklands war, yet all official files relating to the visit have been destroyed.[104]

There are no records, therefore, of the advice given to Foreign Secretary David Owen before Massera's visit, but his decision not to meet the Argentine naval chief—because he was a 'complete shit', Owen said later—was bitterly criticised, particularly by MOD sales officials and business leaders.[105] L. Salthouse of the MOD's sales department complained of 'the unfavourable political climate created by official attitudes towards Argentina'.[106] The British naval attaché in Buenos Aires attributed the failure to win the frigate contract to 'the Falklands issue; our treatment of Chile and anti-Argentine attitudes in Britain'.[107] Meanwhile, Lord Nelson, the chairman of GEC, said in a letter to the permanent under-secretary of the FCO, that the cool reception he had received in Britain had made 'a very sour impression' on Massera.[108] Edmund Dell told Owen that several business leaders, at a dinner he had recently attended had 'expressed concern about the effect which our stance on human rights was having...on our trade interest there.'[109]

Stung at the loss of frigate contracts, the MOD and Department of Trade then began to lobby the FCO to invite the head of the Argentine Air Force, General Orlando Agosti, to Britain, in the hope of persuading him to buy Hawk trainer jets.[110] Lord Nelson wrote to the permanent under secretary at the FCO, Michael Palliser, warning that if Owen blocked Agosti's visit, it would be 'disastrous to our prospects of obtaining contracts for the Air Force.'[111] Meanwhile, Sir Denis Spotswood, the former chief of the British Air Staff and now vice-chairman of Rolls Royce, rang the MOD to say on a recent visit to Argentina he had met Agosti, who was a 'very nice chap and not averse to the UK'.[112] (Agosti, a junta member, was later convicted and imprisoned for the torture of eight people). Both Defence Secretary Mulley and Trade Secretary Dell argued in favour of inviting Agosti.[113] Under such pressure, David Owen agreed to invite the Argentine air force commander, but, at the last minute, Agosti pulled out of the trip for domestic reasons. Owen, who had written a book on human rights while he was foreign secretary, had not changed the broad policy towards Argentina but even token gestures, such as refusing to meet Argentine officers, generated criticism from those departments—such as the DoT and MOD—with the closest links to business, as well as from some Foreign Office officials.[114]

Although the Agosti visit was cancelled, there were numerous other visits by Argentine officers to the UK during Labour's period of office and many British defence officials visited Argentina—but it is impossible to have a complete picture because numerous British files on military visits have been destroyed.[115] Three Argentine air force brigadiers came to Britain in June 1977, where they met Air Marshall P.D.G. Terry, vice chief of the air staff, and visited the RAF Valley station in Anglesey. They also met representatives of Marconi Radar Systems and Cossor Electronics, while Hawker Siddeley Aviation gave a 'dinner for the guests and their ladies' at the Café Royal.[116] The leader of the Argentine delegation, Brigadier Miguel Ángel Osses, was indicted in 2009, accused of involvement in 100 cases of kidnapping and torture.[117] An assistant Argentine naval attaché visited the Royal Marines base in Devonport in November 1977 and was particularly interested in the Commandos' anti-terrorist strategies.[118] Colonel L. E. Hudson of

British Commando forces reported: 'He strongly supported the coup in Argentina and believed very tough measures should be taken against terrorists... [he] showed a keen interest in all aspects of our work.'[119] The second-in-command of the Argentine navy, Vice Admiral Armando Lambruschini, was also invited to Britain. The FCO's Hugh Carless confirmed that Lambruschini and other senior Argentine naval officers had accepted an invitation from British Shipbuilders to tour British shipyards in the spring of 1978.[120] There are no other official documents relating to his visit because the 1978 FCO file on military visits has been destroyed. However, *The Daily Telegraph* reported that three Argentine vice-admirals were shown round shipyards in Southampton and Devonport and were introduced to chief of the naval staff, Admiral Sir Terence Lewin, as well as Sir Anthony Griffin of British Shipbuilders.[121] Lambruschini went on to become head of the navy and, after the fall of the junta, was imprisoned for torture and kidnapping.

On the British side, officials and business leaders made numerous trips to drum up interest in arms sales. Vice Admiral Sir Philip Watson, Director General Weapons (Naval), accepted an invitation in October 1976 to visit top officials in the Argentine navy because he had been 'personally involved in giving weapons advice...particularly the missile and other weapons systems' on the two Type 42 destroyers that Britain had sold and on the Type 21 frigates it hoped to sell.[122] The chairman of British Shipbuilders, Sir Anthony Griffin, visited twice in 1978. On the second occasion, accompanied by the chairman of Vickers, William Richardson, he gave a presentation to Argentine naval officers which began: 'We, as friends of Argentina and the Argentine navy, feel we must tell you all we know.'[123] In the same year, the deputy chairman of British Aerospace, Allen Greenwood, went to Argentina to tout the Hawk trainer jets to the air force.[124] Roger Harding of the MOD's defence sales department made three trips to Argentina between 1977 and January 1979, in which he met senior officers from all branches of the Argentine armed forces. An ever-vocal enthusiast for promoting arms, he reported to London: 'I gain the overwhelming impression that Argentina is very much a "land of opportunity" for sales of defence equipment if political difficulties can be overcome.'[125] The defence sales department were assiduously focused on selling arms, chafing against any restrictions and keen to take up any opportunity regardless of the human rights concerns or strategic implications. On one occasion, they asked

8 BUSINESS AS USUAL: ARMING THE JUNTA (1976–1979)

that the Argentine navy be allowed to test Exocet missiles in Cardigan Bay, because 'unless we demonstrate to the Argentinians our willingness to be helpful in all requests of a military nature then our chances of securing the substantial military contracts likely to be awarded in the future are considerably diminished'.[126] The French-made Exocet missiles were, of course, used to lethal effect against British forces in the Falklands war.

The question of selling arms to Argentina was a difficult issue for the Labour government because, as Ted Rowlands told one deputation of backbenchers, many jobs were at risk in the manufacturing industry, particularly in Britain's declining shipbuilding sector.[127] The Labour secretaries of employment, industry and trade had lobbied for the government to take exceptional measures to win the frigate contract on the grounds of jobs, and the Northern Ireland minister argued strongly, in November 1978, to be given the go-ahead to sell blowpipe surface-to-air missiles and firing units to Argentina in order to protect employment at the Shorts Brothers factory in Belfast—a request that the Labour government approved.[128]

But the government came under increasing pressure to act—hundreds of letters were received from student unions, Amnesty international groups, religious organisations and trade union branches. The Labour Party NEC passed a motion calling for a halt to arms sales; Labour MPs made deputations to ministers, and Liberal peer, Lord Avebury, tabled a question on arms sales in the House of Lords. When Rowlands and Owen decided, in late 1978, to review their policy, the head of the FCO's Latin American department wrote a cautious memo emphasizing the risks of imposing an arms embargo, which included souring 'the climate' of talks over the Falklands and provoking 'a major reaction' from the Argentine government and UK arms manufacturers 'who have invested considerable time and effort in negotiations'.[129]

Nevertheless, Labour decided that arms sales should be more closely scrutinized. In January 1979, David Owen informed the MOD of new guidelines; the government should not approve the sale of the following type of armaments:

1. Equipment which could be directly used for internal repression.
2. Equipment which could threaten the Falkland Islands.[130]

Guidelines of this type had only been imposed once before—on South Africa in 1961—and they were an important step forward in the regulation of the British arms trade, introducing a mechanism that was commonly used in the future. The guidelines, however, were applied very loosely in the case of Argentina; export licences for tanks and bomber planes, for example, were approved under the Thatcher government. In fact, as soon as they were introduced, Labour's defence secretary, Fred Mulley said that, while he accepted the guidelines, each order should be looked at on a case by case basis, because 'we would be reluctant to take any action which would seriously damage our prospects of obtaining at least a reasonable share of this market'.[131] Mulley then asked the FCO to approve sales of ammunition by British companies for use with weapons that had already been sold.[132] Owen agreed to the sale of such ammunition, despite the possibility it could be used for internal repression—the first of many instances when the guidelines were bent.[133]

Restoring an Ambassador

The Foreign Office had suggested reinstating a British ambassador to Argentina less than a month after the March 1976 coup, but Labour minister Ted Rowlands wanted to wait to see how talks on the Falklands progressed.[134] Towards the end of Labour's period of office, Argentina expressed an interest in restoring ambassadors. The head of the FCO's Latin America department, John Ure, advised that reinstating ambassadors could facilitate talks over the Falklands, but that such a move could provoke criticism from the 'human rights lobby' and the 'Falkland islanders and their lobby'.[135] He suggested that Argentina be invited to appoint an ambassador to Britain, after which the British would consider re-appointing their ambassador. David Owen approved this, although his political advisor told FCO officials that this needed 'very careful press handling'.[136] But a leaked press report, announcing that an exchange of ambassadors had been agreed to, led to an angry response from the Labour party. The party's national executive passed a resolution calling it 'totally inappropriate'. With just weeks to go until the general election, the British ambassador was not reinstated until the Conservatives came to power, but Labour ministers had not objected, in principle, to the move.

Conclusion

Just before leaving office, Ted Rowlands held a lunch in honour of the outgoing Argentine chargé d'affaires. The FCO gave him speaking notes that suggested he should say:

> If [the Argentine chargé d'affaires] has any doubts left about the affection and esteem in which his nation is held here, he should remember that the British spend a great deal of their waking hours thinking about either football or girls or both, and they are not unmoved by the spectacle of a nation which wins the World Cup and the Miss World competition both in the same year![137]

On the memo Rowlands wrote: 'and in our nightmares we dream of disappeared persons!!'[138]

There was, then, a difference of tone between Labour ministers and their officials. The FCO played a moderating role, as it had with Chile, continually downplaying the responsibility of the Argentine state in human rights abuses and emphasising British business opportunities. It advised against condemning Argentina in international fora and against restrictions on arms sales. But there was not the continual friction on policy between officials and ministers that there had been over Chile, because Labour was not under the same political pressure to take radical action over Argentina. The ousting of a repressive and corrupt Peronist president had not generated the same outrage in the labour movement as the overthrow of a democratically elected socialist. The human rights campaigners, journalists and exiles who campaigned on behalf of Argentina did not have the institutional leverage—such as the support of backbench MPs or major trade unions—to force the government to take action. Some Labour ministers even argued strongly in favour of arms sales to Argentina on the grounds of job creation. As awareness of human rights abuses grew, Labour took two small steps: extending the refugee programme to Argentines and introducing guidelines on arms sales, but the timidity of its measures was in stark contrast to its policy on Chile.

The Labour government also accepted the FCO's argument that Britain needed to pursue good relations with Argentina in order to resolve the Falklands dispute—ignoring the party's official policy that the Islanders should not be handed over to a regime that abused human rights.

But while the FCO argued that the Falklands dispute made Argentina a special case, British policy towards Argentina was not exceptional, since it adopted a similar policy of pursuing good relations with the dictatorships of Brazil, Uruguay and Paraguay. This indicates that, in the absence of political pressure, the default policy of the FCO was to promote British business interests and encourage trade and investment regardless of regime type.

Notes

1. John Shakespeare to Counsellor C. [sic], Mr. Butler Madden, Mr. Bicheno, Mr. Pearce, 4 March 1976, The National Archives (TNA): FCO7/3027.
2. 'Argentina's Flight from Freedom', report by Shakespeare, 1 April 1976, TNA: FCO7/3027.
3. Note by Robin Edmonds, FCO, 6 May 1976, on A.J. Sindall to Edmonds, 5 May 1976, TNA: FCO7/3034.
4. Shakespeare to FCO, 24 April 1976, TNA: FCO7/3034.
5. Ibid.
6. Colonel R.W. Millo to MOD, 30 April 1976, TNA: FCO7/3022.
7. D. Keeling to J. Lamont, 13 July 1976, TNA: FCO7/3031. See also Background Notes for Mr. Luard, FCO, 28 September 1976, TNA: FCO7/3035.
8. 'Notes for Supplementaries' attached to Hugh Carless to Edmonds, 15 December 1976, TNA: FCO7/3030.
9. Shakespeare to British Embassies, 25 June 1976, TNA: FCO7/3037.
10. An embassy official reported that up to 15,000 people might have disappeared, the first of many chilling despatches sent to the FCO by embassy staff: Hugh Bicheno to Mr. Thompson, 7 October 1977, TNA: FCO7/3276.
11. Report of the National Commission on the Disappearance of Persons, 1984: http://www.desaparecidos.org/nuncamas/web/english/library/nevagain/nevagain_001.htm; 30,000 figure attributed to human rights groups cited on Argentine government website: http://www.me.gov.ar/efeme/24demarzo/dictadura.html.
12. Carless to Mr. Larmour, 26 March 1976, TNA: FCO7/3027.
13. The National Archives contain only one MP's letter written immediately after the coup: Stan Newens MP to James Callaghan, 25 March 1976, TNA: FCO7/3029.
14. Shakespeare to FCO, 26 March 1976, TNA: FCO7/3027; FCO to British Embassy, Buenos Aires, 26 March 1976, TNA: FCO7/3027.
15. 'Argentina's Flight from Freedom', 1 April 1976, TNA: FCO7/3027.
16. Carless to PS/Mr. Rowlands, 24 May 1976, TNA: FCO7/3029.

17. Ibid.
18. See Carlos Escudé and Andrés Cisneros, *Historia General de Las Relaciones Exteriores de la República Argentina, Tomo XIV* (Buenos Aires: CEPE/CARI/Nuevohacer, 2000), p. 273; David Rock, *Argentina 1516–1987: From Spanish Colonization to Alfonsín* (Berkley: University of California Press, 1987), p. 369.
19. Shakespeare to FCO, 7 June 1976, TNA: FCO7/3031.
20. Ibid.
21. Eric Anglin to M.J. Treble, 2 July 1976, TNA: FCO7/3031.
22. 'Lunch with the Argentine Minister of the Economy', report by Steve Matheson, Treasury, 20 July 1976, TNA: FCO7/3031.
23. Lamont to Anglin, 3 August 1976, TNA: FCO7/3031.
24. Ibid.
25. Programme for the visit of the Mission led by Dr. José Martínez de Hoz, July 1976, TNA: FCO7/3031.
26. Briefing by Guy Huntrods, Lloyds Bank International, July 1976, TNA: FCO7/3031.
27. Ibid.
28. Figures from 'Visit by Dr. Martínez de Hoz' briefing by Keeling, FCO, 1 September 1976, TNA: FCO7/3031; Anglin to Lamont, 20 August 1976, TNA: FCO7/3031.
29. Figures from 'Visit by Dr. Martínez de Hoz' briefing by Keeling, 1 September 1976, TNA: FCO7/3031.
30. R.B. Birchmore to PS/Minister of State, 19 October 1976, TNA: DEFE 24/1416.
31. 'Argentina's Offshore Hydrocarbon Activities', report by K.P. Forrest, DoE, 30 December 1976, TNA: FCO7/3409.
32. 'Programme for Captain Noe Guevara', September 1976, TNA: FCO7/3035.
33. J.A. Heap to Carless, 28 September 1976, TNA: FCO7/3035.
34. Anglin to M.J. Treble, 21 May 1976, TNA: FCO7/3034.
35. Anglin to Lamont, 20 August 1976, TNA: FCO7/3031.
36. Anglin to Sindall, 2 June 1976, TNA: FCO7/3034.
37. Ibid.
38. Ibid.
39. Keeling to Sindall, 6 October 1976, TNA: FCO7/3041.
40. Ibid.
41. Note by FCO official on 'Refugees: Note of a Meeting on 26 October 1976', TNA: FCO7/3041; Sindall to Shakespeare, 22 October 1976, TNA: FCO7/3041. For chargé's response see: Shakespeare to Sindall, 3 November 1976, TNA: FCO7/3041.

42. FCO photocopy of Robert Cox, 'Argentina without Shadows', *Buenos Aires Herald*, July 1978 [day not specified], TNA: FCO7/3455.
43. Ibid.
44. J. Illman to Keeling, 26 June 1978, TNA: FCO7/3454.
45. Carless to J.H.G Leahy, 20 July 1978, TNA: FCO7/3455.
46. J.R. Cowling to J.B. Ure, 1 August 1978, TNA: FCO7/3455.
47. Illman to Keeling, 27 July 1978, TNA: FCO7/3455; D. Ankerson to J.N. Elam, FCO, 22 August 1978, TNA: FCO7/3456.
48. Shakespeare to Carless, FCO, 29 March 1977, TNA: FCO7/3276.
49. Ibid. *The Times* stringer was Andrew Tarnowski. He went on to become a Reuters correspondent for 30 years.
50. John Shakespeare to Ure, 22 September 1977, TNA: FCO7/3276.
51. Ibid.
52. Ure to Leahy, 21 September 1977, TNA: FCO7/3276.
53. Leahy to Ure, 23 September 1977, TNA: FCO7/3276.
54. Shakespeare to Ure, 4 October 1977, TNA: FCO7/3276.
55. Author's interview with Gordon Hutchison, 6 October 2014.
56. Paul Hoeffel, 'Argentina Calm if Not Prosperous', *The Guardian*, 26 March 1976.
57. Oscar Arévalo, *El Partido Comunista* (Buenos Aires: Centro Editor de América Latina, 1981), p. 135; Norberto Galasso, A*portes Críticos a la Historia de la Izquierda Argentina*, Tomo II, *1961-2001* (Buenos Aires: Nuevo Tiempos, 2007), p. 156.
58. See Nicola Miller, *Soviet Relations with Latin America* (CUP: Cambridge, 1989); Fernando Nadra, *La Religión de Los Ateos: Reflexiones sobre el estalinismo en el Partido Comunista Argentina* (Buenos Aires: Puntosur, 1989); and Otto Vargas et al., *La Trama de Una Argentina Antagónica: del Cordobazo al fin de la Dictadura* (Editorial Agora: Buenos Aires, 2006), p. 159.
59. 'New Argentina President?', *The Morning Star*, 25 March 1976.
60. Author's interview with Christopher Roper, 27 March 2017.
61. This meeting was held on 11 March 1976, according to *Report of British Argentina Campaign's First National Conference*, Liverpool, 2nd December 1978, Senate House Library archives, London (SH): N320 PAM/3/09.
62. Ibid.
63. *Argentina: The Trade Unions Fight On*, British Argentina Campaign pamphlet, c1978, SH: N320 PAM/4/03.
64. 'Interim Report: Committee for Human Rights in Argentina', July 1978, by Richard Whitecross, TNA: FCO7/3585. Author interview with Cristina Whitecross, 3 May 2017.
65. Carless to Mr. Dales, 1 September, 1976, TNA: FCO7/3038.

66. Sheila M. Griffith-Jones to Mr. Hall, 3 September 1976, TNA: FCO7/3038.
67. Ibid.
68. Note by Mr. Collins, 6 September 1976 on Griffith-Jones to Hall, 3 September 1976, TNA: FCO7/3038.
69. Keeling to Carless, 7 September 1976, TNA: FCO7/3038.
70. Sindall to Mr. Edmonds, 7 February 1977, TNA: FCO58/1165.
71. Ibid.
72. Ibid.
73. Keith Unwin to Ivan Callan, 10 February 1977, TNA: FCO58/1165.
74. Ibid.
75. Callan to Unwin, 17 February 1977, TNA: FCO58/1165.
76. Shakespeare to FCO, 21 October 1976, TNA: FCO7/3039. The victim was congressman Mario Abel Amaya.
77. 'Record of a Meeting on 12 April 1978', TNA: FCO7/3455; 'Record of a Meeting 31 January 1979', TNA: FCO7/3584.
78. *Foreign Policy*, Labour Party Campaign Handbook, 1978, Peter Shore Archive, Shore 12/71.
79. 'Argentina'78: Politics and Football: the XIth World Cup', report by Carless, 6 July 1978, TNA: FCO7/3467.
80. TNA: FCO7/3467; TNA: FCO7/3466; FCO7/3465. Five of the 1978 FCO folders containing letters from the public on human rights have been destroyed.
81. FCO briefing sent to J. Noulton, 1 June 1978, TNA: FCO7/3467.
82. Scottish Office Press Release, 'Secretary of State will See Scotland in Argentina', May 24 1978, TNA: FCO7/3467.
83. 'Argentina'78: Politics and Football: The XIth World Cup', 6 July 1978, TNA: FCO7/3467.
84. 'Argentina two years after the coup—A Terrorist State', Labour Party International Department, ID/1977-78/134, 4 April 1978, Peter Shore Archive, Shore 12/71.
85. *Foreign Policy*, Peter Shore Archive, Shore 12/71, p. 28.
86. Speaking Notes attached to Sindall to PS/Mr. Rowlands, 30 January 1979, TNA: FCO7/3584.
87. Author's interview with Gordon Hutchison, Joint Working Group for Refugees, 6 October 2014.
88. G. Hutchison to T. Malcolmson, 11 March 1979, TNA: FCO7/3584; C.H. Thompson to Malcomson, 8 May 1979, TNA: FCO7/3585; and Ure to A.R. Murray, 26 March 1979, TNA: FCO7/3584.
89. G. Lankford to Malcolmson, 18 January 1979, TNA: FCO7/3584.
90. D.C. Ankerson to Malcolmson, 23 February 1979, TNA: FCO7/3584.

91. Author's interview with British official in the embassy, who prefers not to be named, 17 December 2014.
92. Author's interview with British embassy official, who prefers not to be named, 17 December 2014.
93. Argentina: Annual Review for 1976, by Shakespeare, 10 January 1977, TNA: DEFE 24/1417.
94. 'Record of Meeting Between PUS, HDS and Lord Nelson, 9 May 1978', TNA: DEFE 24/1313; Brief by R.J. Harding, Director Sales 2, for PS/HDS, 8 May 1978, 'HDS Meeting with Lord Nelson', TNI: DEFE 68/377.
95. Argentina: Annual Review 1979 and Valedictory Despatch of HM Chargé d'Affaires, 1980, TNA: FCO7/3725.
96. *Overseas Transactions, Business Monitor* (London: HMSO, 1979, 1982, 1984.) IMF Direction of Trade Statistics, 1979, 1980; for lamenting the failure to win large contracts, see Annual Review for 1978, Argentina, 1979, TNA: FCO7/3572.
97. 'Speaking Notes for Secretary of State, OPD (76) 14: The Falkland Islands: Future Policy 10 March 1976' [drafted by A.J. Collins, FCO, 8 March 1976], TNA: FCO7/3198.
98. Anthony Griffin to Eric Varley, 16 February 1978, TNA: DEFE 68/376.
99. Bruce Millan to Mulley, 7 March 1978, TNA: DEFE 68/376; Edmund Dell to Mulley, 7 March 1978, TNA: DEFE 68/376.
100. D.R. Marsh, DS5, to Mat. Co-ord. (N), 21 February 1978, TNA: DEFE 24/1416; R.J. Harding to Mat. Co-ord. (N), 22 February 1978, TNA: DEFE 24/1416. Harding was commenting on a later version of the draft MOD paper.
101. Chief of Staff Committee, Ministry of Defence, Confidential Annex to COS 6th Meeting 78 held on Tuesday 28 February, 1978, TNA: DEFE 24/1416. See also: 'Meeting Held to discuss the diversion of a RN ship to Argentina', 2 March 1978, TNA: DEFE 68/376; Mulley to Varley, 7 March 1978, TNA: DEFE 68/376.
102. David Owen to Varley, 13 March 1978, TNA: DEFE 68/376; Record of a Meeting between the FCS and the foreign minister of Argentina on Friday 29 September 1978, TNA: FCO7/3466.
103. Answering a parliamentary question, Defence Secretary Fred Mulley confirmed Lewin met Massera on 3 July at an Argentine embassy reception. *Hansard*: HC Deb., 13 July 1978, Vol. 953 c717W.
104. In response to a Freedom of Information request by the author, the FCO stated 'files not selected for permanent preservation, have all been destroyed in compliance with the Public Records Act. This included the 1978 file on military visits to and from Argentina, which was not

8 BUSINESS AS USUAL: ARMING THE JUNTA (1976–1979)   159

selected for permanent preservation.' 4 September 2014. The MOD also confirmed they hold no records of the visit.
105. Owen's comment is from an interview with the author. 3 November 2014.
106. L. Salthouse to PS/Minister of State, 26 September 1978, TNA: DEFE 68/377.
107. D.S. Leggatt, Captain R.N., to Carless, 31 August 1978, TNA: FCO7/3450.
108. Lord Nelson to Michael Palliser, 15 September 1978, TNA: DEFE 68/377.
109. Dell to Owen, 3 November 1978, TNA: DEFE 68/377.
110. R.J. Harding to Sindall, 27 October 1978, DEFE 68/378.
111. Nelson to Palliser, 15 September 1978, TNA: DEFE 68/377.
112. Note for the File by J. O'Mahony, PS/HDS, 27 November 1978, DEFE 68/378.
113. Dell to Owen, 3 November 1978, TNA: DEFE 68/377.
114. Carless to FCO, 9 October 1979. DEFE 68/378.
115. In response to a Freedom of Information request by the author, the FCO revealed that files giving information about military visits from and to Argentina for the years 1976, 1978, 1979, 1980 and 1981 had been destroyed. Freedom of Information Request to the FCO, reference 1014–14, 12 June 2015.
116. 'Visit by Officers of the Argentine Air Force, 13–15 June 1977', MOD brief, 13 June 1977, TNA: DEFE 68/376.
117. 'Megacausa por violación a los DDHH: alto jefe aeronáutico se negó a declarar', ámbito.com, 20 July 2009: http://www.ambito.com/noticia.asp?id=471848.
118. Note by Col. L.E. Hudson, 'Visit of the Argentinian Assistant Naval Attaché, Commander Juan A. Dover', 3 November 1977, TNA: DEFE 24/1417.
119. Ibid.
120. Carless to Ure, 'Visit of Admiral Lambruschini: 28–31 May', 28 April 1978. DEFE 24/1313.
121. John Petty, 'Naval secrets on show in ship sales drive', *The Daily Telegraph*, 30 May 1978.
122. Vice-Admiral Watson accepted the invitation. It is not clear from the files whether the visit went ahead. Philip Watson to HDS, 13 August 1976, TNA: DEFE 68/376; Watson to Carlos Torlaschi, 29 October 1976, TNA: DEFE 68/376.
123. 'Presentation by Admiral Sir Anthony Griffin, to Vice Admiral Oliva, Director General of Naval Material and ARA Officers on Wednesday 25 October 1978', TNA: DEFE 68/377.

124. Allen Greenwood to Palliser, 18 September 1978, TNA: DEFE 68/377.
125. 'Visit to the Argentine 22–28 January 1979', report by Roger Harding January 1979, TNA: DEFE 68/378; Report of a Visit to Argentina by R.J. Harding, 14 March 1978, TNA: DEFE 68/376; and R.J. Harding to AUS (Sales), 12 December 1977, TNA: DEFE 68/376.
126. R.J. Spencer to Keeling, 'Argentine Request for use of UK range for launching Exocet', October 1978 [Day illegible, appears to be 12 October], TNA: DEFE 68/377. There is no reply from the FCO to this request in the files, so we cannot be certain what the outcome was.
127. 'Record of a Meeting Between the Minister of State and Members of the International Committee of the Labour Party on 12 April 1978', TNA: FCO7/3455.
128. J.D. Concannon to Rowlands, 3 November 1978, TNA: DEFE 68/377; Rowlands to Concannon MP, 10 November 1978, TNA: DEFE 68/378.
129. Ure to Hall, 12 December 1978, TNA: FCO7/3579.
130. Owen to Mulley, 26 January 1979, TNA: FCO7/3579.
131. Mulley to Owen, 7 February 1979, TNA: FCO7/3579.
132. Ibid.
133. Owen to Mulley, 30 March 1979, TNA: FCO7/3579.
134. Carless to Larmour, 12 April 1976, TNA: FCO7/3029; J.R. Young to Carless, 15 April 1976, TNA: FCO7/3029.
135. Ure to Hall, FCO, 2 February 1979, TNA: FCO7/3573.
136. Note by David Stephen, 6 February 1979, on Ure to Hall, 2 February 1979, TNA: FCO7/3573.
137. Ure to PS/Mr. Rowlands, 6 March 1979, TNA: FCO7/3590.
138. Note by Rowlands on Ure to PS/Mr. Rowlands, 6 March 1979, TNA: FCO7/3590.

CHAPTER 9

Oil, the Islands and the Falklands Lobby (1976–1979)

Was the Falklands conflict a war for oil? Some on the British Left—including former Energy Secretary Tony Benn—thought so. Certainly, many Argentine politicians and scholars believe Britain retains the islands for economic and strategic gain. Oil has never been Britain's primary reason for maintaining sovereignty, but this chapter shows that the British government and British oil companies have taken a keen interest in the potential oil reserves around the Islands since the 1970s. It examines the influence of British corporations—and particularly oil companies—on the Labour governments' attitude towards sovereignty talks with Argentina. It then considers why those talks failed. Given that there was no room for compromise because Argentina was unwilling to accept any other solution except the transfer of sovereignty of the Falkland Islands, the overriding factor preventing British politicians from reaching a deal was the fear of parliament's reaction. The fact that domestic political constraints were crucial provides an opportunity to look at the circumstances in which a campaigning group—in this case the Falkland Islands Committee—can be successful.

The Business Lobby and the Decision to Negotiate with Argentina

Both Conservative and Labour governments had felt it necessary to negotiate with Argentina since 1965, when the United Nations General Assembly passed a resolution which declared its 'cherished aim of bringing to an end everywhere colonialism in all its forms, one of which covers the case of the Falkland Islands (Malvinas)', and called on Britain and Argentina to negotiate a peaceful solution to the dispute.[1] The cabinet minutes for the period 1976–1979 show that the primary reason ministers gave for negotiating was to avoid escalating tension and possible military conflict with Argentina, given that the cost of defending the islands—the so-called 'Fortress Falklands' policy—was viewed as unacceptably high. This conclusion is supported by the secondary literature. However, other reasons for negotiating with Argentina included the desire to exploit the economic resources around the islands, particularly oil, British commercial interests in Argentina and Latin America, and concern about the economic decline of the Islands themselves.

Large British corporations with investments in Latin America argued that Britain's commercial interests were being put at risk by the failure to resolve the sovereignty dispute with Argentina. This was the argument put forward by executives of Barings Bank, Lloyds Bank and a former director of Shell at a secret seminar on the Falklands organised by the FCO on 8 May 1975.[2] The only business executive at the meeting who was in favour of maintaining the status quo was the chairman of the Falkland Islands Company. The Latin American Dining Club, a group of British businessmen interested in trade with Latin America, also lobbied for an end to the dispute; at a dinner in 1976, the main speaker declared 'the time had come to "treat with" Argentina'.[3] Meanwhile the Anglo-Dutch multinational Unilever, interested in the fishing prospects in the South Atlantic, wrote to the FCO saying: 'We support wholeheartedly your attempts to keep friends with Argentina.'[4] Representatives of Canning House—the centre of Anglo-Latin American business and diplomatic exchange—were also vocal supporters of rapprochement. The Conservative peer Viscount Montgomery, a former chairman of Canning House's economic committee, tabled numerous questions in the Lords advocating a resolution to the dispute and Robert McAlpine, another Canning House notable and Barings executive, also argued in favour of resolving the dispute.[5]

OIL AND THE FALKLAND ISLANDS DISPUTE

One of the most vocal business lobbies was the oil companies. Although there is a danger of over-emphasising the question of Falklands oil, it is worth examining in some depth, because it is an issue that has been overlooked by British historians and over-played by some Argentine commentators, and there is a need for a nuanced assessment of what role the discovery of oil played in the policy-making process.[6]

There had been a series of diplomatic initiatives on the Falklands before Wilson's Labour government came to office in 1974 (see Table 9.1). By the mid-1970s, oil had become an important new factor in the dispute. Oil companies had started enquiring about exploration licences from the British government since 1969.[7] In 1971, the government commissioned a geology expert, Professor D.H. Griffiths of Birmingham University, to carry out a geological survey of the waters around the Islands. Griffiths reported in early 1975 that the prognosis was 'sufficiently promising to encourage further commercial exploration'.[8] The government submitted the findings to Sir Peter Kent, a former chief geologist at BP, who agreed that some areas were 'decidedly

Table 9.1 Anglo-Argentine negotiations on the Falkland Islands 1966–1982

1966–1968:	**Talks Leading to a Draft Memorandum of Understanding (1968) on Transferring Sovereignty** Abandoned after Islander/parliamentary opposition leads Britain to insist any deal must be subject to the 'wishes' of the Islanders
1969–1975:	**Talks about Economic Cooperation** • 1971 Anglo-Argentine Communications Agreement • 1972 Argentine-built airstrip opens • 1974 Argentine state-owned oil company to supply fuel to islands • 1974 Conservative and Labour governments consider proposing a condominium but the idea is abandoned because of Islander opposition
1976–1981:	**Talks on Sovereignty—Leaseback** • Labour cabinet agrees in 1976 to explore leaseback, but leaseback was not formally proposed to Argentina, because of the fear of public opposition • Thatcher government agrees to explore leaseback and it was discussed with Argentina in secret talks in 1980, but idea is abandoned because of Islander/parliamentary opposition
Early 1982:	Argentina and UK agree to keep talking

promising' and predicted that there would be 'brisk competition from industry for small selected parts'.[9] The Department of Energy, which was being lobbied by energy companies and eager to see the results of the survey, wrote to the FCO saying: 'Our ministers are very interested in the possibility of exploiting offshore oil around the Falkland Islands.'[10] Among the companies requesting licences were the Canadian corporations Ashland Oil and Kelvin Resources.[11] BP and Shell, meanwhile, kept in regular informal contact with the Department of Energy and FCO.[12] While smaller oil companies lobbied for immediate licences, large companies like BP believed that exploring for oil in Falklands waters without the agreement of Argentina could lead to legal disputes and prejudice their business in Latin America. Taking into account corporate concerns, FCO officials drafted a paper in which they concluded: 'Of one thing we can be certain: there can be no exploitation of any oil there may be around the Falklands except in collaboration with the Argentines.'[13]

Foreign Secretary James Callaghan wrote to the prime minister in early 1975 warning that if Britain refused to talk to Argentina, not only would it lead to confrontation, but it 'would also preclude any possibility of exploring or exploiting either oil deposits on the Falkland Islands Continental Shelf or the resources of the South West Atlantic as a whole.'[14] The paragraph on oil in this letter is completely redacted—as are many of the references to oil in the National Archives' collection of government papers, indicating the continuing sensitivity of the subject. Callaghan suggested using oil as a 'constructive input in a fresh Anglo-Argentine dialogue', in which joint oil exploration would be the first step. This proposal was put to the Cabinet's Defence and Oversea Policy (DOP) Committee in July 1975 and approved by ministers. A memorandum for the meeting noted that oil companies would need to be assured of 'peaceful access to the area for a period (10–20 years) sufficient to enable them to recoup the heavy investment. No company will operate in the area in the face of Argentine opposition.'[15]

The Argentines, however, would not accept a discussion of joint oil exploration without also discussing sovereignty. Tensions rose when Britain commissioned a Labour peer, Lord Shackleton, to carry out an economic survey of the Islands in early 1976. In protest, the Argentines withdrew their ambassador and fired on a British research ship. It was in this context of rising tension that the Labour cabinet agreed, in March 1976, to offer talks on sovereignty or 'the nature of a hypothetical future constitutional relationship', with a view to offering Argentina a leaseback.[16] The cost of defending the Islands and the likelihood of military conflict were the primary reasons for this move, but the question of oil continued to play a large part in subsequent discussions.

While all politicians and officials agreed that British oil companies, Islanders and perhaps the Treasury could potentially benefit from the exploitation of oil round the Falklands, there was a difference of emphasis between the FCO and the Department of Energy. Some in the FCO saw oil primarily—in the words of one official—as 'a lever to cajole the Islanders into accepting that there could be…benefit from closer relations with Argentina'.[17] However, the Department of Energy consistently lobbied for British companies to get the maximum benefit from the oil and against Britain giving up its rights to the Continental Shelf. An FCO official characterised the Department of Energy's position as 'every square inch of sea bed must be fought for with the utmost robustness and vigilance.'[18]

The Department of Energy initially viewed Falklands oil as a long-term prospect because recent North Sea oil finds had given Britain sufficient oil for the immediate future, but during the 1970s, oil companies became increasingly interested in South Atlantic oil.[19] World oil prices quadrupled between 1973 and 1974 following an embargo by Arab oil-producing countries, making areas previously thought uneconomical worth exploring. Interest was further fuelled by newspaper articles, supposedly based on a CIA report, which erroneously claimed that the waters around the Falklands contained three times more oil than the North Sea.[20] The Griffiths report, in fact, estimated that the Falklands waters had one tenth of the amount of oil as the North Sea. Burmah Oil, Home Oil Ltd., William Press Group and Worley Engineering Ltd were among the companies which contacted the FCO about oil prospects in the region in 1977.[21] But BP—a company in which the British government had a majority shareholding—had the most weight with officials. At the suggestion of Sir Jack Rampton, the Permanent Under-Secretary at the Department of Energy, two BP executives visited Argentina in late 1976, where they met the junta's energy minister and representatives of Argentine oil companies.[22] Keen to start operations in the South Atlantic, BP met twice with FCO officials in early 1977 and in May, BP's technical director, Dr. J. Birks, wrote to Foreign Office minister Ted Rowlands, asking for an indication of the government's attitude towards BP setting up a consortium with Argentine companies to search for oil around the Falklands and off the coast of Argentina.[23] Birks added that the Falkland Islands Company had expressed an interest in joining such a consortium.[24]

Meanwhile, Argentina began to show an interest in exploring for oil and commissioned two US companies to carry out seismic surveys of the waters off the Argentine coast in early 1977, as a first step towards issuing oil-exploration licences.[25] Multinational interest in the area was reflected by the fact that one of the surveys was underwritten by BP, Chevron, Mobil, Elf, Aquitaine and Total.[26] The British were concerned that the Argentine-sponsored seismic studies would cross the (unofficial) median line in the sea between Argentina and the Falkland Islands (This fact was pointed out to the FCO by Labour MP and geologist Colin Phipps, who after the Falklands War set up Desire Petroleum, a company which began drilling for oil around the islands in 1998).[27] Although the British government had not formally claimed the waters beyond the 200-metre isobath from the Islands, it wanted to reserve its rights to up to 200 miles of the continental shelf. A Department of Energy official urged the FCO to protest at Argentina's actions. 'The worst thing would be to do nothing,' he wrote, as this could lead to 'our giving up without so much as a whisper the title to any oil which might lie beneath the sea outside the 200 metres line'.[28] The FCO also feared that inaction would weaken Britain's sovereignty claim, so in May 1977, it instructed its chargé d'affaires to deliver a formal protest to the Argentine government, noting: 'We must make sure that we do not prejudice our rights...over the Falkland Islands Continental shelf in advance.'[29] But the FCO came under pressure from companies, including BP and Western Geophysical, to allow the seismic surveys so they could have a clear idea of the oil deposits in the Southwest Atlantic.[30] Energy Secretary Tony Benn also urged that the surveys should go ahead as soon as possible and suggested that British companies should form a consortium with Argentina's state oil company YPF to explore for oil.[31] Given that Argentina had ignored Britain's protest, the FCO negotiated directly with the two American companies, belatedly authorising them to carry out their seismic studies. In return, the companies promised to give a copy of their data to the British government.

During the 1970s, the United Nations was coordinating negotiations on a new Convention on the Law of the Sea, which included the concept of an Economic Exclusion Zone (EEZ) in which a sovereign state had the right to explore and exploit the maritime resources within 200 nautical miles from its coast. Although negotiations on the Convention

(UNCLOS) did not end until 1982 and it did not come into force until 1994, the concept of 200-mile maritime zones was very much in the minds of officials considering the Falkland Islands in the 1970s. The Foreign Office discussed with other government departments how the renewed interest in oil and the emerging concept of 200-mile Economic Exclusion Zones should affect formal negotiations with Argentina. At a cross-departmental meeting in May 1977, Hugh Carless explained that the FCO envisaged splitting British possessions in the South Atlantic into four areas of consideration: the Falklands Islands; the 200 miles of sea around the Falkland Islands including their maritime and subterranean resources (oil and fish); the Dependencies of the Falkland Islands (South Georgia and the Sandwich Islands); and their 200-mile maritime zones. While leaseback would be the most appropriate solution for the Falkland Islands themselves, said Carless, there should also be a separate leaseback arrangement for the maritime zones, 'which would allow Britain to exploit the resources of the area'.[32] In regard to the Dependencies and their maritime zones, Britain's aim should be 'to retain access to the economic resources'.[33] During the meeting, the representative of the Department of Energy emphasised that 'we would not wish to write off any potentially interesting areas as world oil resources were finite and declining'.[34]

FCO officials drew up a draft paper for ministers which stated with regard to economic resources: 'Our principal objective is preferential access to oil deposits and royalty income derived from future exploitation of these deposits.'[35] However, Foreign Secretary David Owen felt that in order to secure the main objective of retaining the sovereignty over the Falkland Islands themselves, Britain should be prepared to concede sovereignty over the Dependencies and the maritime resources of both the Islands and the Dependencies. He ordered a re-draft of the paper ahead of the cabinet's Defence and Oversea Policy (DOP) Committee meeting.[36] In speaking notes prepared for Owen, his case was made more explicit:

> We have to get it across to Argentina that we are not after economic advantage at their expense, and that our concern for the Islanders is our real and genuine concern. I do not in any case believe that it is right for us to seek to secure for ourselves, economic resources 7000 miles away...we should not lay ourselves open to accusations...that we are economic imperialists.[37]

Despite intending to cede rights to the oil and fish resources, these speaking notes suggest that Owen still envisaged some sort of cooperation:

> What I hope we can achieve is some arrangement which gives benefit to the Islanders from offshore economic activity in the area, and which also gives the maximum opportunity to British companies to take part in economic activities in the area.[38]

A proposal to offer 'concessions over maritime resources' was put to the cabinet's Defence and Oversea Policy Committee in July 1977.[39] The Department of Energy was vehemently against this; a briefing paper for Tony Benn noted that separating the continental shelf from the Islands could set a dangerous precedent for British claims in other areas of the world and warned that Britain could lose out on valuable oil business in the South Atlantic.[40] In his diary, Benn described Owen's proposals as a 'sell-out' and said that the Department of Energy briefed him strongly against them.[41] (It was perhaps because Benn witnessed the strong oil lobby while Secretary of State, that he later viewed the 1982 conflict as a war for oil.) But it was not only the Department of Energy that was concerned; the cabinet secretary, in a memo to Prime Minister Callaghan, wrote: 'The concessions proposed are both substantive and potentially of considerable economic importance. To make them now in return for what may be only a tactical and short term objective would seem to involve playing a valuable card to take only a very small trick.'[42]

The minutes and memoranda of the DOP meeting remain closed to the public, but other archival sources show that ministers raised concerns about Owen's proposal to cede the rights to the maritime zones and that the Prime Minister ordered legal advice to be sought 'on the implications of the total abandonment of our claims to fisheries and continental shelf rights around the Falkland Islands'.[43] David Owen's DOP paper argued that if concessions on maritime resources were not enough, Britain should consider offering full leaseback of the Islands themselves.[44] Ministers, concerned that this would be unpopular with parliament, asked the FCO to 'play for time' in the next round of negotiations, rather than make precise proposals.[45] During subsequent talks in July and December 1977, the British put forward the 'mixed approach' in general terms (i.e. separating the Islands from their maritime zones and from the Dependencies), but did not make a specific offer to cede the sovereignty of the maritime zones.[46] FCO briefing notes for the minister made clear that Britain's aim remained 'to try to ensure that the UK and the Falkland Islands obtain as great a share as possible in any development of oil resources which may take place in the area'.[47] The 'mixed approach' concept bemused the Argentine delegation, which continued to demand sovereignty over the whole area, and any idea of treating the maritime zones separately ran into the sand in 1978 when the Argentines refused to accept that the Falkland Islands generated their own continental shelf.[48]

That the Foreign Office considered ceding the sovereignty rights over oil and fish resources, in exchange for retaining sovereignty over the Islands themselves, suggests that oil was not Britain's primary interest in retaining the Falkland Islands (or the primary reason for going to war in 1982). However, the strong protest from the Department of Energy, and to a lesser extent the Cabinet Office, against giving up oil rights, and the fact that Britain never formally offered to cede the maritime zones to Argentina, indicate that there was a strong business-influenced counter lobby within the government, which aimed to ensure that the British government and British companies achieved the maximum benefit possible from the potential oil reserves. While oil did not determine the British government's policy towards the Falklands, it is not correct to conclude that the British government or British companies were not interested in the oil: they clearly were. It should be remembered that during the 1970s, oil companies were in favour of a deal with Argentina, without which, they believed, it would be legally and politically impossible to explore for oil. The calculation was that getting some of the oil was better than getting none. In the changed geopolitical circumstances after the Falklands war, the British government felt politically strong enough to declare a unilateral 200-mile economic exclusion zone around the islands, and when talks on joint oil projects with Argentina in the 1990s failed, the Falkland Islands Government went on to grant oil exploration licences unilaterally in 1996 and 2010. It is notable, however, that major oil multinationals continued to be wary of drilling in contested waters and the licences have been bought by small venture capitalist companies (Table 9.2).

Table 9.2 British oil exploration around the Falkland Islands since 1982

1986:	150-mile fisheries zone declared by Falkland Islands Government
1993:	200-mile economic oil exploration zone declared by Falkland Island Government
1995:	Joint oil cooperation agreement signed by Argentina and UK, but no joint exploration takes place
1996:	The Falkland Islands Government sells seven production licences
1998:	Drilling begins in waters around the Falkland Islands. No major discoveries are found and the low oil price deters further investment
2010:	The Falkland Islands Government launches a new offer of oil exploration licences. All licences were bought by small companies, including Rockhopper, Desire Petroleum, Falklands Oil & Gas and Borders and Southern Petroleum. 21 exploratory wells were drilled. Some modest oil and gas discoveries were announced. Development work on these discoveries was continuing in 2017
2016:	The UN Commission on the Limits of Continental Shelf rules that the Falkland Islands lie in Argentine waters. The UK government says the decision is not binding
2016:	Argentine and UK governments pledge to cooperate on economic issues, including oil and gas

THE POLITICAL PRESSURES AGAINST A SETTLEMENT

Large British companies may have been in favour of a rapprochement with Argentina, but trade with Latin America made up just 3% of Britain's total trade in 1975, which weakened the business lobby's weight and made it less able to counter the strong feeling in parliament in favour of keeping the Falklands.[49] The fear of a 'political storm' was uppermost in ministers' minds throughout the dispute.[50] Every cabinet meeting which discussed the Falklands problem during Callaghan's period of office discussed the possible reaction of parliament.[51] Ministers, aware that the defence of British citizens and sovereign territory were issues that struck a patriotic chord with many MPs, were terrified of a humiliating mauling in parliament. David Owen said he watched the Falklands 'like a hawk' after seeing the colonial secretary Fred Lee suffering at the hands of MPs over the question of Gibraltar. 'I've never forgotten it. If they can pull a minister down they'll do so. There is a streak in the House Commons of "Get the bastard!"'.[52] Similarly, one of Ted Rowlands' abiding memories was, as a junior backbencher, watching Labour minister Michael Stewart 'being almost torn limb from limb in the House' when previous Falklands talks had become public.[53]

On numerous occasions during the Callaghan government, ministers slowed the pace of negotiations because of the likely reaction in the House of Commons; for example, in December 1976, cabinet ministers noted that if they were to 'state plainly' their intention to talk to Argentina, there would be a 'political storm', so they agreed instead to play for time.[54] Similarly, in 1978, David Owen wrote to the prime minister that it was difficult to maintain 'our strictly rational approach' in the face of opposition from parliament and the press.[55] As a high-ranking FCO official put it: 'The Falklands problem taken as a whole is complicated, but the nub of it is simple: Parliament.'[56]

Opposition to a Falklands 'sell-out' was expertly mobilised by the Falkland Islands Committee, a lobby group formed in 1968. The fate of a small British community under threat from an aggressive neighbour had such an emotive and nationalistic appeal to MPs and the right-wing press that parliament would probably have been sceptical of any Falklands deal even without the encouragement of the Committee, but their activities ensured that parliamentarians were constantly reminded of the Islanders' predicament. Although the Committee worked hard to win cross-party support, it had far greater numbers of Conservative MPs backing it than Labour MPs. Nevertheless, there were enough Labour MPs willing to vote and speak in favour of the Falkland Islanders to risk eliminating Labour's slender three-seat majority in parliament. The Callaghan administration became even more susceptible to pressure in November 1976 when, after by-election defeats, it became a minority government. Nor did Labour ministers want to be tarred as anti-patriotic by Conservative MPs or the popular press.

The Labour MPs who supported the Falkland Islands Committee—such as Bernard Conlan, Eric Ogden and James Johnson—came from the right wing of the party. They had developed an interest in the Falkland Islands through the Commonwealth Parliamentary Association (CPA), which brought together MPs who had an interest in former colonies. The CPA organised cross-party trips to the Falkland Islands and became one of the channels through which the Falklands lobby worked. The Labour politicians who backed the Falkland Islands Committee came from a different faction of the party from the left-wing MPs who had been most vocal about human rights abuses in Argentina and Chile. Many of the campaigners for human rights in Argentina were not, in fact, aware of, or interested in, the Falklands issue until 1982.[57] Neither the Argentina Support Movement nor the Committee for Human Rights in Argentina took a position on the Falklands, although the short-lived British Argentina Campaign did take a stance, calling for no talks on the Islands while the military ruled Argentina.[58]

The Falklands question was not widely discussed by Labour backbenchers before the Argentine invasion and they had no clearly articulated position. Frank Hooley was the only Labour MP who, during the 1970s, repeatedly espoused the view that Britain should renounce its claim to the Falklands on the grounds of anti-imperialism. It was a complex question for the Labour left because its strong tradition of anti-colonialism clashed with its horror at the human rights abuses being perpetrated by the Argentine regime. And while Argentine progressives unanimously viewed the Falklands as a clear-cut case of imperialism, in Britain many noted that there was no oppressed indigenous population and felt sympathy for the British-descended Islanders' demand for self-determination. This lack of a clear Labour-Left position led politicians to take a variety of, sometimes contradictory, positions. Tony Benn, who later became a prominent opponent of the war, took a more nationalist-sounding approach in his diary in 1977:

> The Argentine Government is determined to get hold of the islands even though they are 400 miles away and the arms trade, the total spinelessness of the Foreign Office and the general decay of Britain will have combined to put us in a position where we will be unable to do anything to defend the 1950 people who live there.[59]

Tam Dalyell MP, who also came to prominence as an anti-war MP, did not take a close interest in Falklands issues before 1982, making only one—broadly pro-Islander—contribution to the debates in parliaments in the decade before the invasion.[60] Meanwhile, those who had campaigned most vigorously on the question of human rights in the 1970s, such as Stan Newens MP and Judith Hart MP, went on to take opposing positions when the war broke out: Newens backed the British task force on the grounds that the Islanders should be defended against aggression, while Hart advocated a negotiated solution.

The Labour Party's National Executive Committee passed a resolution, in 1977, which attempted to reflect both the growing concern about human rights violations in Argentina and the unease that the Islanders could be transferred to such an abusive regime:

We call on the government to ensure that under no circumstances will the inhabitants of the Falkland Islands be handed over to any Argentine regime which violates human and civil rights.[61]

This position on the Falklands was restated in the Labour Party's Foreign Policy Campaign Handbook the following year. Labour ministers had sympathy with this perspective; Callaghan reportedly expressed them in a characteristically pithy manner after reading a human rights report from Buenos Aires in 1976. 'I'm not handing over a thousand eight hundred Britons to a gang of fucking Fascists,' a former embassy official records him as saying.[62]

So while the Labour party's official statements did not persuade ministers to halt talks with Argentina, they did make them more cautious in their approach because they knew that they reflected a growing distaste among Labour MPs about dealing with the Argentine dictatorship. The Falklands Islands lobby, therefore, had significant leverage during the Labour years because a minority government was caught by a pincer movement in parliament, comprising nationalistic Tory and right-leaning Labour MPs of the Falkland Islands Committee on one side, and the left-wing, anti-junta wing of the Labour party on the other.

The UK Falkland Islands Committee was influential in other ways. It had considerable support from establishment figures; its chairman was a baronet, its vice chairman a Knight Commander of the Order of the British Empire and its letterhead displayed among its supporters two Commanders of the Order of the British Empire (CBE), a Member of the same order (MBE), a dame, two QCs, a Royal Navy captain and a justice of the peace.[63] The campaign could count on informal advice from former ministers on parliamentary tactics and it was also very well-funded. The Committee established and financed a Falkland Islands Office at a cost of £35,000 a year, employed a full-time public relations officer and paid for the services of a PR company, Sallingbury Limited.[64] They also hired a parliamentary draftsman, who drafted all their parliamentary questions.[65] Much of the funding initially came from the Falklands Island Company, owned by fuel company Coalite, but, according to an FCO analysis, by the mid-1970s the campaign had a wide cross-section of support and had outgrown its initial dependence on the company, although it continued to pay a substantial subscription. Another commercial backer was Alginate Industries Ltd., which had an interest in developing chemicals from the seaweed around the Falklands.[66]

The Committee's relationship with the Foreign Office was contradictory because, while there was a feeling of mutual suspicion and some antagonism between Committee members and officials, the campaign was nevertheless very influential. The antagonism derived from the campaign's propaganda, which centred on the accusation that the Foreign Office was secretly trying to persuade ministers to 'sell out' the Falklands—a charge FCO officials resented.[67] FCO correspondence is peppered with remarks which show their wariness of the committee such as: 'If the Falkland Islands Committee are not cooking up trouble, it will be a historic first.'[68] FCO officials also believed that Committee members misrepresented what officials said in private meetings. FCO official Hugh Carless, for example wrote: 'Several Committee members are skilled and persistent interrogators, and some of them have a reputation for embroidering what ministers and officials tell them.'[69] They were so wary of the Committee's secretary Bill Hunter Christie—a barrister and former Foreign Office official, whom they described at various times as 'rather touchy', 'impertinent', 'intolerable' and 'neurotic'—that the FCO had an informal rule that no official should meet him alone.[70] But the Foreign Office, nevertheless, recognised that the campaigners had significant parliamentary support, an official noting that 'their ability to manipulate a dedicated and vocal parliamentary lobby could limit severely HMG's room for manoeuvre.'[71] As well as recommending that the minister of state, Ted Rowlands, should accept delegations from the Committee and attend their functions, FCO officials also proposed more informal ways of influencing the campaigners. David Hall, head of the FCO's Falkland Island Department wrote:

> We should not underestimate these people. They are skilled and persistent interrogators…But they have a human weakness for flattery—which, to be of use, must be subtle and I would like to see a rather broader based contact with them in future. A little pretence of consultation and some modest hospitality…might pay dividends.[72]

It was not just their strong parliamentary support that gave the Falkland Islands Committee influence in the FCO; they also had informal access to FCO officials because they operated in the same upper and upper-middle class social networks. The FCO's David Hall complained it was hard to keep to the rule of not meeting Hunter Christie alone because he belonged to the same private club.[73] To Hall's embarrassment, the Falkland Islands Committee held a cocktail party in honour of his retirement to which all FCO officials working on the Falklands and Latin America were invited. While this was clearly a lobbying tactic, it also showed the social access the Falkland Islands Committee enjoyed. In contrast, the trade-union dominated Chile Solidarity Campaign did not have the social contacts (or the desire) to hold a soirée for diplomats.[74] On another occasion, in order to 'get some idea of their thinking and to maintain our contacts with them', the FCO invited the chairman of the Falkland Islands Committee, Sir John Barlow, and two other committee members, to an informal dinner with FCO officials at the Cavalry Club in Piccadilly.[75] Meanwhile Robin Edmonds, an assistant under-secretary at the FCO, noted that he had recently invited Sir John Barlow to a private dinner.[76]

The Falklands lobby was wider than the Falkland Islands Committee itself; the 'Friends of the Falklands' was a less overtly political organisation which brought together people with an interest in the Falklands. Many of the 'Friends' were influential establishment figures, such as the Labour peer Lord Shackleton and Viscount Boyd of Merton, a former Tory Secretary of State for the Colonies, who had easy access to FCO officials and could influence policy both formally and informally. Members of this organisation were not necessarily opposed to cooperation with Argentina, but did want to ensure that the Islanders' interests were not forgotten. They had a less antagonistic relationship with the Foreign Office—FCO official David Hall, for example, was happy to join the Friends on his retirement.[77] Another 'Friend of the Falklands', Sir John Lapsey, a former Royal Air Force commander, had a regular dialogue with the FCO and asked them if it would be useful for him to join the Committee to persuade them to take a less extreme stance.[78]

The broad Falkland Islands 'lobby' had both parliamentary leverage and informal social access to influence policy makers. It was strong enough to make ministers and officials extremely cautious in negotiations with Argentina and helped to ensure that no agreement on sovereignty was ever reached. Although the cabinet had agreed in principle to explore leaseback, it was never formally proposed to Argentina during Labour's period of office. Lawrence Freedman has pointed out that the Falklands lobby 'had sufficient clout to stop a British government abandoning the islanders but not enough to ensure that they were properly cared for.'[79] It is true that while the Labour government were willing to pay for a more robust defence policy than the Conservatives, sending a task force and maintaining *HMS Endurance* as a naval presence in the area, the Falklands lobby could not persuade them to spend the much larger amounts needed to permanently reinforce the military garrison on the Islands, or build a longer runway, which would have made the islanders less commercially dependent on Argentina. It is important to emphasise that the Falklands were not a priority for governments of either party before the 1982 conflict. The issue was not important enough either for politicians to risk their political credibility by pushing an unpopular deal through parliament, or important enough for governments to spend the money needed to protect the islands from a possible military incursion. Ultimately the talks failed because the threat of military conflict was judged to be remote enough to be able to risk delaying a settlement, while the British business lobby, including oil companies, in favour of rapprochement with Argentina was not weighty enough to persuade ministers to stand up to parliamentary opposition.

Notes

1. UN Resolution 2065, 16 December 1965.
2. Record of a Meeting Held by the Minster of State on 8 May 1975, The National Archives (TNA): FCO7/2958.
3. Robin Edmonds to Mr. Young, 7 July 1976, TNA: FCO7/3200.
4. F. Martin, Unilever, to Hugh Carless, 13 September 1976, TNA: FCO7/3035.
5. Carless to Mr. Edmonds, 18 January 1977, TNA: FCO7/3373.
6. See Introduction, including note 90, for discussion of secondary sources on oil and strategic issues.
7. Draft FCO Paper, 'Assessments of the oil potential of the Falkland Islands continental shelf'. No date [*circa* January 1976, in accordance with other documents in the file], TNA: FCO7/3234.
8. 'Geology of the Region Around the Falkland Islands: Summary of report by P.F. Barker, J. Burrell, F. Simpson and D.H. Griffiths', date of covering letter 11 April 1975, TNA: FCO 96/369.
9. 'Review of Birmingham Report of Geology of the Falkland Islands Region, Summary', by Peter Kent, 2 June 1975, TNA: FCO 96/369.
10. E.J. Lindley, to Carless, 20 January 1975, TNA: FCO 96/369.
11. Colin M. Evans, Ashland Oil Canada Ltd., to David Ennals, 19 August 1975, TNA: FCO 96/369.
12. See note by Carless, 19 January 1976, on J.A. Heap to Mr. Hall, 15 January 1976, TNA: FCO7/3234; note by Carless on Heap to Carless,

21 January 1976, TNA: FCO7/3234, 1976; note by Edmonds on Heap to Carless, 21 January 1971, TNA: FCO7/3234.
13. A.J. Coles to Mr. Collins, 26 March 1975, TNA: FCO 96/369; Draft DOP paper, attached to Coles to Edmonds, 1 April 1975, TNA: FCO 96/369.
14. James Callaghan to Harold Wilson, PM/75/38, 14 May 1975, TNA: FCO7/3373.
15. DOP Committee: Falkland Islands: Dispute with Argentina, Memorandum by the Foreign and Commonwealth Secretary, 3 July 1975, Annex B: Falkland Islands Oil, TNA: CAB 148/155.
16. Cabinet, minutes, 18 March 1976, TNA: CAB 128/58/11.
17. Heap to Hall, 15 January 1976, TNA: FCO7/3234.
18. R.A. Burrows to Mr. Buxton, 4 May 1977, TNA: FCO76/1616.
19. 'Bilateral talks with Argentina, Paris, 10 July 1976, Falkland Islands: Oil', briefing by the Department of Energy, DRAFT, 28 June 1976, TNA: FCO76/1616.
20. D.J. Harding to D. Hall, 27 April 1977, TNA: FCO7/3409; Hall to PS/Mr. Rowlands, 5 May 1977, TNA: FCO7/3409.
21. R.A. Fowle, Burmah Oil Trading Ltd., to C.W. Osborne, 9 February 1977, TNA: FCO7/3409; A.W. Haydock, Home Oil (UK) Ltd., to Osborne, 20 April 1977, TNA: FCO7/3409; and D.S. Keeling to Eric Anglin, 24 February 1977, TNA: FCO7/3409.
22. 'Argentina's Offshore Hydrocarbon Activities—Future Activities', report by K.P. Forrest, DOE, 30 December 1976, TNA: FCO7/3409.
23. Hall to Anglin, 7 January 1977, TNA: FCO7/3409; 'Offshore Falkland Islands Exploration', briefing by M. Pennell, Deputy Chairman, BP, 11 February 1977, TNA: FCO7/3409; BP Brief on Hydrocarbon Prospects of Marine Areas Surrounding the Falkland Islands, TNA: FCO7/3409; 'Record of a Meeting Between Mr. J. Grundon and Mr. D. Oliver of BP and Hugh Carless', 3 May 1977, TNA: FCO7/3409; Jack Birks, BP, to Ted Rowlands, 9 May 1977, TNA: FCO7/3409; and Birks to Rowlands, 11 July 1977, TNA: FCO7/3410.
24. Birks to Rowlands, 9 May 1977, TNA: FCO7/3409.
25. Geophysical Services International and Western Geophysical.
26. Anglin to FCO, 28 June 1977, TNA: FCO7/3410.
27. Colin Phipps to Rowlands, 31 January 1977, TNA: FCO7/3409.
28. G. Brown, to H. Cortazzi, 6 May 1977, TNA: EG14/38.
29. FCO to British Embassy, Buenos Aires, 31 May 1977, TNA: FCO7/3409.
30. Anglin to FCO, 28 June 1977, TNA: FCO7/3410; Birks to Rowlands, 11 July 1977, TNA: FCO7/3410; Adrian Sindall to John Ure, FCO, 19 July 1977, TNA: FCO76/1616.
31. J.R. Bretherton to PS/Minister of State, FCO, 3 August 1977, TNA: FCO7/3410.

32. 'Record of a Meeting to discuss Anglo/Argentine Negotiations on the Falkland Islands Dispute', FCO record, 18 May 1977, TNA: EG14/38.
33. Ibid.
34. Ibid.
35. Draft Outline DOP paper, 'Falklands/Argentina'. No date [*circa* 5 May 1977—deduced from position in file], TNA: FCO7 76/1615.
36. Secretary of State's Meeting on the Falkland Islands: Monday 13 June, FCO record, 17 June 1977, TNA: FCO76/1616.
37. Draft Speaking Notes: DOP Meeting—Anglo Argentine Negotiations on the Falkland Islands, FCO. No date [*circa* 30 June 1977—deduced from date of officials' comments written on this draft and contents of the draft], TNA: FCO76/1616.
38. Ibid.
39. The minutes and memoranda for the DOP meeting of 4 July 1977 are closed. 'Concessions over maritime resources' comes from 'Draft Passage for Secretary of State's Speaking Note for DOP on the Falkland Islands', drafted by the Maritime and General Department of the FCO, 29 June 1977, FCO76/1616. It is also the phrase used by official historian Lawrence Freedman and the official report by Lord Franks, both of whom had access to government papers.
40. DOP (77) 15, Cabinet DOP Committee, 'The Falkland Islands: Strategy for Anglo-Argentine Negotiations', Brief for the Secretary of State, FCO, 1 July 1977, TNA: EG14/38.
41. Tony Benn, *Conflict of Interest, Diaries 1977–80* (London: Hutchinson, 1990), pp. 184–185.
42. John Hunt to Callaghan, 1 July 1977, TNA: PREM 16/1504.
43. R.A. Burrows, FCO, to Mr. Buxton, FCO, 7 July 1977, TNA: FCO76/1616. Minutes for the DOP Committee discussions on the Falkland Islands on 4 July and 15 November 1977 are closed (TNA: CAB 148/167/1). The DOP Committee memorandum on the continental shelf is also closed (Memorandum: Falkland Islands: The Legal Implications of a possible cession of continental shelf rights, Note by the Secretaries, 18 November 1977 (item 33), TNA: CAB 148/167/1). The minutes for the DOP Committee of 21 November 1977, are open. These minutes show that the Attorney General advised the DOP committee that ceding rights to the Falkland Islands Continental Shelf would probably not set a dangerous precedent for British claims elsewhere and that ministers accepted his conclusions. TNA: CAB 148/167/1.
44. Hunt to Callaghan, 1 July 1977, TNA: PREM 16/1504.
45. Hunt to Callaghan, 14 November 1977, TNA: PREM 16/1504.
46. FCO Record of Anglo-Argentine Negotiations, Rome 13–15 July 1977, TNA: FCO76/1617. For details of what was discussed at the December 1977 talks, see note from Owen to Callaghan, 22 December 1977, TNA:

PREM 16/1504. See also Freedman, *The Official History*, Vol. I, p. 80; and Donaghy, *The British Government*, p. 155.
47. FCO Steering Brief, 'Anglo-Argentine Negotiations: Second Round in New York from 13 to 15 December 1977 and Meeting with the F.I. Councils Delegation, 18 December 1977', TNA: FCO7/3395, 1977.
48. Owen to Callaghan, 7 April 1978, TNA: PREM 16/1504.
49. Trade figures from FCO Briefing, November 1977, TNA: FCO49/740.
50. The phrase 'political storm' is found in the cabinet minutes of 16 December 1976, TNA: CAB128/60/20.
51. Cabinet minutes, 16 December 1976, TNA: CAB128/60/20; cabinet minutes, 3 February 1977, TNA: CAB/128/61/4; and cabinet minutes, 3 March 1977, TNA: CAB 128/61/9. See also cabinet minutes,18 March 1976, TNA: CAB 128/58/11.
52. Interview with David Owen by the author, 3 November 2014.
53. British Diplomatic Oral History Programme, Churchill College, Cambridge, interview with Adrian Sindall, p. 36.
54. Cabinet DOP Committee, minutes, 8 December 1976, TNA: CAB 148/161; cabinet minutes, 16 December 1976, TNA: CAB/128/60/20.
55. Owen to Callaghan, 6 February 1978, TNA: PREM 16/1504.
56. Note by Edmonds on Carless to Edmonds, 8 October 1976, TNA: FCO7/3201. See also Rowlands to Callaghan, 14 October 1976, TNA: FCO7/3201.
57. Author's interviews with: Stan Newens MP, 17 June 2015; Ann Wright, Argentine Support Movement, 25 March 2015; Julia Napier, Cambridge Committee for Human Rights in Argentina, 17 November 2014; Gordon Hutchison, Joint Working Group for Refugees, 6 October 2014; and Mike Gatehouse, Chile Solidarity Campaign, 13 June 2013.
58. *Argentina: The Trade Unions Fight On*, British Argentina Campaign pamphlet, *circa* 1978. Senate House archives, N320 Pam/4/03.
59. Benn, *Against the Tide*, p. 185.
60. *Hansard*, HC Deb., 2 February 1977, Vol. 925, cc550–561.
61. 'Argentina, Chile, Brazil: A statement by the NEC of the Labour Party', July 1977, Peter Shore Archives, Shore 12/71.
62. Hugh Bicheno, *Razor's Edge: The Unofficial History of the Falklands War* (London: Weidenfeld & Nicholson, 2006), p. 27. Former embassy official Bicheno said that the remarks were reported in a private letter to him from the head of the FCO's Latin America Department.
63. Letterhead of the UK Falkland Islands Committee, 10 March 1976, TNA: FCO7/3232.
64. Figures for Falkland Islands Office and employees from D.G.F. Hall to Sindall, Carless and Edmonds, 12 May 1977, TNA: FCO7/3405; M. Hickson to Sindall, 30 June 1977, TNA: FCO7/3405.

65. Hall to Sindall, Carless and Edmonds, 12 May 1977, TNA: FCO7/3405.
66. 'The Falkland Islands Committee', FCO Briefing, attached to Hall to D.A. Fish, 11 June 1976, TNA: FCO7/3232.
67. See for example letter from Leif Barton to Hugh McCartney MP, 31 March 1977, TNA: FCO7/3405.
68. Note by Edmonds on Hall to Edmonds, 2 March 1976, TNA: FCO7/3232.
69. Carless to Edmonds, 14 July 1976, TNA: FCO7/3232. See also Hall to Carless, 23 January 1976, TNA: FCO7/3232.
70. Hall to Sindall, 29 April 1977, TNA: FCO7/3405; E.N. Larmour to Carless, 8 January 1976, TNA: FCO7/3232; Hall to Collins, 2 March 1976, TNA: FCO7/3232; H. Pearce to Keeling, 12 July 1977, TNA: FCO7/3405, 1977; and Keeling to Pearce, 30 June 1977, TNA: FCO7/3405.
71. Hall to Carless, 23 January 1976, TNA: FCO7/3232, 1976. See also TNA: FCO briefing, attached to Hall to Fish, 11 June 1976, TNA: FCO7/3232.
72. Hall to Sindall, Carless and Edmonds, 29 June 1976, TNA: FCO7/3232.
73. Hall to Sindall, 29 April 1977, TNA: FCO7/3405.
74. Elena Butler to Keeling, 20 June 1977, TNA: FCO7/3405.
75. Hall to Carless, 1 December 1975, TNA: FCO7/3232; Hall to Carless, 3 February 1976, TNA: FCO7/3232.
76. Note by Edmonds, 26 January 1976; on Hall to Carless and Edmonds, 23 January 1976, TNA: FCO7/3232.
77. Hall to Sindall, 12 May 1977, TNA: FCO7/3405.
78. Sindall to PS/PUS, 15 June 1977, TNA: FCO7/3405.
79. Freedman, p. 17.

CHAPTER 10

Befriending 'Common or Garden' Dictators (1979 to 2 April 1982)

Margaret Thatcher may be remembered for bringing down General Galtieri—a 'common or garden dictator' as she described him—but her government had sought to strengthen commercial and diplomatic ties with the dictatorship before the Falklands war.[1] A British ambassador was reinstated in Buenos Aires within months of her government taking office, arms sales accelerated and the number of British trade missions to Argentina sharply increased. Cecil Parkinson became the first government minister to visit Argentina in ten years. Meanwhile Labour's refugee programme for Argentines fleeing persecution was ended. The right wing of the Conservative party approved of the junta's neoliberal economic policies and the Argentine finance minister was delighted to be granted a personal audience with Mrs. Thatcher, but the British right never developed as close a relationship with the Argentine junta as they had with the Pinochet regime.

British diplomats believed that a Conservative government would be sympathetic to their desire for a more pragmatic, business-friendly approach to Argentina and lost no time in promoting a less abrasive relationship with the junta. Two months before the May 1979 election, when the opinion polls showed a Conservative victory was almost certain, Hugh Carless, the chargé d'affaires in Buenos Aires, wrote to London, urging officials to recommend to the incoming administration a more 'forward looking policy' towards Argentina, that would focus less on human rights and more on strengthening business ties.[2] Carless wrote again soon after Margaret Thatcher's election, saying: 'Since the British elections...the concept of Argentina opting for a closer relationship with Britain would seem to have gained ground here.' He suggested that in exchange for granting Argentina 'political recognition as a valid partner', sharing military and nuclear technology, and a 'symbolic' agreement on the Falklands, British business could win lucrative contracts.[3]

Although officials in London were more sensitive to public criticism of Argentina's human rights record, within days of the new government taking office they recommended that Britain exchange ambassadors with Argentina. John Ure, the head of the South America department, argued that 'the advantages in terms of enhanced effectiveness in political negotiation and trade promotion outweigh the disadvantages of having to answer misdirected criticism.'[4] His superior noted that Argentina had been involved in 'thousands of abductions and the widespread use of torture' and ministers should expect protests from human rights campaigners, but nevertheless concluded that there was 'really no question of our snubbing Argentina about their request to send an ambassador'.[5] Nicolas Ridley and Lord Carrington agreed, noting only that timing and publicity should be carefully handled. The decision to restore ambassadors was announced in parliament in July 1979, less than three months after the Conservatives took office.

Downgrading Human Rights

Minister of State Nicholas Ridley sympathised with the most conservative diplomats' desire for a less moralistic foreign policy. One of his first acts was to close the refugee programme for those fleeing persecution from Latin America, commenting in an internal memo: 'We can't accept all political detainees just because they are sponsored by any old UK organisation...I think the criteria should be tightened up.'[6] British diplomats in Buenos Aires responded by proposing a reduction in human rights work by the embassy. The head of chancery recommended that in the light of the 'modified emphasis on the issue of human rights on the part of Her Majesty's Government', the embassy should stop making enquiries about detainees or disappeared persons who did not have a direct connection to Britain.[7] Chargé d'affaires Carless meanwhile, in a long submission, took the opportunity to argue once again for a 'low key' approach to human rights, on the grounds that 'strident foreign criticism...is not likely to be productive'.[8] Some officials in London argued that the embassy should continue to follow up cases of disappeared persons and were very critical of the regime's human rights abuses in internal memos. But the new head of the Latin American Department, Robin Fearn, agreed with Carless that 'we should avoid strident criticism' as 'counterproductive'.[9]

There was a convergence of outlook, therefore, between high-ranking FCO officials and Conservative ministers; human rights should be subordinated to improving commercial ties with Argentina. During the Conservative period of office, Britain made no formal protest about human rights to the Argentine government, although human rights were usually mentioned during talks with Argentine ministers or officials. The last formal démarche to Argentina on human rights by Britain and her EEC partners before the Falklands invasion was in 1978. Britain did co-sponsor a resolution on the disappeared at the United Nations General Assembly in 1980 and a resolution at the UN Commission of Human Rights a year later but, as an FCO briefing in early 1982 made clear, 'in practice we…adopt a very low profile' on Argentine human rights.[10]

The most important factor influencing policy towards Argentina was the Falklands dispute. It dominated the time of Ridley, and later Luce, as ministers for Latin American affairs and it was the only subject relating to Argentina that cabinet discussed. The Foreign Office argued that good relations with Argentina were necessary in order to resolve the dispute—an assertion with which Nicholas Ridley agreed—noting, in an early meeting with officials, that it might be possible to persuade Argentina to accept a continuation of British sovereignty 'if we acted in a friendlier fashion and tried to help them in other areas'.[11] A counter argument could have been made that the fate of the Islanders should not be discussed with Argentina while it was governed by a regime responsible for gross violations of human rights, but instead both Conservative and Labour politicians used the dispute as a justification for diluting their criticism of Argentina's human rights record.

Business Interests

The second most important factor influencing policy towards the Argentine dictatorship was the desire to take advantage of opportunities for British business. The FCO's priority in Latin America was to promote trade and investment. This was supported by a small but vigorous lobby of British manufacturers and bankers interested in selling to, or investing

Table 10.1 British interests in Argentina in 1981 according to the FCO

In order of priority, unchanged since 1977
  (i) Falkland Islands
  (ii) Trade
  (iii) British Antarctic Territory [Argentina and Britain had conflicting territorial claims in Antarctica, see next chapter]
  (iv) Investment
  (v) Consular activities
  (vi) Defence sales
  (vii) Human rights

Source FCO country assessment paper[13]

in, Argentina, as well as the Departments of Trade and Industry, and the Ministry of Defence. The Conservatives were receptive to the concerns of British business. They lifted capital controls on overseas investment and sought to promote exports, particularly arms exports, in Latin America and elsewhere. Early on in her government, Margaret Thatcher told cabinet colleagues that 'a more determined effort must be made to sell more defence equipment overseas…by easing the political constraints which sometimes inhibited sales'[12] (Table 10.1).

Fêting the Argentine Finance Minister

One way in which officials, businessmen and politicians tried to encourage trade with Argentina was by fêting the junta's finance minister José Martínez de Hoz. The minister arrived for his third visit to London since the coup, in May 1979, as a VIP guest of the British Board of Trade. As his visit coincided with the British general election, no politician could see him, but he met Sir Anthony Parsons, the deputy under-secretary at the Foreign Office and had dinner at the Savoy with chargé d'affaires Hugh Carless. Martínez de Hoz also met the governor of the Bank of England and many company directors, including representatives of BAE, GEC, Shell, Rolls Royce, Plessey and Tate & Lyle. An anglophile who loved the pursuits of the English upper class, he had mixed with British diplomats so much that they referred to him by his English nickname. 'Joe has many friends in Britain, including Evelyn de Rothschild, who is taking him to the 2000 guineas [horse race],' wrote Carless in a letter to Sir Anthony Parsons.[14] The focal point of the trip was Martínez de Hoz's address to an audience of 300 businessmen and diplomats at Canning House, an event organised by the business-backed Latin American Trade Advisory Group and sponsored by the FCO. The meeting was chaired by the Tory peer, Viscount Montgomery, who held numerous company directorships and was a vocal advocate for strengthening British ties with South American dictatorships. In an article in *The Guardian* Montgomery wrote:

> One problem confusing the development of constructive dialogue on Latin America has been the demagoguery of 'human rights'. This has become a much over used political slogan, as frequently the people for whom the 'rights' are demanded are no more than urban terrorists…It is very important to understand that the whole attitude to authoritarian governments is quite different in Latin America from that in Britain.[15]

His article prompted numerous letters, including one from a reader who wrote:

> Please convey my congratulations to Viscount Montgomery. His sane and practical views on South America went down very well here at the Anglo-Hispanic Loco Club, I can tell you. It was high time that a fellow Loco like young Monty stood up and told these Johnnies from llama-land that a good dose of dictatorship is the only way to set the economy to rights.[16]

Martínez de Hoz returned to London the following year. With the elections over, he was welcomed by a host of ministers. An FCO official noted that the free-market policies of Martínez de Hoz, were 'in several respects similar to those on which the Conservative Party fought the election', and a number of Conservative ministers found common ideological ground with the Argentine finance minister.[17] A Department of Trade official wrote that his encounter with trade ministers, John Nott and Cecil Parkinson, was 'very much a meeting of minds' and the discussion was 'particularly lively and friendly'.[18] Meanwhile, the Chancellor of the Exchequer, Geoffrey Howe, told the minister, who represented a regime that had banned independent trade unions and killed hundreds of shop-stewards, that 'in the UK, trade unions had become one of the major fossilisers of the economy'.[19] Martínez de Hoz also met the energy secretary and Foreign Secretary Lord Carrington—the only minister to mention human rights—but he was most keen to see Margaret

Thatcher. The FCO lobbied hard for an appointment with the prime minister; the private secretary wrote to Downing Street, describing the Argentine as 'an international figure of considerable standing in the economic world'.[20] Martínez de Hoz met Margaret Thatcher in Downing Street on 5 June 1980. Planned as a very brief courtesy call, the meeting overran despite a scheduled cabinet meeting, as the Argentine finance minister described his economic policies which, he said, were 'very similar to those being pursued by the prime minister'.[21] She later wrote to him saying she had very much enjoyed the meeting and Martínez de Hoz professed himself 'delighted' with the 'welcoming atmosphere' he had encountered during his visit to London.[22]

All officials spoke in glowing terms about Martínez de Hoz. At the FCO Colin Bright wrote: 'The success of the visit serves to demonstrate the impact a man of Dr Martínez de Hoz's calibre can have.'[23] Another official described him as 'an impressive and persuasive spokesman for Argentina', while Hugh Carless claimed he was 'the most encouraging and attractive personality produced by Argentina since the war, who is trying...to push this country out of its comfortable *Peronista* mould of isolation'.[24] Martínez de Hoz resigned in 1981 after his experimental policies sparked one of Argentina's worst financial crises in modern history. The country suffered a wave of bankruptcies and was left with a multi-million dollar foreign debt. After the fall of the dictatorship, Martínez de Hoz was indicted for human rights abuses in 1988, but was pardoned by the president after only 77 days in jail. He was re-arrested in 2010 and died under house arrest in 2013, charged with involvement in the kidnapping and extortion of a textile-mill owner and his son.

Trading with the Junta

As part of the Conservative drive to encourage Argentina to do business with British companies, the trade minister Cecil Parkinson visited Buenos Aires in August 1980. Accompanied by a group of company directors, from Lloyds, Plessey, Hawker Sidley, GEC and Wimpey, Parkinson encouraged Argentine ministers to award British firms contracts and even offered to share Britain's nuclear expertise. Cecil Parkinson had a personal audience with the head of the junta, General Videla, and met all of the regime's key economic ministers. British officials had taken great care to ingratiate themselves with their hosts, suggesting Parkinson give a book on horse-breeding to economy minister Martínez de Hoz, and a work outlining Conservative party philosophy, signed by Margaret Thatcher, to the Argentine trade minister.[25] Once again, officials noted that the visit took place 'in a notably cordial atmosphere', and Parkinson told his hosts that the Thatcher government and the Argentine junta 'shared a similar approach to economic policy'.[26] The British ambassador noted: 'Neither the Falkland Islands nor human rights featured strongly in discussions… Human rights were raised indirectly and informally on a number of occasions, but at no time became an issue.'[27]

The following year, Peter Walker, the agriculture minister, also visited Argentina. The drive to capture more of Argentina's lucrative market was reflected in the growing number of British trade missions sent to Argentina in the Thatcher years: these rose from four in 1978 to eight in 1979, and ten in 1980. But although Argentina's imports from Britain more than doubled between 1978 and 1981 to US$389m, and British companies' net earnings in Argentina rose by 45% in the same period, British diplomats continued to lament that the Falklands factor inhibited trade and prevented British companies from winning large state contracts from the regime.[28] There was, however, a sharp rise in lending and investment by British banks and, by the end of 1981, UK banks' claims on Argentina were US$5.8bn.[29]

The new British ambassador, Anthony Williams, who arrived in Buenos Aires in February 1980, was a consistent advocate of closer ties with Argentina. In one of his first diplomatic reports entitled 'A New Look at Argentina', he claimed that the military regime, having used 'horrific' methods to defeat the opposition, was now 'more nannyish than oppressive', and concluded: 'Argentina is a very interesting market, as British businessmen are coming to realise.'[30] In his end-of-year despatch, he wrote: 'Five years of sobering military administration and of Dr Martínez de Hoz's liberal monetarism has made Argentina a much more possible country to deal with.'[31] Content that Anglo-Argentine relations were improving, he lamented that 'the need to be sufficiently active on the human rights front to satisfy public and parliament opinion in the UK will still be a continuing, though minor, irritation.'[32]

One such irritation was the *Financial Times* journalist Hugh O'Shaughnessy, who was commissioned to write a supplement to accompany an *FT* conference on the benefits of investing in Argentina, an event at which ambassador Anthony Williams was due to speak. Rather than producing a puff piece, O'Shaughnessy's report highlighted the economy's weaknesses and the regime's human rights abuses. Williams was furious and demanded that the FCO complain to the editor about publishing 'this kind of drivel'.[33] When officials in London suggested that this could misfire, the ambassador wrote a letter lambasting the FCO news department saying: 'I was an Information Officer when most of them were in their cradles and, if they are not nowadays able to drop a hint to a 'trusty' like the *Financial Times*, that's where, it seems to me, they should still be.'[34] But officials in London did, in fact, try, as they had done before, to shape the news coverage in a subtle way, through casual conversations with journalists and editors. An FCO press officer spoke to O'Shaughnessy—who would not be budged—and another official was able 'to raise the matter informally', when an *FT* news editor dropped into the Department of Trade for a chat.[35]

If the ambassador was prepared to give cautious praise to the authoritarian government, the British counsellor, David Joy, who arrived at the embassy in early 1982 was more effusive, writing:

> Although I am all for human rights…I am already beginning to have more than a sneaking suspicion that the country is more likely to progress materially under the present regime which re-established order and government, than any government elected by the rabid communist/left-wing Peronist taxi driver who drove me to the office this morning. It does seem to me that the best policy for an Argentine Government today to pursue is that of gradual—even very gradual—liberalisation. The pure air of democracy, applied too early, could well result in a further bout of inebriation.[36]

MILITARY VISITS AND TRAINING

While most British officials did not enthuse so fulsomely about the merits of the Argentine military dictatorship, they shared the business community's view that a stable regime provided opportunities to promote British trade and investment. The sector most eager to sell to Argentina was, predictably, the arms industry, backed by the defence sales department of the MOD and the Department of Trade. The Conservative government maintained the guidelines introduced by Labour under which no equipment or weapons that could be used for internal repression or threatened the Falklands should be sold. However, because the Conservative cabinet had also agreed to vigorously promote arms sales by removing 'political constraints', the Foreign Office interpreted the guidelines in an extraordinarily loose way.

One way to promote arms sales was to invite Argentine military personnel to Britain. Admiral Massera, the head of the Argentine Navy, responsible for the torture and disappearance of thousands of people at the notorious naval mechanical school and a known hardliner on the Falklands, had retired in 1978 but remained an influential figure on the Argentine political scene. Ahead of his planned tour of Europe in 1979, FCO and embassy officials recommended that Conservative ministers meet Massera, pointing out that he could influence defence contracts and that he had resented being snubbed by Labour ministers on his previous visit.[37] Ridley met Massera in October 1979. During their meeting, the retired Admiral told Ridley that 'in ideal "military terms", Argentina wanted to "take" the Islands', but as this was 'unrealistic' they were seeking a compromise with Britain.[38] The Foreign Office hosted a lunch for Massera at the Savoy and among the invitees were Admiral of the Fleet Peter Hill-Norton and retired Air Marshal Sir Denis Spotswood, now deputy chairman of Rolls Royce.[39] 'Massera seemed a little taken aback at the effort to which we had gone,' reported one official.[40]

Large Argentine military delegations attended the Farnborough air shows and British Army Exhibitions in the years preceding the Falklands war, but the FCO insisted that high-ranking personnel should not be invited because this could be 'awkward' for the British Government.[41] This did not prevent the MOD asking, in January 1982, if it could invite the head of the Argentine Air Force to the British Army Equipment Exhibition—a request the FCO turned down.[42] A number of Argentine military personnel were trained in Britain: more than 80 attended courses in 1980 and 67 in 1981. When an FCO official enquired on 30 March 1982, three days before the invasion of the Falklands, whether such training places should be withdrawn in order to convey a signal of displeasure to Argentina, the defence department of the Foreign Office replied: 'Any action in this area would risk damaging UK commercial interests.'[43]

Arms Sales and the Falklands

The combination of arms manufacturers and the MOD defence sales department made a powerful lobby that persuaded ministers to approve export licences for equipment that clearly posed a threat to the Falklands, as was the case with the Stingray light-weight torpedo, even though its state-of-the-art technology had been classified by the Ministry of Defence as a matter of national security. The MOD's defence policy staff had initially turned down Marconi's request to promote Stingray in Argentina, arguing that as Britain's nuclear submarines were one of the principal deterrents to an Argentine attack on the islands, 'it would seem imprudent to provide them with a potent anti-submarine capability.'[44] An MOD sales representative responded by saying: 'I was surprised to see you making so much of a military threat against the Falkland Islands,' adding: 'I was under the impression that...we had accepted that the Argentinians could take the Falkland Islands at any time they wish.'[45] Marconi executives wrote several times to the MOD emphasising that it was a 'matter of extreme urgency if we are to realise this first overseas serious potential order'.[46] Supported by strong lobbying from the MOD sales team, ministers gave approval to promote a sanitised version of the anti-submarine torpedo in March 1980. The vice chief of the British naval staff, however, remained concerned that promoting the classified torpedo could 'not only imperil our security but allow potential customers to abscond with our technology'.[47]

The Foreign Office was under constant pressure from other government departments and manufacturers to relax the arms-sales guidelines. When the nationalised company British Shipbuilders asked for permission to supply a dock-landing ship and an assault ship to Argentina, the ministers of trade, industry and defence all argued that the company should be allowed to tender, despite the fact that the vessels posed—in defence minister Lord Strathcona's words—'a very obvious threat to the Falkland Islands'.[48] Cecil Parkinson, the trade minister, who went on to be a member of the Falklands war cabinet, argued in favour of the bid, saying that 'our competitors will be delighted to supply...The value of these orders to our hard pressed shipbuilders will be obvious.'[49] However, despite the lobbying, Nicholas Ridley refused to allow the company to tender, much to the chagrin of the head of the defence sales, Sir Ronald Ellis, who wrote: 'Can we point out to the minister that the Argentinians have a British Type 42 which can be used against the Falklands—what then!'[50]

On another occasion, the World War II hero Sir Douglas Bader, who had become the director of an arms-manufacturing company, lobbied hard to be able to supply cannons for Argentine Pucara ground-attack planes.[51] He was backed by right-wing journalist, Harry Chapman Pincher who wrote a letter to Defence Secretary Francis Pym, complaining that 'a promising export order to the Argentine' had been blocked by 'Whitehall bumbledom'.[52] An invasion of the Falklands was very 'unlikely', added the journalist, who specialised in intelligence matters. Sir Douglas had handed a personal note to Lord Carrington while at a boat show and Chapman Pincher had heard about the export order while on a shooting party—an illustration of the personal links between the commercial and political elites. The personal lobbying persuaded Pym, who asked the FCO to approve the sale of the cannon.[53] But once again, the Foreign Office turned down the request, Nicolas Ridley insisting: 'We must stick to our guns.' He went on: 'The prime minister was most insistent when I saw her about the Falkland Islands that we should not sell Argentina any arms.'[54]

But while Margaret Thatcher took a very staunch pro-Islander view whenever the Falklands was brought to her attention, she did not keep a close eye on the matter. Furthermore, her comments contradicted her government's stated policy of promoting arms sales and the Foreign Office came under strong pressure from other departments to take a more relaxed attitude. Defence minister Lord Strathcona, with the backing of Francis Pym, sought a meeting with the Foreign Office in 1980 to express his concerns about the constraints on arms sales to Argentina. Meanwhile, the head of the chancellery at the British embassy in Buenos Aires wrote to complain that 'our credibility as defence salesmen' was being damaged by such a 'negative' stance.[55] One reason for this attitude was that officials did not think an invasion of the Falklands was likely. Although every British intelligence and military report published in the 1970s and 1980s had indicated that an invasion of the Falklands was possible, it was believed that Argentina would be more likely to increase the pressure gradually, by taking a series of escalating steps such as a withdrawal of services from the Islands and a blockade. The Foreign Office, therefore, under pressure from the commercial lobby, approved export licences for several items which violated their own guidelines on the Falklands and human rights.

A common reason for justifying arms sales was that other countries would supply them if Britain didn't. But a more circuitous argument used by officials was that Britain had sold so many arms in the past to Argentina that selling more would not affect her offensive capacity. This was the main justification for approving the sale of four new Canberra bomber planes, as well as refurbishment kits for eleven Canberras that had been previously supplied to Argentina. The head of the FCO's Latin American department, Robin Fearn, recommended granting an export licence in 1980, saying that the bomber planes could 'theoretically, play a direct role in any Argentine attack against the Falklands', but 'Argentina already possesses a more than adequate Canberra capability for use in any attack on the Islands, if desired.'[56] He added: 'To refuse this sale could, moreover, do damage to our reputation in Argentina as an arms supplier and more generally to our bilateral relations. It could seriously prejudice other sales prospects to the Argentine arms force.'[57] Nicholas Ridley approved the licence and ministers revalidated their approval in July 1981. British Aerospace signed a contract for the sale of two Canberras and the refurbishment of ten others soon after, but continued to negotiate to try to sell the Argentines up to nine more bombers. Even in mid-March 1982, just two weeks before the invasion of the Falkland Islands, when the Canberra bombers came to be considered again, officials still did not refuse an application. 'At a time of increasing tension, it would seem inappropriate to supply medium bombers which could be deployed against the Falklands,' wrote one official. He added:

However, before endorsing rejection it would be wise to consider whether the arguments used to justify previous sales retain any validity. The previous arguments were:

1. As the Argentines already have many suitable aircraft including 15 Canberras, another few could make no real difference to their capability,
2. A refusal to carry on selling previously approved equipment would call into question our reliability as an arms supplier...
3. Political damage such a policy reversal would have on Anglo Argentine relations.[58]

Rather than blocking the sale, the official suggested delaying a decision until the situation in the Falklands was clearer.[59]

The granting of political clearance for Canberra bombers was used to justify the sale of other equipment that threatened the Falklands. In late 1981, the FCO's Robin Fearn, recommended that ministers approve the sale of an ex RAF Vulcan bomber plane to Argentina. 'A Vulcan bomber could clearly be used in an attack on the Falklands...It would therefore breach the guidelines,' he wrote, 'however...it would be inconsistent to permit the sale of Canberras but prevent the purchase of a Vulcan.'[60] Fearn's superior, Sir Derek Day, expressed reservations about the proposal: 'I ask myself why the Argentinians could possibly want a single second-hand strike role Vulcan bomber...Do the Argentinians really need such an aircraft for defensive purposes?' But the new Conservative minister of state at the Foreign Office, Richard Luce, gave the go-ahead for the Vulcan.[61] In February 1982, Luce also approved a licence for the sale of Infra-Red Linescan, an airborne surveillance device for the detection of vehicles or personnel on the ground. Luce had initially queried the sale asking: 'surely it could be used against us in a possible defence of the Falkland Islands?'[62] But an FCO official pointed out, once again, that the government had already approved the sale of Canberra aircraft, Lynx helicopters and Type 42 destroyers.[63] He added: 'It might be difficult to explain to the Ministry of Defence why we were prepared to sell the Argentines such major military items as fighter/bombers and warships, but not surveillance equipment.'[64] Satisfied, Luce approved the sale.[65]

But if officials and ministers in London were not alert to the coming storm, neither were the British military attachés in Buenos Aires. Just three days before the invasion of the Falkland Islands, a British military attaché informed London that he planned to meet the Secretary General of the Argentine Air Force the following week to discuss the sale of bomber planes. He wrote:

> There is an interest in acquiring extra squadron of bombers during the 1980s.... Relationship with BAE [British Aerospace] has undoubtedly improved: ...if all goes well here BAE could move further up the class in time.[66]

The British defence attachés were decorated after the war and military attaché Colonel Stephen Love was praised for sending a prescient letter to the Falkland Islands governor in March 1982 warning that the Argentines could invade the Falklands.[67] However, Love, and the other British military attachés, were vigorous proponents of arms sales to Argentina, sending a constant stream of telegrams to London reporting sales opportunities and meetings with military buyers. Among the sales to Argentina proposed by the British military attachés in 1981 were tanks, armoured cars, and, most extraordinarily of all, an aircraft carrier and Harrier jets.[68] The MOD sales team in London followed up the Argentine interest in aircraft carriers suggesting that *HMS Hermes*—which played a vital role for Britain in the Falklands conflict—could be sold to Argentina or a new Invincible-class carrier could be built for them. As part of the sales-pitch, the Argentine naval attaché in London, Rear-Admiral Walter Allara, was invited aboard *HMS Invincible* to watch Sea Harriers in operation in September 1981.[69] Love and the other British military attachés regularly mixed socially with Argentine officers and had a visibly cordial relationship with them; a guest at a grand dinner at Love's palatial home in Buenos Aires recalled military officers boasting over champagne about their exploits in the 'dirty war'.[70] While this might be defended on the grounds of intelligence gathering, the telegrams the attachés sent to London expressed no qualms about selling arms to the Argentine military (Tables 10.2 and 10.3).

Arms Sales and Human Rights

The Conservative government also approved several licences for military hardware that violated its own guidelines on internal repression. Ministers made clear to officials that commercial, strategic and political considerations were more important than human rights concerns. This was illustrated in late 1980 when the Argentine armed forces sought to buy British machinery for the manufacture of machine-gun ammunition. The Foreign Office recommended refusing a licence on human rights grounds, but Nicolas Ridley argued the company should be allowed to tender.[72] Although he accepted that an ammunition factory 'would appear to contravene both criteria Ministers have agreed to apply to arms sales to Argentina', his private secretary noted that 'Mr Ridley is anxious not to irritate the Argentines at this stage.'[73] The Conservative steer was made even clearer following the cabinet's Defence and Oversea Policy (DOP) Committee's decision to remove 'political constraints' on arms sales, which led the Foreign Office, in early 1981, to introduce a looser interpretation of the guidelines on human rights and 'adopt a more generous approach to arms sales' in Argentina and Chile.[74]

Commercial and political considerations were also decisive when ministers gave permission for Vickers to promote and supply a main battle tank to Argentina, a vehicle that could clearly be used to subdue the civilian population. Officials had noted in their submission that although the tank could 'theoretically be used for internal repression', this was unlikely and an order would help employment in the depressed area of Newcastle.[75] Nicolas Ridley approved the tanks for Argentina, even though in the same year he turned down a request to sell battle tanks to Chile. In the latter case, 'particular, domestic, political sensitivities'

Table 10.2 British arms sales to Argentina 1967–1982

Equipment	Date of contract	Date of delivery
6 ex-Royal Navy TON class minesweepers	Not available	1967
44 Seacat and 135 Tigercat surface-to-air missiles	Not available	1968–1971
8 ex-RAF Canberras	1968	1970
2 Type 42 destroyers	May 1970	1st commissioned 1976
(the second destroyer was built in Argentina with UK technical support)		2nd commissioned 1980
1 HS 125 transport aircraft	June 1970	1971
5 Skyvan transport aircraft	September 1970	1971
113 sub machine guns to navy/army/police	1975	*
2 Lynx ASW helicopters	January 1976	2 delivered in 1979
Electronic warfare equipment for Argentine navy (Decca Ltd) (£2m)	1976	**
370 army vehicle radios	March 1976	1976–1978
40 sub-machine guns to navy	1976	*
33 sub-machine guns, plus 509,000 rounds of 9mm ammunition to police and navy	1977	*
42 Sea Dart surface-to-air missiles	1st batch: November 1969	1977–1981
	2nd batch: August 1979	
44 sub-machine guns to navy and army	1978	*
Blowpipe anti-aircraft missile system and 120 Blowpipe Missiles	1978	1978
Laser rangefinder for Argentine army (£2.4m)	1978	**
100 Seacat & Tigercat surface-to-air missiles (Shorts Bros, £3.6m)	1978	**
Head Up display equipment for air force (pilot navigational aids etc.) (Marconi, £10m)	1979	**
Ejector seats for air force (£2m)	1979/1980	**
Missile control system (£1m)	1980	**
Drivers periscopes for army (£2m)	1980	**
Radar system for navy (Plessey) (£1m)	1980	**
Kit for 4 German-built frigates (mainly engines and gearing) (£40m)	1981	**

*no date of delivery, but sources suggest that the arms were delivered
**contract signed, sources do not state whether the arms were delivered
Source FCO and MOD[71]

Table 10.3 Major defence items agreed by British ministers for sale to Argentina 1980–1982 which were either not bought by that country or were not delivered

Equipment	Date of ministerial agreement	Comments
Stingray lightweight torpedo	March 1980	
8 Lynx helicopters (£34m)	Date of contract: 1980[a]	Due for delivery July 1982
Spares for Browning machine guns	March 1980	
Canberra aircraft and refurbishment kits	April 1980	
Vickers main battle tank (MBT)	June 1980	Approved by Britain but Argentina chose another supplier
Shipborne torpedo launching system	February 1981	
Modification kit to enable 20 mm Oerlikon cannon to be fitted to Argentine-manufactured armoured personnel vehicles	March 1981	
Centaur half-track Land Rovers	April 1981	Approved by Britain but Argentina chose another supplier
Participation in construction of TNT plant in Argentina	May 1981	
20 mm naval guns for FRG-built patrol craft (Argentine coastguard)	July 1981	
Canberra aircraft and refurbishment kits (revalidation of April 1980 agreement)	July 1981	
Ex-RAF strike-role Vulcan bomber	September 1981	Approved by Britain, but Argentina chose another supplier
Infra-red linescan (airborne surveillance equipment)	February 1982	

[a] Date of ministerial approval not specified
Source FCO and MOD[71]

prevented him from approving a licence, providing a clear example how the relative strength of human rights campaigns can affect policy.[76] In the case of Argentina, the campaign was weak, and ministers believed they could approve arms sales without a political outcry. As negotiations over the tanks developed, an Argentine army colonel led a delegation of military personnel to the British factories of Vickers and Lairds in April 1981, and expressed an interest in buying 38 tanks and 19 Centaur armoured personnel carriers.[77] In advising ministers on the armoured car, the FCO's Robin Fearn noted its sale 'would be open to criticism on human rights grounds because of its capability for repressive use', but he judged that contingency 'unlikely' and once again used the logic of previous arms sales authorisations, pointing out that ministers had already approved the sale of the tank.[78] Ministers agreed and authorised the sale of armoured personnel carriers to Argentina in 1981. However, Argentina eventually chose an Austrian supplier, leading the British military attaché Colonel Love to lament that the 'deal has come to naught'.[79]

Ministers also approved a licence for Royal Ordnance Factories to act as consultants in the construction of a TNT explosive plant in Argentina. As part of the contract, the company planned to send advisors to Buenos Aires and train Argentines at their factory in Bridgewater. In their submission to ministers, FCO officials noted: 'The use for internal repression of TNT (which is used for making shells…) is an unlikely contingency, although clearly not impossible.'[80] Among the other equipment that was approved by ministers were spares for Browning machine guns and modification kits to enable Oerlikon guns to be fitted to Argentine armoured cars. When recommending approval of the kits to minister, Fearn argued:

> Armoured personnel vehicles have clear implications for human rights and we might be criticised if we were to be involved at any stage in their construction or armament. It is however, unlikely that our involvement would ever become known.[81]

The deals on some of the larger items—the battle tanks, Centaur armoured cars and the Vulcan bombers—fell through only after Argentina chose other suppliers, much to the disappointment of British manufacturers and defence-sales officials, who had done all they could do win the orders.

The desire to sell arms to Argentina was primarily driven by commercial interests, to win big export orders and secure jobs in Britain. This goal was shared by ministers and officials from the Foreign Office, the MOD, and the Departments of Trade, Industry and Employment, whose social contacts with business leaders enabled them to discuss deals informally. The Falklands Islands lobby was of concern to Conservative ministers, but even though officials did question whether particularly controversial deals—such as the sale of bomber planes—would be defensible in parliament, the commercial case was judged to be so strong in many instances—and the possibility of an invasion of the Falklands so small—that export licences were approved. Ministers and officials also followed the twisted logic that Britain needed good relations with Argentina in order to resolve the Falklands dispute and therefore arms sales should be encouraged as a way of improving relations, even though those arms could potentially increase the threat to the Islands. Meanwhile, human rights campaigns on Argentina were small and unable to influence arms sales decisions—in contrast to the much larger trade-union backed Chile campaigns which acted as a powerful counter lobby. Officials therefore felt able to approve the sale of military equipment that could clearly be used for internal repression in Argentina without fearing that such a decision would spark a political outcry.

HUMAN RIGHTS CAMPAIGNS

The publicity surrounding the 1978 World Cup had led to a greater awareness of human rights abuses in Argentina and campaigning organisations such as the British Argentina Campaign and the Committee for Human Rights in Argentina won the backing of several NGOs, church groups and local trade union branches. In parliamentary terms, however, the campaign remained weak, its appeal limited mainly to MPs and peers who already had an interest in Latin America, such as Labour's Judith Hart, Michael Flannery, Stan Newens, Liberal peer Eric Avebury and—on the Conservative side—Bernard Braine. And even if a growing number of Labour MPs now knew about 'the disappeared' and the Mothers of the Plaza de Mayo, their ability to influence the government was drastically reduced as the Conservative government had a large majority. The Labour Party general secretary wrote to Lord Carrington in 1979, calling on the government 'to make known to the Argentine authorities its deep concern' about human rights abuses, and the Labour National Executive Committee passed a resolution with the same demand, but the Conservatives felt no compulsion to act on the request and no formal complaint to the Argentine government was made.[82] Campaigners working on both Chile and Argentina noticed immediately that the Conservative government had a less responsive attitude; one of those who met Ridley described him as 'disdainful'.[83] In contrast to Labour ministers, Nicholas Ridley met very few delegations of campaigners. On one occasion, he met the exiled Argentine senator, Hipólito Solari Yrigoyen, along with a member of Amnesty International. Ridley told the senator that whilst in Buenos Aires 'he had gained the impression that the Government enjoyed a measure of popular support' because they had 'suppressed terrorism' and managed the economy well, suggesting this was positive because governments with public backing were more likely to call elections.[84] The senator replied that the Argentine government was 'totally tyrannical' and 'had no intention of handing power back to the people'.[85] Ridley's successor as FCO minister, Richard Luce, met no human rights delegations, turning down a request from a Labour MEP, even though FCO officials had recommended that Luce receive him.[86]

While human rights became a lower priority under the Conservative government, FCO officials at desk level continued to give sporadic help to human rights campaigners, on several occasions allowing the Joint Working Party for Refugees to send sensitive lists of detainees' names through embassy channels. Although the criteria for accepting refugees were tightened up and sponsorship by a British organisation was no longer sufficient grounds for a security-cleared Argentine exile to be granted access to the UK, British embassy staff did continue to follow up several enquiries about detainees sent by the numerous church groups, trade union branches and human rights groups that 'adopted' political prisoners. Trying to glean information about prisoners, however, was a laborious and sobering experience, as it became clear that many of the 'disappeared' had been murdered by the authorities. Of the estimated 140 prisoners 'adopted' by British organisations in 1979, 52 were given clearance for entry to Britain, but by 1981, only four had been freed without conditions.[87] A further nine were released under surveillance. Human rights campaigners, therefore, came up against three problems during the Conservative period of office—the ongoing difficulty of explaining the complex Argentine political situation to a wide audience, a British government unreceptive to their concerns, and a chilling wall of silence from the Argentine dictatorship—a frustrating experience that exhausted many of the activists.[88]

Conclusion

In the years preceding the Falklands war, the Conservative government tried to improve relations with the Argentine dictatorship. The Foreign Office and Conservative ministers shared a pro-business outlook and there was little friction between officials and politicians over policy. Ambassadors were exchanged, ministerial visits were resumed and the number of trade missions to Argentina increased. It was believed that good Anglo-Argentine relations were needed to resolve the Falklands dispute and there was also a strong commercial lobby—backed by the Departments of Trade, Industry, and Employment—which believed a stable military regime provided opportunities for British business. The arms industry, encouraged by the MOD's sales department and Britain's military attachés, was particularly eager to export to Argentina, and the government violated its own guidelines on defence sales in an effort to win contracts. While Conservative ministers and officials were acutely aware of the Falklands Islands lobby, particularly its support among Tory backbenchers, they took little notice of non-governmental organisations working on human rights in Argentina and the predominantly left-leaning campaigners had virtually no leverage over the government. Human rights were, therefore, subordinated to commercial interests and the government imposed no sanctions against Argentina before the invasion of the Falkland Islands.

Notes

1. Margaret Thatcher, *The Downing Street Years* (London: Harper Collins, 1993), p. 181.
2. Hugh Carless to J.B. Ure, 30 March 1979, The National Archives (TNA): FCO7/3573.
3. Carless to FCO, 11 June 1979, TNA: FCO7/3573.
4. Ure to Sir Anthony Parsons and PS/Mr. Ridley, 9 May 1979, TNA: FCO7/3573.
5. Note by G.E. Hall on Ure to Parsons and PS/Mr. Ridley, 9 May 1979, TNA: FCO7/3573.
6. J.W. Yapp to Mr. Shepherd, FCO, 4 June 1979, TNA: FCO7/3585.

7. A.R. Murray to T.H. Malcomson, 30 November 1979, TNA: FCO7/3586.
8. 'Subversion, Repression and Human Rights in Argentina', FCO report, 15 November 1979, TNA: FCO7/3586.
9. Robin Fearn, FCO, to Carless, 10 December 1979, TNA: FCO7/3586.
10. 'Anglo-Argentine Relations', FCO briefing [Date of covering note: 23 February 1982], TNA: FCO7/4906.
11. Minister of State's meeting, minutes, 16 May 1979, TNA: FCO7/3573.
12. DOP Committee, minutes, 3 December 1979, TNA: CAB 148/183.
13. Country Assessment Paper: Argentina [no date, c1981 deduced from content], TNA: FCO7/3869.
14. Carless to Parsons, 20 April 1979, TNA: FCO7/3581.
15. 'A Continent Condemned out of Hand', David Montgomery, *The Guardian*, 4 June 1979.
16. Letter from K. Jinks to *The Guardian*, 7 June 1979.
17. Carless to Lord Carrington, 18 May 1979, TNA: FCO7/3581. The quotation reads: '...on which the Conservative Party policy [sic] fought the election.'
18. Telegram no. 67 from DTI, to British Embassy, Buenos Aires, 9 June 1979, TNA: FCO7/3727.
19. 'Note of a Meeting Held at No. 11 Downing Street on 5 June 1980' Chancellor of the Exchequer's Office, 13 June 1980, TNA: FCO7/3727.
20. R. Lyne to Michael Alexander, 26 February 1980, TNA: FCO7/3727.
21. Alexander to Lyne, 6 June 1980, TNA: PREM 19/140.
22. Margaret Thatcher to José Martínez de Hoz, 11 June 1980, TNA: PREM 19/140. Martínez Hoz's thoughts reported in FCO to Buenos Aires, 10 June 1980, TNA: FCO7/3727.
23. C. Bright, FCO, to Murray, 11 June 1980, TNA: FCO7/3727.
24. FCO to Buenos Aires, 10 June 1980, TNA: FCO7/3727; Carless to Parsons, 20 April 1979, TNA: FCO7/3581.
25. British Embassy, Buenos Aires, to DoT, 14 July 1980, TNA: FCO7/3728.
26. Anthony Williams to FCO, 11 August, 1980, TNA: FCO7/3728; 'Meeting with Dr. Walter Klein, 6 August 1980', FCO record, TNA: FCO7/3728.
27. Williams to FCO, 11 August, 1980, TNA: FCO7/3728.
28. IMF Direction of Trade Statistics, 1979, 1980, 1981; *Overseas Transactions, Business Monitor* (London: HMSO, 1982).
29. DOP Committee, 'Argentina: Economic Retaliation against the United Kingdom', Note by the Secretaries, 16 April 1982, TNA: CAB 148/206.
30. 'A New Look at Argentina', by Anthony Williams, 4 September 1980, TNA: FCO7/3724.

31. Argentina: Annual Review for 1980, 23 January 1981, TNA: FCO7/3870.
32. Ibid.
33. Williams to Fearn, 16 January 1981, TNA: FCO7/3875.
34. Ibid.
35. Mr. McCrory to Bright, 9 February 1981, TNA: FCO7/3875.
36. David Joy to Fearn, 3 March 1982, TNA: FCO7/4073.
37. Ure to G.W. Harding, FCO, 11 October 1979, TNA: FCO7/3589; Carless to FCO, 17 October 1979, TNA: FCO7/3589.
38. K.D. Temple to Ure, 31 October 1979, TNA: FCO7/3589.
39. 'Programme for Admiral Massera's Visit', FCO record, October 1979, TNA: FCO7/3589.
40. G.A. Duggan, FCO, to Carless, 5 November 1979, TNA: FCO7/3589.
41. Draft paragraphs for a brief on defence sales, attached to Bright to H.R. Owen, 15 July 1980, TNA: FCO7/3728, 1980.
42. Lieutenant-Colonel P.S.D. Griffin (retd) to Meryl Cowley, 21 January 1982, TNA: FCO7/4085.
43. C. Hulse to Giffard, 30 March 1982, TNA: FCO7/4085.
44. J.R. Hill to The Secretary RMI Sub-Committee, MOD, 21 August 1979, TNA: DEFE 68/378.
45. Stephen F. Smith to DoDP (C), 11 September 1979, TNA: FCO7/4078.
46. D. Evans, Marconi Space and Defence Systems Ltd., to Roger Harding, 25 February 1980. TNA: DEFE 68/378; See also D. Evans to Rear Admiral A.A. Murphy, MOD, 25 February 1980, TNA: DEFE 68/378; Sir Robert Telford, GEC-Marconi Electronics, to Ronald Ellis, 29 August 1979, TNA: DEFE 68/378.
47. V.C.N.S. [Anthony Morton] to Ellis, 17 March 1980, TNA: DEFE 68/378.
48. Lord Strathcona to Ian Gilmour, January 1980 [no specific day on document] TNA: DEFE 68/378. Adam Butler to Gilmour, 14 January 1980, TNA: DEFE 68/378.
49. Cecil Parkinson to Gilmour, 15 January 1980, TNA: DEFE 68/378.
50. Note by Ellis on Ridley to Francis Pym, 15 January 1980, TNA: DEFE 68/378.
51. Sir Douglas Bader to Carrington, 7 January 1980, TNA: DEFE 68/378; 'Note of a Meeting Between Export Licensing Branch and Sir Douglas Bader', 21 December 1979, TNA: FCO7/3730; Record of a Call by Sir Douglas Bader on the Minister of State, Monday 18 February 1980, FCO7/3730.
52. Chapman Pincher to Pym, 28 December 1979, TNA: DEFE 68/378.
53. J.D.S. Dawson to Lyne, 22 January 1980, TNA: FCO7/3730; Dawson to Head of DS13, MOD, 1 February 1980, TNA: DEFE 68/378.

54. Notes by FCO official G.W. Harding and by Nicholas Ridley on Fearn to G.W. Harding, FCO, and PS/Mr. Ridley, 'Argentina: arms sales',14 January 1980, TNA: FCO7/3730.
55. Duggan to G.W. Harding and PS/Mr. Ridley, 18 February 1980 TNA: FCO7/3730; David Jones, PS, MOD, to Michael Richardson, 13 February 1980 TNA: FCO7/3730; and Murray to Duggan, 18 March 1980 TNA: FCO7/3730.
56. Fearn to G.W. Harding, FCO, and PS/Mr. Ridley, 23 April 1980, TNA: FCO7/3730.
57. Ibid.
58. R.J. Chase to Fearn and Bright, 16 March 1982, TNA: FCO7/4088.
59. Chase to Fearn and Bright, 16 March 1982, TNA: FCO7/4088.
60. Fearn to Derek Day and PS/Mr. Luce, 17 September 1981, TNA: FCO7/3874.
61. Note by Day, 22 September 1981, on Fearn to Day and PS/Mr. Luce, 17 September 1981, TNA: FCO7/3874. Derek Day was a Deputy Under Secretary at the FCO responsible for the Americas. For Luce's approval see handwritten note by official [appears to be 'P.B.'—P. Bean/APS/Mr. Luce], 29 September 1982, on note from Fearn to Day and PS/Mr. Luce, 17 September 1981, TNA: FCO7/3874, 1982.
62. J.M. Cresswell to Fearn, 22 February 1982, TNA: FCO7/4088.
63. Chase to PS/Mr. Luce, 24 February 1982, TNA: FCO7/4088.
64. Ibid.
65. Note by official [appears to be 'P.B.'—P. Bean, APS/Mr. Luce] to Chase, 26 February 1982 on Chase to PS/Mr. Luce, 24 February 1982, TNA: FCO7/4088.
66. British defence attaché, Buenos Aires, to MOD, 'for Jones D. Sales 2—Canberras', 29 March 1982, TNA: FCO7/4088.
67. Stephen Love to Rex Hunt, 2 March 1982, TNA: FCO7/4916.
68. Telegram no. 9/1530z from BRITNAV, Buenos Aires, to MODUK, 9 January 1981, TNA: FCO7/3874; Telegram no. 18/1435z from BRITDEFAT Buenos Aires to MODUK, 18 November 1981, TNA: FCO7/3874, 1981; Telegram no. 01/1345z of from BRITDEFAT Buenos Aires to MODUK, 4 November 1981, TNA: FCO7/3874; and Love to J. Wade, 12 June 1981, TNA: FCO7/3874.
69. David G. Jones to Fearn, 16 July 1981, TNA: FCO7/3874. See also Jimmy Burns, *The Land that Lost its Heroes* (London: Bloomsbury, 2002), p. 139.
70. Author's interview with Jimmy Burns, 3 March 2015. See also Jimmy Burns, *The Land that Lost its Heroes*, pp. 163–164.
71. R.M. Jackson to PS/Mr. Onslow, 21 July 1982, TNA: FCO7/4078; Draft reply to Parliamentary Question on arms sales, attached to

D.G. Jones to Head of DS13, 20 April 1982, TNA: FCO7/4621; 'Argentina: Major Arms Contracts 1976–1979', FCO record attached to J.R Cowling to Fearn, 28 November 1979, TNA: FCO7/3579; R. Harding to Fearn, 24 January 1980, TNA: FCO7/3730; 'Sales of Defence Equipment to Argentina', attached to B.J. Todd, MOD to T.H. Malcolmson, 28 March 1980, TNA: FCO7/3730; and 'Major Sales of Defence Equipment to Argentina' attached to R.H. Smith to Ure and PS/Mr. Ridley, 11 February 1981, TNA: FCO7/3874.
72. Fearn to PS/Mr. Ridley, 4 December 1980, TNA: FCO7/3730.
73. K.D. Temple, PS/Mr. Ridley, to Fearn, 5 December 1980, TNA: FCO7/3730.
74. Note of a meeting of the FCO Arms Sales Group on 15 December 1980, FCO, 12 January 1981, TNA: FCO7/3874.
75. Fearn to G.W. Harding, FCO, and PS/Mr. Ridley, 6 June 1980, TNA: FCO7/3730.
76. Fearn to Ure and PS/Mr. Ridley, 28 April 1981, TNA: FCO7/3874.
77. Fearn to Ure and PS/Mr. Ridley, 28 April 1981, TNA: FCO7/3874.
78. Fearn to Ure, Day and PS/Mr. Ridley, 29 April 1981, TNA: FCO7/3874.
79. Love to J. Wade, 12 June 1981, TNA: FCO7/3874.
80. Fearn to Day and PS/Mr. Ridley, 1 May 1981, TNA: FCO7/3874.
81. Fearn to Ure and PS/Mr. Ridley, 25 March 1981, TNA: FCO7/3874.
82. Ron Hayward to Carrington, 30 August 1979, FCO7/3585.
83. Author's interview with Mike Gatehouse, 13 June 2013.
84. 'Call on the Minister of State by Dr Hipólito Solari Yrigoyen, 28 August 1979', FCO, TNA: FCO7/3586.
85. Ibid.
86. Fearn to PS/Mr. Luce, 13 October 1981, TNA: FCO7/3876; P.L. Bean to Fearn, 15 October 1981, TNA: FCO7/3876. The MEP was Ken Collins.
87. Committee on Human Rights in Argentina newsletter, June 1979, TNA: FCO7/3876. Ridley to Eric Avebury, 7 September 1981; TNA: FCO7/3876; Richard Luce to Avebury, 5 January 1982, TNA: FCO7/3876.
88. Author's interviews with Ann Wright, 25 March 2015, and Julia Napier, 17 November 2014.

CHAPTER 11

Antarctica, Oil and Leaseback: Britain's Strategic Interests in the Falklands (1979 to 2 April 1982)

Margaret Thatcher's victory in the Falklands war overshadowed the policy errors that preceded the invasion. The official inquiry into the causes of the conflict detailed the failure to draw together intelligence, the misreading of Argentine intentions, and, crucially, the sending of a series of signals which gave Argentina the impression that Britain did not intend to defend the Falklands—the most important of which during the Thatcher years was the withdrawal of the only British naval vessel in the South Atlantic, *HMS Endurance*.[1] The British Nationality Bill (1981) which stripped Islanders of automatic British citizenship and the reluctance to invest in the Falklands' infrastructure may have also suggested to the Argentines that the Islanders were a low priority for the British government.

The report concluded that it would have been impossible to have foreseen that the invasion would take place on 2nd April 1982, but while it is true that the exact date would have been hard to pinpoint—not least because General Galtieri brought the plan forward—intelligence reports for decades had indicated an invasion was a possibility. British diplomats had mixed socially with Argentine military officers, but this had given them no insight into their intentions: the policy of strengthening commercial ties with the junta and muting criticism of its human rights abuses did nothing to deter the invasion. An 'un-ethical' policy had reaped no rewards.

This is not an exhaustive account of the causes of the Falklands war, which have been debated elsewhere. Instead this chapter looks closely at Britain's economic and strategic interests in the Islands and considers whether these affected the UK's stance in the pre-war negotiations with Argentina, a suggestion that has been downplayed or rejected in the British literature but heavily emphasised by many Argentine commentators.[2] Archival records show that while oil companies favoured a deal with Argentina during the 1970s, the Department of Energy urged caution during the Thatcher years, as it became concerned that a leaseback might not provide British oil corporations or the Exchequer with a sufficient share of the oil wealth. New evidence presented here also shows that politicians feared that losing the Falklands could weaken Britain's claim to Antarctica. While parliamentary concern about the fate of the Islanders was the main reason that politicians were reluctant to cede the sovereignty of the Islands, Britain's economic and strategic interests should not be discounted when analysing events leading up to the Falklands conflict.

Did the Foreign Office pursue the policy of leaseback against the wishes of its political masters? The question raises the issue of political agency—that is: who makes policy, un-elected bureaucrats or politicians? The charge that the FCO was trying quietly to reach a deal with Argentina has been made by historians, such as Bicheno, and some Conservative politicians not least Margaret Thatcher, who criticised their 'flexibility of principle'.[3] Foreign Office minister Richard Luce also criticised the FCO.[4] But this chapter shows that Margaret Thatcher and her ministers approved leaseback—albeit reluctantly. While the Foreign Office did favour making a deal with Argentina, in all its briefings, it provided at least two options: either come to a negotiated settlement or reinforce the defences of the Islands. The problem was that the Thatcher government abandoned the leaseback option but took no counter-balancing contingency measures, leaving the Islands vulnerable to attack. The Falkland Islands Committee, a social movement with close links to the elite, expertly marshalled domestic opposition to a settlement, but could not persuade Thatcher's neoliberal government to spend more on defending the Islands. This was a failure of the politicians, not the officials. This book has also considered whether the social class of FCO officials coloured their advice. It concludes that a simple binary opposition between a corporate-class and a working-class perspective is not sufficient to explain divisions over the Falklands, which are better understood through an examination of splits within the elite.

Economic Interests in the Falklands

The prohibitive cost of defending the Islands against potential Argentine economic or military aggression was the main reason Thatcher's ministers agreed to negotiate with Argentina. A memorandum by Foreign Secretary Lord Carrington in late 1979 warned that if Britain refused to negotiate, the Islands could be blockaded or even invaded. But he also argued that if an agreement was not reached with Argentina, the Islands could fall into economic decline, British trade with Argentina could be damaged and that it would be impossible to exploit the economic resources (primarily oil and fish) of the South Atlantic.[5] Long annexes attached to the memorandum outlined not only the cost of defending the Islands militarily, but also the threat to British commercial interests in Argentina, in particular, the loss of large potential defence and nuclear contracts, if no agreement was reached. Margaret Thatcher and members of the cabinet's Defence and Oversea Policy (DOP) Committee accepted these arguments and agreed, in July 1980, to begin exploratory discussions on a solution that could include a 'surrender of sovereignty and simultaneous leaseback arrangements' (Table 11.1).[6]

Table 11.1 Anglo-Argentine talks on the Falkland Islands 1979–1982

September 1979	Lord Carrington recommends leaseback as the best option, in a memo to the prime minister and to members of the Cabinet's Defence and Oversea Policy (DOP) Committee
January 1980	Cabinet's DOP Committee agrees to seek Islanders' agreement to start talks with Argentina
April 1980	Nicholas Ridley holds exploratory talks with Islanders and Argentines
July 1980	Cabinet's DOP Committee agrees to talks with Argentina, which could include a 'surrender of sovereignty and simultaneous leaseback arrangement'
September 1980	Nicholas Ridley proposes leaseback to the Argentine deputy foreign minister in secret talks
November 1980	Cabinet's DOP Committee agrees to recommend leaseback to Islanders
November 1980	Nicholas Ridley visits Islands; a majority of Islanders undecided about leaseback, some strongly opposed
2 December 1980	Nicholas Ridley announces leaseback in parliament and is heavily criticised by MPs

(continued)

Table 11.1 (continued)

January 1981	Islanders demand a freeze on sovereignty talks
January 1981	Cabinet's DOP agrees to continue talks in the hope that Islanders will eventually back leaseback
February 1981	Nicholas Ridley and Islanders meet Argentines, who reject a freeze
September 1981	Lord Carrington meets Argentine foreign minister and asks for new Argentine proposals
February 1982	Richard Luce and Islanders meet Argentines and agree to set up negotiating commission to resolve dispute

THE BUSINESS LOBBY

The FCO had long been aware that British business leaders with interests in Latin America regarded the Falklands dispute as an impediment to trade. Lord Nelson, the chairman of GEC, for example, met the chief of the Argentine air force in July 1979 to discuss a nuclear contract and was told that 'Britain would never win any major contracts in Argentina unless progress were made over the Falkland Islands'—comments that were relayed back to the British embassy and the FCO.[7] More than 100 British businessmen gave the Argentine ambassador a rapturous welcome—'the equivalent of a Canning House standing ovation'—in March 1980, at a seminar in Belgravia when he outlined investment opportunities in Argentina.[8] 'He clearly had most of his audience eating out of his hand,' commented one FCO official.[9] A member of the audience had queried whether the problem of the Falklands still remained, prompting the FCO official to comment: 'There is clearly a danger that British businessmen will side with Argentina because they view the problem simply as an obstacle to good trading relations.'[10] As tension rose in the weeks leading up to the Argentine invasion, Guy Huntrods, a director of Lloyds Bank International, expressed concern 'at the implications for British commercial and financial interests in Argentina'.[11] Meanwhile, Viscount Montgomery a Tory peer with business interests in Latin America, made several speeches in the Lords during the Thatcher years, arguing that it was in Britain's interests to do a deal with Argentina over the Falklands.[12]

OIL AND THE FALKLANDS

Oil companies interested in exploring the waters around the Falklands had been keen advocates of rapprochement with Argentina in the 1970s. During Thatcher's period of office, large oil companies continued to believe that it would be legally and politically difficult to exploit Falklands oil without resolving the sovereignty dispute, but they were no longer clamouring for immediate access to the waters around the Islands. BP, which had lobbied hardest to start exploring the area in the 1970s, became less enthusiastic after viewing the geological survey data, which became available in 1979.[13] BP believed that the data showed the most promising areas were around the shores of Argentina, rather than the Falklands. So too, did Shell and Esso, which bought licences from Argentina to prospect offshore for oil in 1979–1982. Oil companies also pointed out that the technology needed to access many of the deep-water hydrocarbon deposits in the South Atlantic would not be available for ten to fifteen years.[14] Finally, BP was heavily involved in the development of North Sea oil so, although it did not rule out exploring the Falklands area in the future, it was not an immediate priority. Smaller firms interested in exploration or surveying work, however, continued to lobby hard for immediate access to Falklands waters, including a company owned by the Labour MP Colin Phipps, which was given permission by the FCO to carry out an aero-magnetic survey in early 1979.[15] Meanwhile, the British National Oil Corporation (BNOC), a state-owned company established in 1975, began to take an interest in the Falklands, investing £250,000 in purchasing the geological survey data and meeting representatives of the state-owned Argentina oil company YPF in Buenos Aires to discuss joint exploration in 1979.[16] But although it concluded that the Falklands area would warrant further investigation, as a new company, it forecast that it would need at least ten years or more before it had the capacity to operate overseas as a leading player.[17] The Department of Energy, which voiced the concerns of the larger British oil companies, as well the British state's interests in oil assets, therefore repeatedly called for a cautious and gradual approach to the negotiations over leaseback, anxious that Britain's rights to any potential oil deposits should not be signed away. The Department lobbied for British companies to get the most preferential deal possible, on a timescale that best suited their interests.

When, in late 1979, Lord Carrington proposed a 99-year leaseback formula, the Secretary of State for Energy, David Howell, wrote to Margaret Thatcher saying: 'We ought to be very careful about adopting a course which could lead to British oil companies losing a favourable position they might otherwise have had'.[18] He called for a full discussion on the economic implications of leaseback, warning that if sovereignty was transferred 'it could also involve a substantial loss to the British economy if oil were found'.[19] The Chancellor of the Exchequer, Geoffrey Howe, agreed with Howell that the costs and benefits needed to be examined, while Sir Kenneth Berrill, head of the Cabinet Office's Central Policy Review Staff, said that the terms of any negotiations would need to be looked at carefully because Argentina would want to see 'the benefits of any oil discoveries going to the Argentine, rather than to the Falkland Islands and United Kingdom companies'.[20] Margaret Thatcher never took a close interest in the issue of Falklands oil; on Carrington's letter, in which he proposed creating a 200-mile exclusion zone for fishing and oil which would be leased to Britain for 99 years, she wrote 'Why can't development proceed now?' But this was her only comment on the issue in the pre-war years.[21] She was much more exercised by the political principle of transferring sovereignty to Argentina and wrote angry notes on Carrington's draft rejecting the entire leaseback idea, although just a few months later she was persuaded of the case.[22]

Britain's objectives in the dispute were outlined by Carrington in October 1979 in a memorandum to DOP cabinet colleagues. These included defending the right of the British settlers to remain under British administration and ending a dispute which was damaging to the Islands economy, UK trade with Argentina and Britain's international relations. Another key objective, however, was to 'to ensure that the UK derives advantage from economic resources of the area, possibly oil and certainly fish'.[23] In a note to Margaret Thatcher, the cabinet secretary, Robert Armstrong, emphasised that, as well as discussing the military defence of the Falklands, ministers needed to consider 'the possible oil and fishery benefits at stake' and 'the implications for our oil and fishery interests elsewhere of the possible cession of UK sovereignty over the Falkland Islands continental shelf'.[24]

Department of Energy officials, however, were concerned that the commitment to preserving Britain's oil rights was not strong enough when ministers agreed, in January 1980, to start exploratory ministerial talks with Argentina. An official urged the energy secretary to write to ministers again reminding them 'of the importance we attach to preserving access to any oil in disputed waters'.[25] He added:

> The revenue from oil would clearly benefit ourselves and the Islanders... In addition, British companies...would gain an inside track for the related development business which could be very valuable.[26]

Energy Secretary David Howell duly wrote to Lord Carrington, in February 1980, stating: 'I hope...you will not lose sight of retaining, if at all possible, access for the UK to any oil or gas which might be found in Falkland Island waters.'[27] To drum home the point, the Department of Energy wrote to the Foreign Office ahead of talks between Nicholas Ridley and the Argentine deputy foreign minister asking to have inserted into Ridley's briefing notes the phrase: 'The Department of Energy attach importance to our retaining, if at all possible, access for the UK to any oil or gas which might be found in Falkland Islands waters.'[28] Britain's economic and oil interests were, then, taken into account during the deliberations over the Falklands in the years preceding the outbreak of war.

Leaseback and Oil

Ridley, like the Foreign Office, saw oil as a way of resolving the dispute through Anglo-Argentine economic cooperation and, when he met Argentine deputy foreign minister Carlos Cavandoli, in April 1980, he proposed joint exploration of Falkland waters, remarking: 'Oil today was the same as gold had been to the Spaniards. We should hasten.'[29] But Argentina would only consider it as part of an overall deal on sovereignty. Ridley took a close interest in the question of oil, asking officials who would benefit from any potential exploration and to draw up a detailed oil licensing regime.[30] A Foreign Office official explained to him that although, by precedent, the revenues from oil exploration would go to the Falkland Islands government, not the British Exchequer, he added: 'In practical terms, we ought to be able to ensure...that we get a substantial share of the action and the profit.'[31]

Nicholas Ridley was authorised by ministers in July 1980 to hold secret talks with the Argentine deputy foreign minister. He met Cavandoli in September 1980 and proposed the idea of transferring the sovereignty of the Islands and a 200-mile exclusion zone to Argentina, which would then be leased back to Britain. The Argentine minister approved of the idea in principle but proposed a 24-year lease, whereas Nicholas Ridley suggested a 250-year lease (with a view to accepting 99 years).[32] On his return, Margaret Thatcher and the Defence and Oversea Policy (DOP) Committee agreed to seek the Islanders' approval of leaseback.[33] During this DOP meeting, ministers also noted: 'It would be important to make satisfactory arrangements for any oil that might be discovered...further thought should be given to ways in which the United Kingdom might be guaranteed entitlement to a substantial part of the revenues.'[34] Once again, oil was not the primary consideration, but was part of ministers' calculations. The leaseback plan, however, was effectively killed on 2 December 1980 when MPs from all parties reacted with horror when it was proposed by Ridley in the House of Commons (see below).

The Islanders and Oil

Oil was never the key issue for the residents of the Islands. Two Islanders, accompanied by Nicholas Ridley, met Argentine ministers in New York in February 1981. The Argentine ambassador promised the Islanders all sorts of advantages if sovereignty was transferred, but Falkland Islands councillor Stuart Wallace impressed on the Argentines that the Islanders 'were primarily concerned with the structure of their way of life; that came before any economic benefit.'[35] The UK-based Falkland Islands Committee, however, did emphasise the economic potential of the Islands and lobbied in favour of oil exploration. This was partly because the Committee had close links with the Falkland Islands Company, and other business interests, such as Alginate Industries, the Falkland Sheep Owners Association and the wool merchants Jacomb, Hoare and Co, which would benefit, directly or indirectly, from increased economic activity in and around the Islands. But the committee also highlighted—and exaggerated—the economic potential of the Islands in an effort to win political support in Britain, going so far as to add a masthead to its note-paper reading: 'the Falklands Islands: the new North Sea'.[36]

Oil Companies' Concerns About Leaseback

Despite domestic opposition, ministers continued to believe that leaseback, in the long-run, would be the best solution and officials continued to discuss how it might work out in practice. Robin Fearn, head of the South American Department, set out the FCO's objectives for a possible oil regime:

1. We get the maximum possible preferential treatment for British companies in the issue of the licences...
2. British equipment is used as much as possible.
3. A share of the oil goes to the UK...
4. FIG [Falkland Islands Government] obtain an appropriate share of the proceeds consistent with its developmental needs and its capacity for absorption...
5. The impact of oil related development on the Islanders traditional way of life should be kept to a minimum.
6. The Argentines should not benefit to any greater extent than we can help...[37]

But the state-owned British oil company, BNOC, and the Department of Energy were concerned that Britain could be ceding too much and took a more cautious approach. During a meeting at the FCO, a BNOC executive emphasised: 'The Government should be careful not to give away what could be of great worth i.e. the prospects for oil finds in the Falklands Continental Shelf.'[38] The chairman of the company, Philip Shelbourne, added: 'Above all BNOC did not want to wake up one day to find that someone else had picked up concessions in Falkland Islands waters without their having been given a chance to compete.'[39]

Meanwhile, the Department of Energy questioned whether Britain should include the Falkland Islands continental shelf in the leaseback deal at all, an official noting, 'Such a surrender of sovereignty must surely make more difficult...an oil regime which secures HMG control over those rights (e.g. to petroleum exploration and production activities).'[40] The Department recommended that, if the continental shelf were included in the leaseback, then Britain should have the 'exclusive' right to explore for oil within it and that there should be no joint administration with Argentina.[41] Another Department of Energy official, in a long internal memo, outlined why it would be in the interests of

Britain's oil companies not to rush into a deal. North Sea oil would be providing the Exchequer with revenues and oil for at least two decades, while 'the most attractive areas' around the Falklands were in waters that could not be developed using existing technology, he wrote.[42] Although large oil companies believed that an agreement with Argentina was necessary to make oil exploration politically and legally viable, the Falklands area was not their top priority; they could afford to wait until the best deal was negotiated and more advanced technology became available. So while British oil companies had been a lobbying force for a sovereignty deal with Argentina in the 1970s, they had now become, if anything, a gentle brake on the process.

Most large oil companies were more interested in bidding for the licences to explore off Argentina's coast that were put up for auction by the Argentine state oil company in 1981. In another example of the British determination to preserve its rights to the oil, the Foreign Office lodged a formal protest because the exploration blocks crossed over the putative median line between Argentina and the Falklands. The British government also placed an advert in the *International Herald Tribune* and oil journals, in April 1981, warning oil corporations that the tender area went over the median line. Emphasising the need for action, a Foreign Office official wrote: 'We must maintain that any oil in the Falkland Islands continental shelf is British, without specifying whether we mean HMG or Falkland Islands have the right to exploit it. The important point is that it is ours not Argentine.'[43]

It is clear, then, that the British government had shown an interest in exploiting the oil around the Falklands for many years and, although oil was never the most important consideration, at every stage of the negotiation Britain's access to the potential oil deposits was considered by ministers and officials. While the Foreign Office believed oil exploration would be impossible without an agreement with Argentina, it nevertheless aimed to achieve an oil regime that would most benefit British companies, the British exchequer and the Islanders. The Department of Energy was even more insistent that British rights to oil deposits should be preserved and for that reason was cautious about the leaseback proposal, and in particular, the ceding of sovereignty of the Falkland Islands continental shelf to Argentina. Just three months after the Falklands war, when British sovereignty had been conclusively asserted through military means, the new energy secretary, Nigel Lawson, sought to encourage oil and gas companies to start exploring in waters around the Falklands.[44]

Geopolitical Strategic Interests

In the decades after the Second World War, Britain passed from being a leading world power to become a 'great power of second rank', with a drastically diminished global role.[45] Most of Britain's colonies won independence, leaving Britain with a small rump of isolated imperial possessions, such as Hong Kong, Gibraltar and the Falklands, while the demise of the Overseas Sterling Area (1968) and the collapse of the Bretton Woods agreement (1971) ended Britain's co-sponsorship of the international currency system. As Britain's imperial role diminished, defence spending was cut and its naval forces were reduced.

The Falkland Islands may have once had a strategic military value to Britain when it was a global power, but after 1945 Britain accepted that the South Atlantic was a US sphere of influence.[46] British military leaders argued that there were no separate British defence interests in the South Atlantic, and that UK forces should be concentrated in the NATO area of responsibility.

The South Atlantic had been a low priority for the United States and Western powers in the years following the Second World War, but during the 1970s, it became an increasingly important trade route. The closure of the Suez Canal (1967–1975) forced ships to sail round the southern tip of Africa and almost all oil shipments to the US and Europe went through the South Atlantic in this period.[47] Even after 1975, it remained a busy trade route as super-tankers were too large to fit through the Canal. The United States and NATO also became increasingly concerned about the growing Soviet presence in the South Atlantic as the number of Soviet naval and fishing vessels rose and the USSR strengthened economic ties with Argentina, Brazil and other Southern Cone countries.[48]

Meanwhile, the freedom of manoeuvre of the USA and the UK in the South Atlantic had been curtailed by the ending, in 1975, of the Anglo-South African Simonstown agreement, which had given British vessels the right to dock at ports along the coast of South Africa. Furthermore, as a result of the Portuguese revolution and the subsequent independence of Portugal's African colonies, Western powers had lost access to other bases and ports in southern Africa.[49] The instability in southern Africa caused by the liberation wars in Angola, Mozambique, Namibia and Rhodesia and the anti-apartheid struggle in South Africa added to the strategic concerns of the United States and Britain.

However, the US response to the perceived Soviet threat in the South Atlantic was to try to build an anti-communist alliance with the dictatorships of Argentina, Brazil and Chile. The Reagan administration considered creating a South Atlantic Treaty Organization (SATO), which would include the military regimes of Argentina and Brazil, as well as South Africa. While the United States' close ties with Argentina caused friction with Britain after the invasion of the Falkland Islands in 1982, before the war Britain accepted that building an anti-Soviet alliance in the South Atlantic was a necessity.

In the years before the outbreak of hostilities, neither FCO, nor cabinet nor MOD papers suggest that Britain saw the Falklands as a strategic military asset. On one occasion in 1976, Hugh Carless, head of the FCO's Latin America Department, suggested that Britain and Argentina could have a joint military base on the Falklands to combat the Soviet threat, but the Ministry of Defence (MOD) and the FCO's defence department objected on the grounds that the South Atlantic was outside the NATO area and establishing a base would stretch Britain's defences. During a meeting to discuss the naval base proposal, an MOD official said that Britain 'had no basic defence interest in the area', while an official from the FCO's defence department said: 'There would be serious objections in principle to any extension of the British defence effort in the South Atlantic—any strategic role would be hard to justify and it could lead to trouble with the US'.[50] South American countries should see off the Soviet threat in the area, an FCO Defence Department paper argued.[51]

During the Thatcher years some critics of the leaseback policy suggested that sovereignty should not be ceded because the Islands had strategic value, prompting a Foreign Office official to propose the commissioning of a study, noting: 'We have tended to take the view that the Islands have little strategic significance nowadays…but…no one has ever looked at the problem with an expert eye.'[52] However, the idea was rejected by the FCO on the grounds that 'the conventional wisdom' that the Islands had no strategic value was correct. 'Demonstrably the Royal Navy do not value the Islands very highly or they would be using facilities there at present,' wrote an official.[53] The evidence, therefore, suggests that neither the British government nor the defence establishment considered the Falklands to be a potential strategic military asset and such considerations played no role in the breakdown of sovereignty talks with Argentina prior to the 1982 invasion.

During the war, however, Mrs. Thatcher did emphasise the military strategic importance of the Islands during a phone call with President Ronald Reagan, as part of her effort to persuade the US to support the British war effort.

> The prime minister said…the Falkland Islands were of strategic importance. If the Panama Canal was closed, it would be important that Port Stanley and South Georgia should be in the hands of a friendly power. This had been very significant in the last two World Wars. Argentina was getting very close to the Soviet Union…The last thing anyone would want is the Russians in both Cuba and the Falkland Islands. South Georgia, as an ice-free port, was important to the future of Antarctica.[54]

But while the United States agreed that they would not want the Falkland Islands to fall into the hands of the Soviets, they continued to believe that the best way of combating the perceived Communist threat in the South Atlantic was through an alliance with the Argentine junta and the other South American dictatorships.[55]

Antarctica

One geopolitical factor considered by British officials, however, was Britain's access to Antarctica. Britain's objectives in Antarctica were spelt out to cabinet ministers in a confidential memorandum from the foreign secretary and energy secretary in 1982:

1. Securing the largest possible share of any benefits from the development of hydrocarbons and minerals in the area.
2. Maintaining the Antarctic Treaty system as a guarantee for the continued peace of the area.[56]

The impact of Britain's Antarctic interests on relations with Argentina was complex because while Britain, Argentina and Chile had competing claims on Antarctic territory, they also had a common interest against most other countries of the world, which did not recognise any national territorial claims. Only four other nations claimed territory in Antarctica: Australia, New Zealand, Norway and France. All territorial claims to Antarctica had been legally frozen by the Antarctic Treaty that came into force in 1961, but during the 1970s and early 1980s, as Antarctic Treaty members prepared to discuss their attitude to the resources in the area, Britain sought to make an alliance with Argentina on the basis that they both agreed that nation states should be able to claim parts of Antarctica. As Sir Kenneth Berrill of the Cabinet Office made clear:

> On Antarctica there is a possibility—no one can put it any higher at the moment—that significant volumes of oil will be found…But all the pressures internationally are to stop the United Kingdom from getting full benefits from such discoveries. If we are to resist such pressures, we need to adopt a single-minded and robust stance in international negotiations over the years ahead and such a policy would be more likely to succeed if we worked closely with Argentina (and Chile) whose interests are similar to our own.[57]

During the Antarctic Treaty talks of 1979, the British and Argentine delegations informally consulted each other and during Anglo-Argentine talks on the Falklands in 1980, Nicholas Ridley highlighted the Antarctic as an area where the two countries had joint interests and could cooperate.[58] As late as 26 March 1982, in the midst of the South Georgia crisis, Argentine and British officials met in Buenos Aires to discuss their approach to an upcoming meeting of Treaty signatories to discuss mineral rights in Antarctica.[59]

Britain was determined to preserve its rights to oil and mineral resources in Antarctica and, once again, the Department of Energy was the strongest lobbying force. When an MP suggested to Lord Carrington that the Falklands dispute could be resolved if Britain ceded some of British Antarctic Territory to Argentina in exchange for Argentina dropping its claim to the Falklands, the FCO rejected the suggestion as against the 'national interest'. It noted the 'promising' geological prospects, adding;

> The FCO has already come under strong pressure from the Department of Energy and the [Cabinet Office's] Central Policy Review Staff…Both argue that the UK should hold out for full rights over all minerals in the British Antarctic Territory…Both would resist even more strongly a proposal to give up sovereignty over the British Antarctic Territory.[60]

During the Anglo-Argentine negotiations over the Falklands in 1979– 1981, neither the Department of Energy nor the Foreign Office raised concerns that ceding sovereignty over the Falklands could have a bearing on Britain's claim to Antarctica because they were confident that, legally, these were separate issues, and that the Antarctic Treaty protected (and froze) all nation states' territorial claims in Antarctica. Ministers also ignored those—such as Lord Buxton, a peer and Anglia TV executive who took close interest in Falklands issues—who argued that the Islands and their dependencies could be used as 'forward bases' for oil exploration in Antarctica.[61]

However, after the Argentine invasion on 2 April 1982, ministers did express fears that if Britain gave up the Falkland Islands, that might weaken its claim to Antarctica. A memorandum by Foreign Secretary Lord Carrington and energy secretary Nigel Lawson, dated 16 April 1982, published here for the first time, outlined the potential oil and mineral resources in the Falklands and in Antarctica, and warned:

> Surrender of our sovereignty in the Falklands and their dependencies might be interpreted as indicating lack of resolution to press our claim to any Antarctic hydrocarbons.[62]

It added:

> If, in the longer term, Argentina concluded that it had been worsted in their adventure in the Falkland Islands and Dependencies, our long term position in the British Antarctic Territory would probably be politically strengthened. The converse, however, is also likely to be true.[63]

An annex to another memorandum by the foreign secretary and energy secretary written on 4 June, ten days before Britain's final victory, once again noted: 'Any transfer of sovereignty of the Falkland Islands (or the Dependencies) would be seen by the Argentines as strengthening their claim to parts of the British Antarctic Territory.'[64]

Meanwhile, during the hostilities, Mrs. Thatcher met Lord Shackleton and Lord Buxton to discuss the economic future of the Islands. Lord Buxton repeated his view that the Islands were a gateway to Antarctica and Lord Shackleton said that Antarctic oil prospects were Argentina's real interest in the area. At their suggestion, the prime minister met members of the British Antarctic Survey, to discuss the future development of the Falkland Islands and the British Antarctic Territory, including the prospects for oil.[65]

Before the war, Britain's interests in Antarctica may not have had a strong bearing on its negotiations with Argentina over the Falklands, because they believed they could reach a consensual agreement and that

Britain's wider interests were protected by the Antarctic Treaty. But once the two countries came into conflict, ministers clearly saw a link between Britain's claim to the Falklands and its rights in Antarctica, and feared that, despite the protection that the Antarctic Treaty afforded, ceding sovereignty over the Falklands could jeopardise British access to valuable mineral and hydrocarbon resources in Antarctica.

This examination of Britain's economic and strategic interest in the Falklands indicates that the British government did not view the Islands as a military asset but was interested in the oil potential of the Islands. It also shows that Britain wanted to protect its claim to British Antarctic Territory but, until the invasion of the Falklands, had sought to do this through an alliance with Argentina. Strategic and economic factors did, therefore, play a part in Britain's calculations before the Falklands war and should not be overlooked when examining British pre-war policy towards Argentina.

Divisions Within the Elite

This study has proposed that social class played a part in shaping the views of FCO officials and, in particular, led them to sympathize with the outlook of the business community. While it is true that the FCO agreed with British companies that the Falklands dispute was hindering trade with the Latin America, the main opposition to this perspective did not come from the labour movement, as the Labour Left did not have a coherent position on the Falklands. The key divisions over the Falklands during the Thatcher years were within the elite. Some of the most vocal opposition to the idea of giving up the Falklands came from Tory MPs and Establishment figures with a nostalgia for empire. These individuals often came from the upper class, from military families or from families with a background in the colonial service. While British military leaders might have accepted that the South Atlantic was a US sphere of influence, these empire-nostalgics continued to believe that Britain was a world power in its own right and might need strategic outposts. In addition, during the Thatcher years, senior naval officers opposed to proposed cuts to the surface fleet became a sectional interest that bolstered the Falklands cause. The divisions within the elite were complex, overlapping and shifting. British oil companies, for example, which in the 1970s had been eager for a deal with Argentina in order to explore the hydrocarbon deposits around the Falklands, during the

Thatcher years took a more cautious, long-term perspective. Meanwhile, the UK-based Falkland Islands Committee, which represented business interests around the Islands, switched from opposing leaseback to privately supporting it during the Thatcher years, as the best way of protecting their economic interests. The splits in the elite remained even after the invasion—a *Financial Times* editorial in April 1982, for example, questioned the wisdom of dispatching a task force. Nevertheless, British victory in the Falklands served to unite most of the elite, including the Conservative party, military leaders and diplomats, behind a re-assertion of British global and military power. Margaret Thatcher, for example, wrote afterwards:

> The significance of the Falklands war was enormous, both for Britain's self-confidence and for our standing in the world. Since the Suez fiasco in 1956, British foreign policy had been one long retreat. The tacit assumption made by British and foreign governments alone was that our world role was doomed to steadily diminish... Victory in the Falklands changed that.[66]

In addition, Thatcher's Falklands victory consolidated in power a free-market, anti-union government which benefited British corporate interests. For many companies, this consolidation of neoliberalism in Britain came to outweigh the potential damage to British markets in Latin America, which, after all, made up only 2% of total British trade in 1980.[67]

The Blame Game: Lobby Groups, Politicians and State Officials

But if this book has served to provide a fuller picture of Britain's strategic interests in the Falklands, it should be emphasised that domestic factors were uppermost in politicians' minds in the years preceding the Falklands war. Cabinet minutes, FCO papers, the prime minister's correspondence, as well as politicians' memoirs, all suggest that parliamentary opposition to 'selling out' the Islanders was the main reason that Margaret Thatcher's government did not transfer the sovereignty of the Falklands to Argentina.

There are two moments worthy of closer examination. Firstly, the parliamentary debate on 2 December 1980 when Nicholas Ridley announced the leaseback plan and was attacked by MPs from all sides of the House. This is widely seen as the point leaseback was 'killed'—in

Thatcher's words—because after the Commons debate the Islanders hardened their opposition to leaseback and demanded a freeze on sovereignty talks. Leaseback was never again proposed by ministers in parliament. A second key moment, highlighted in the Franks Report, was the decision by Lord Carrington in mid-1981 not to undertake a public relations campaign in order to revive and promote the leaseback plan because of 'domestic constraints'.[68] By looking more closely at the events leading up to these two key moments, we can assess the role of pro-Falkland lobby groups, officials and politicians, and examine why the leaseback plan failed and why the government was left with a policy of neither negotiating a settlement nor defending the islands adequately.

Some accounts characterise the leaseback idea as a Foreign Office plot to 'sell out' the Islands, or as a scheme backed only by FCO minister of state, Nicholas Ridley.[69] It is, therefore, important to examine Margaret Thatcher's attitude to the scheme. When Lord Carrington first proposed leaseback in late 1979, Thatcher was vigorously opposed, writing 'NO!' on Carrington's memo and: 'I could not possibly agree to the line the foreign secretary is proposing. Nor would it ever get through the H. of C.—let alone the parliamentary party,' comments which her official biographer, Charles Moore, has highlighted.[70] However, in July 1980, she agreed that Ridley should explore leaseback with the Argentines and at a meeting of the Defence and Oversea Policy Committee in November 1980, she accepted that leaseback 'was likely to be the only way out of the present impasse'.[71] She argued that if it were not for 'the power of Argentina to disrupt life in the Falklands' and 'the difficulty and expense…of maintaining an effective defence and providing for the economic development of the Islands', the 'government would not be justified in a surrender of sovereignty'. She added, however, that:

> It seemed likely that, on balance, given the bleakness of their present situation, the majority of the Islanders would be ready to support negotiations with Argentina on the lines proposed, recognising that, while the Government would not go back on its commitment to defend them, it was not able to offer alternative ways of improving their position.[72]

Moore, her biographer, emphasises her doubts about leaseback at this November meeting, not her acquiescence, and quotes her as saying 'We could bomb Buenos Aires if nothing else', a comment that was not included in the official record. Thatcher's own memoirs also emphasise her dislike of the leaseback plan.⁷³ But it is clear from the official record that, while she had misgivings, she saw no other alternative. Nor did any of the other ministers present at the meeting. But when Ridley proposed the plan to the House of Commons three weeks later, no other minister came to his defence.

During the debate, nine Conservative and six Labour MPs spoke against Ridley, led by a hostile intervention from Labour's foreign affairs spokesman Peter Shore, who criticised the leaseback plan, even though the previous Labour government had approved the idea in principle. Almost half the MPs who spoke were supporters of the Falkland Islands Committee or had previously taken a strong interest in the Falklands, which suggests that the Falklands 'lobby' was influential. By 1979, it had written 2000 letters, distributed 6000 pamphlets and leaflets and issued several hundred press releases.⁷⁴ The lobby's success, however, also stemmed from the fact that no Conservative MP was willing to support Ridley. Mrs. Thatcher had approved the leaseback policy but was unwilling to send whips to cajole Tory backbenchers into supporting it. It is noteworthy too that prominent opponents of the Falklands war, such as Tam Dalyell and Tony Benn, who later opposed the sending of a task force on the grounds that there should be a negotiated settlement, did not speak up either.

Islanders' Views of Leaseback

After the Commons debate, the Islanders came out clearly in favour of a freeze on sovereignty talks. There are conflicting accounts of the Islanders' stance before the Ridley debate, some asserting that the population were always steadfastly opposed to leaseback.⁷⁵ The correspondence in the newly-opened FCO files suggest a more mixed response: officials in the British embassy in Buenos Aires reported that four Island councillors would be ready to see leaseback explored, four were undecided and two against.⁷⁶ It also noted:

> Councillors' general assessment was that of those in Port Stanley who had already declared their views the majority was strongly opposed to the leaseback concept... although commercial sectors and those in outlying settlements took more positive view of need for early negotiated solution. There was however real division of opinion and everyone needed more time for thought.⁷⁷

Rex Hunt, the governor, believed it was too early to judge Islander reaction, but concluded: 'Many are considering seriously all possibilities for the Islands' future, including a leaseback arrangement.'[78] There was clearly a vocal group against leaseback, which organised 'Keep the Islands British' protests, and was backed by the local Falkland Islands Committee, but even within this committee, according to Governor Hunt, two were in favour of leaseback and eight against.[79] So while there was certainly no enthusiasm for the leaseback solution, and, as Freedman notes, many were frustrated by the lack of detail provided by Ridley, the evidence suggest that many of the Islanders had not made up their minds until the MPs' debate in London hardened their views.[80]

Some authors suggest that the Foreign Office pushed leaseback because they put commercial interests above the interests of the 1800 Islanders and, in doing so, turned a blind eye to the abuses of the Argentine regime. There is some truth in this argument; as this study has shown, the FCO had sympathy for British businesses' desire to resolve the dispute and some British diplomats did mix with military officers and downplay the junta's human rights violations. A fairer assessment, however, should take into account that other government departments such as Trade and Defence pushed even harder for trade with Argentina, and that, in every Foreign Office policy paper, at least two options were proposed: either Britain should make an agreement with Argentina *or* break off talks and increase the defences of the Islands. The problem was that the Thatcher government allowed the leaseback plan to collapse, but took no precautionary military measures; on the contrary, it announced the withdrawal of the only British naval vessel in the South Atlantic, despite protests from the foreign secretary, over 100 MPs, senior Royal Navy officers and Islanders.

The pro-Islanders' lobby had succeeded in persuading the government to abandon leaseback, partly because the prime minister was well disposed to their cause, illustrating that one important factor for social movement success is having sympathisers in government. But, more importantly, the government—erroneously—judged that the risks of provoking a political row were greater than those of inaction. The government was prepared to make what it regarded as a low-cost concession by dropping the leaseback idea. But it was unbending against appeals to save *HMS Endurance* and to amend the Nationality Act to allow all Islanders residence in Britain because reducing public spending and

Table 11.2 The Falkland Islanders and British citizenship

The British Nationality Act (1981) defined an Islander as a British Dependent Territories citizen, which meant they did not have the automatic right to enter or live in the UK. Only Islanders with British parents or grandparents were granted British citizenship with rights to abode in the UK
The British Nationality Act (1983), passed after the Falklands War, gave all Islanders British citizenship

controlling immigration were two key policy planks for the Thatcher government.[81] Ministers feared that giving all Islanders British citizenship would set a precedent for other British overseas territories; though they did make an exception for Gibraltar—indicating, once again, that the Falklands were not a high priority (Table 11.2).

After the Ridley debate, the government was left with a policy of negotiating with an increasingly impatient Argentina—after 16 years of talks—with nothing substantial to offer, while the Islands remained vulnerable to attack. Fearing that this policy was unsustainable, the Foreign Office held a high-level meeting in June 1981, which was chaired by Nicholas Ridley. It was attended by Governor Rex Hunt; Ambassador Anthony Williams and high-ranking FCO officials, including the permanent under-secretary, Michael Palliser. The ambassador said: 'If we allowed the leaseback initiative to die then we would be left with no way out of our dilemma,' while Assistant Under Secretary John Ure, warned: 'Time is running out.'[82] Ure argued that 'the most important single factor in influencing the Islanders views was the public debate in the UK.'[83] Ridley was insistent that the Islanders should not be seen to be put under pressure, but agreed that a public relations campaign explaining leaseback should be launched.

Ridley wrote to Carrington recommending that a PR campaign should be discussed at a meeting of the cabinet's Defence and Oversea Policy (DOP) Committee.[84] Officials drafted a paper for the committee, which said it was 'increasingly urgent' to find a solution, adding: 'Simply to play for time…is not a viable option.'[85] Three possibilities were outlined:

- to talk to Argentina without Islander concurrence.
- to launch a PR campaign explaining leaseback;
- or to break off negotiations and take contingency defence measures.[86]

But Lord Carrington, after meeting with Ridley and officials, rejected the idea of a PR campaign because of the 'domestic political risk'.[87] The draft DOP paper was not used and neither the DOP Committee—nor the full cabinet—discussed the Falklands again until the crisis began to unfold in March 1982. While officials had thought it urgent that ministers meet to discuss the Falklands, Carrington settled instead for sending a letter to ministerial colleagues, recommending no new initiative except asking Argentina to put forward constructive proposals. Officials had warned that action was urgent and it was clearly a political decision not to act on their advice, a key moment that was highlighted in the Franks report.[88]

The PR drive in favour of leaseback was rejected even though, as newly-opened FCO documents now confirm, many of the government's most vocal critics expressed support for leaseback in private. By October 1981, a majority of the Falkland Islands Committee backed leaseback, Air Commodore Brian Frow, the Committee's secretary, told FCO minister Richard Luce in a meeting.[89] The UK-based Committee was funded by the Falklands Islands Company and other corporations with interests (or potential interests) in the Falklands. Most of its executives had come to the conclusion that the best prospect for business was leaseback. Other prominent supporters of the Islanders' cause, such as Lord Buxton—who had written several letters to the prime minister, urging her to keep *HMS Endurance*—told ministers that he believed leaseback was the only viable solution, and offered to visit the Islands, with Lord Shackleton, and other non-political figures, to raise awareness of the risks of not reaching a settlement.[90] It is possible, therefore, that if the government had promoted leaseback it might have won support. The government believed that domestic opinion constrained their actions, but they made no attempt to influence that opinion.

An alternative—perhaps 'ethical'—policy would have been to refuse to talk to Argentina while the military remained in power, but ministers decided it would be too costly to defend the Islands if the junta responded aggressively. Another option would have been to follow the approach of Callaghan, who had also reluctantly approved leaseback, but backed up negotiations with sporadic naval deployments; but neither Mrs. Thatcher nor Lord Carrington took the same close interest in defence deployments as Callaghan and David Owen. Instead the Conservative government abandoned any serious attempt to reach a negotiated settlement, while failing to take any counter-balancing military contingency measures. On the contrary, they continued to sell arms to the junta and sent a series of signals that they were unlikely to defend the Islands.

Conclusion

This chapter has shown that strategic factors were taken into consideration in the years preceding the Falklands war. Although oil companies had been a lobbying force for a deal with Argentina in the 1970s, during Thatcher's period of office, the Department of Energy grew increasingly concerned that a leaseback deal would not offer sufficient protection for British energy interests, and so became a voice of caution. It was also a key British objective to protect its mineral interests in Antarctica, but in the years preceding the Falklands war, it was believed this was best done through an alliance with Argentina. However, once hostilities began, politicians clearly saw a link between their claims to the Falkland Islands and Antarctica, fearing that if they lost sovereignty over the Falkland Islands, their legal claim to Antarctica would be weakened.

The divisions over the Falklands during the Thatcher years reflected splits within the elite. While companies with interests in Latin America favoured a negotiated settlement with Argentina, this business lobby was relatively weak because Latin America accounted for only 2% of British trade. Many Establishment figures—Conservative politicians, peers, former military leaders and some business leaders—took a broader view of British global interests, believing it vital that Britain retained its status as a global power, which implied not only maintaining the capacity to defend its subjects all over the world, but also retaining a network of military outposts across the globe.

While the Foreign Office did articulate the views of British businesses that wanted a rapprochement with Argentina, and did, as a result, downplay the horrors of the junta's human rights abuses, the Departments of Trade and Employment, and Ministry of Defence also lobbied hard for trade with Argentina. The suggestion that the FCO pursued a policy of appeasement towards Argentina without the knowledge or agreement of Conservative ministers is unsustainable. The official record shows that the prime minister and her ministerial colleagues approved leaseback. Ministers also approved arms sales to Argentina, even when these violated their own guidelines. The FCO presented politicians with clear alternatives: they should either try to reach a settlement or strengthen the Islands' defences, but the Thatcher government failed to do either. Politicians were given the opportunity to make their own decisions; they had political agency. It was not the case that the bureaucratic machine was quietly trying to undermine ministers; on the contrary, the politicians were presented with the facts, but failed to act on them.

The problem was that although intelligence reports had warned for years that an Argentine invasion was a possibility, no one believed them. The Falkland Islands were therefore a low priority. Politicians did not think it was worth risking a political row pushing an unpopular deal with Argentina through parliament. The Falklands lobby were successful in preventing a negotiated settlement with Argentina because it had broad support in the House of Commons, as well as among Establishment figures, such as peers and former military leaders. Also important to the lobby's success was the fact it had sympathisers within government, including Thatcher, who was not prepared to promote a deal she had little enthusiasm for. The crucial factor, however, was the government's erroneous assumption that taking no action was a costless decision because they underestimated the risk of an invasion. The Falklands lobby, despite having a broad coalition of support, was not strong enough to persuade the government to increase spending on the defence of the Islands or amend the British nationality bill, because fiscal tightening and controlling immigration were key elements of the Conservatives' overall political and economic strategy. The result was that no deal with Argentina was reached, but the defences of the Islands were not strengthened and they remained vulnerable to attack.

In the euphoria surrounding Thatcher's victory in the Falklands, the policy blunders that preceded the hostilities may have been forgotten, but it is nevertheless hard not to conclude that the Falklands conflict, in which 907 people died, was an avoidable war.

Notes

1. The Lord Franks, *Falkland Islands Review* (London: HMO: 1983).
2. See Introduction, note 90.
3. Margaret Thatcher, *The Downing Street Years* (London: Harper Collins, 1993), p. 181; Hugh Bicheno, *Razor's Edge: The Unofficial History of the Falklands War* (London: Weidenfeld & Nicholson, 2006). See also Duncan Anderson, *The Falklands War 1982* (Oxford: Osprey, 2002).
4. Richard Luce, *Ringing the Changes, A Memoir* (Norwich: Michael Russell, 2007), p. 147.
5. DOP Committee, Falkland Islands, Memorandum by the Foreign & Commonwealth Secretary (FCS), 12 October 1979, The National Archives (TNA): CAB 148/183.
6. DOP Committee, minutes, Wednesday 2 July, TNA: CAB 148/189. See also DOP Committee, minutes, Tuesday 29 January 1980, TNA: CAB 148/189.
7. Hugh Carless to FCO, 4 July 1979, TNA: FCO7/3574.

8. Thomas Malcomson to Colin Bright, Gordon Duggan and Robin Fearn, FCO, 18 March 1980, TNA: FCO7/3726.
9. Note by Bright on Malcomson to Bright, Duggan and Fearn, 18 March 1980, TNA: FCO7/3726.
10. Ibid.
11. FCO official to Smith and Bright, 'BOTB: 16 March: Falkland Islands' [16 March 1982, date deduced from content], TNA: FCO7/4907.
12. *Hansard*, HL Deb., 3 July 1979, Vol. 401, cc222–224; HL Deb., 16 December 1981, Vol. 426, cc208–237; HL Deb., 28 July 1981, Vol. 423, cc694–732; and HL Deb., 21 April 1982, Vol. 429, cc551–557.
13. File note by D.J. Harding, FCO, 3 October 1979, TNA: EG 14/91; Record of FCO meeting with BP, 9 February 1981, TNA: FCO7/3984; and J.B. Ure to PS/Mr. Ridley, 10 April 1981, TNA: FCO7/3984.
14. DOP Committee, Falkland Islands, Memorandum, by FCS, 12 October 1979, Annex 7: Maritime Area: Economic Potential, TNA: CAB 148/183.
15. T.L. Richardson, FCO, to R. Birchmore, 13 March 1979, TNA: POWE 63/1596.
16. FCO to Buenos Aires, 17 October 1979, TNA: EG 14/92; draft note from M.E. Reidy to PS/Minister of State, 28 September 1978, TNA: POWE 63/1596; and Reidy to PS/Minister of State, 'BNOC: Falkland Islands', 29 September 1978, TNA: POWE 63/1596.
17. Record of Meeting with BNOC on 30 March 1981, FCO, TNA: FCO7/3984.
18. David Howell to Margaret Thatcher, 22 September 1979, TNA: PREM 19/612.
19. Ibid.
20. Geoffrey Howe to Thatcher, 24 September 1979, TNA: PREM 19/656; Kenneth Berrill to Howell, 27 September 1979, TNA: PREM 19/612.
21. Notes by Thatcher on Carrington to Thatcher, 20 September 1979. TNA: PREM 19/656.
22. Notes by Thatcher on Carrington to Thatcher, 20 September 1979, TNA: PREM 19/656.
23. DOP Committee, Falkland Islands, Memorandum, by FCS, 12 October 1979, TNA: CAB 148/183.
24. Robert Armstrong to Thatcher, 25 January 1980, TNA: PREM 19/656.
25. Birchmore to Mr. D'Ancona and PS/Secretary of State, 30 January 1980, TNA: EG 14/92.
26. Ibid.
27. Howell to Carrington, 5 February 1980, TNA: PREM 19/612.
28. P.D. Ivory to D.J. Harding, 10 April 1980, TNA: EG 14/92.
29. Anglo/Argentine Ministerial Talks on the Falkland Islands: New York, 28–29 April 1980, FCO record, TNA: PREM 19/612.

30. Note by Ridley on K.J. Chamberlain to Bright, 16 September 1980, TNA: EG 14/93; note by Ridley Duggan to PS/Mr. Ridley, 29 October 1980, TNA: EG 14/93.
31. Duggan to PS/Mr. Ridley, 29 October 1980, TNA: EG 14/93.
32. DOP Committee, Most Confidential Record, OD (80) 23rd Meeting, 7 November 1980, TNA: CAB 148/196.
33. Ibid.
34. Ibid.
35. Anglo-Argentine Ministerial Talks on the Falkland Islands, 23/24 February 1981, FCO record, TNA: PREM 19/612.
36. Bright to Rex Hunt, 7 May 1980, TNA: EG14/92.
37. Fearn to P. Harding, 2 June 1981, TNA: FCO7/3984.
38. Record of Meeting with BNOC on 30 March 1981, TNA: FCO7/3984.
39. Ibid.
40. H.L.M. Ross to Mary Dickson, 16 June 1981, TNA: EG 14/93. Emphasis in the original.
41. Dickson to Fearn, 22 July 1981, TNA: FCO7/3985.
42. P. Boys to Mr. Priddle [Date of covering letter: 2 July 1981], TNA: EG 14/93.
43. R.H. Smith to A.J. Williams, 4 December 1981, TNA: FCO7/3985.
44. P.W. Heap to Fearn, 22 September 1982, TNA: FCO7/4709; Nigel Lawson to Francis Pym, 18 October 1982.
45. David Sanders, *Losing an Empire, Finding a Role: British Foreign Policy Since 1945* (London: Macmillan, 1990), p. 292.
46. David Thomas 'The United States factor in British relations with Latin America' in Victor Bulmer Thomas (ed.), *Britain and Latin America* (Cambridge: Cambridge University Press, 1989).
47. For more on the strategic value of the South Atlantic see chapters by José Miguel Insulza and Andrew Hurrell in Atilio Borón and Julio Faúndez (eds.), *Malvinas Hoy: Herencia de un Conflicto* (Buenos Aires: Puntosur Editores, 1989).
48. Andrew Hurrell, 'La Importancia Estratégica del Atlántico Sur y Las Malvinas/Falklands' in Borón and Faúndez, p. 255.
49. Ibid., p. 257.
50. Record of a Meeting held in the FCO on 8 June 1976, TNA: FCO7/3204.
51. Draft FCO briefing note 'Possible Argentine interest in acquiring naval facilities in the Falkland Islands' attached to E. Clay to Miss Binns, No date [Date deduced from content: *circa* 20 June 1976], TNA: FCO7/3204. See also P.M. Gowen, R.N., MOD, to DS11, MOD, 29 June 1976, TNA: FCO7/3204; W.J.A. Wilberforce to Carless, 18 June 1976, TNA: FCO7/3204.
52. Bright to Smith and Fearn, 11 December 1980, TNA: FCO7/3801.
53. Note by R.H. Smith, 11 December 1980 on Bright to Smith and Fearn, 11 December 1980, TNA: FCO7/3801.

54. Record of Telephone Conversation Between President Reagan and the Prime Minister on Thursday 13 May 1982, TNA: FCO7/4532.
55. Nicholas Henderson to FCO, 27 April 1982, TNA: FCO7/4534.
56. DOP Committee, 'British Policy in the Antarctic: Minerals', Memorandum, by FCS and Energy Secretary, 24 February 1982, TNA: FCO7/5078. These objectives were also expressed in: DOP Committee, 'British Policy in the Antarctic', Memorandum, by FCS, 1 December 1980, TNA: CAB 148/191.
57. Berrill to Howell, 27 September 1979, TNA: PREM 19/612.
58. Anglo/Argentine Ministerial Talks: New York, 28–29 April 1980, FCO record, TNA: PREM 19/612; UK/Argentine Dispute Over the Falkland Islands: FCO Briefs for Talks 28–30 April, New York, TNA: FCO7/3806.
59. 'Record of Consultations with Argentina', TNA: FCO7/5080, 1982. Consultations with Argentina took place on 25 and 26 March 1982, See also DOP Committee, 'British Policy in the Antarctic: Minerals,' Memorandum by the FCS and Energy Secretary, 24 February 1982, TNA: FCO7/5078.
60. Commentary on Mr. Shersby's Proposals, FCO brief, attached to Fearn to Ure, 26 January 1982, TNA: FCO7/4905.
61. Lord Buxton to Thatcher, 22 September 1981, TNA: FCO7/3974.
62. 'Hydrocarbon, mineral and fisheries potential of the Falkland Islands, their dependencies and Antarctica', DOP Committee Memorandum, Note by the Secretaries, 16 April 1982, TNA: CAB 148/206.
63. Ibid.
64. Cabinet DOP Committee, 'British Policy in the Antarctic: Minerals', Memorandum by the FCS and the Energy Secretary, 4 June 1982, Annex C, TNA: CAB 148/206.'
65. Falkland Islands: Call on the Prime Minister by Lord Shackleton and Lord Buxton, FCO record, 28 May 1982 TNA: CAB 164/1626; note from PS, 10 Downing Street, to John Holmes, 1 June 1982, TNA: CAB 164/1626, 1982; and record of a meeting between Dr. Ady and Dr. Swithinbank of the BAS on Tuesday 1 June 1982 at 10 Downing Street, TNA: CAB 164/1626.
66. Thatcher, *The Downing Street Years*, p. 173.
67. The 2% figure is from Victor Bulmer-Thomas, *British Trade with Latin America in the Nineteenth and Twentieth Centuries* (London: University of London, Institute of Latin American Studies, Occasional Papers No. 19, 1998), Tables 1 and 2.
68. Fearn to Williams, 23 September 1981, TNA: FCO7/3965.
69. Hugh Bicheno's, *Razor's Edge: The Unofficial History of the Falklands War* (London: Weidenfeld & Nicholson, 2006). Richard Luce, *Ringing the Changes, A Memoir* (Norwich: Michael Russell, 2007), p. 137; Charles Moore, *Margaret Thatcher: The Authorised Biography* (London: Allen Lane, 2013), pp. 658–659.

70. Carrington to Thatcher, 20 September 1979, TNA: PREM 19/656; Moore, p. 658.
71. DOP Committee, Most Confidential Record, OD (80) 23rd Meeting, Minute 1, Friday 7 November 1980, TNA: CAB 148/196.
72. Ibid.
73. Moore, p. 659; Thatcher, *The Downing Street Years*, pp. 175–176.
74. Clive Ellerby, 'The Role of the Falkland Lobby, 1968–1990', in Alex Danchev, *International perspectives on the Falklands Conflict: A Matter of Life and Death* (Basingstoke: Macmillan, 1992), p. 96.
75. Moore, p. 659; Thatcher, *The Downing Street Years*, pp. 175–176.
76. British Embassy, Buenos Aires, to FCO, 30 November 1980, TNA: FCO7/3809.
77. British Embassy, Buenos Aires, to FCO, 30 November 1980, TNA: FCO7/3809.
78. Rex Hunt to FCO, 3 December 1980, TNA: FCO7/3809.
79. Hunt to FCO, 11 December 1980, TNA: FCO7/3809.
80. Lawrence Freedman, *The Official History of the Falklands Campaign*, Vol. 1 (London: Routledge, 2005), pp. 128, 130.
81. Letters from several MPs, Lords, Islanders and members of the public against the withdrawal of *HMS Endurance* are contained in: TNA: FCO7/3974; TNA: FCO7/3975; and TNA: FCO7/3976.
82. Record of a Meeting held in 1 Carlton Gardens on 30 June 1981, FCO record, TNA: FCO7/3964.
83. Ibid.
84. Ridley to Carrington, 20 July 1981, TNA: FCO7/3964.
85. Draft, DOP Committee, Falkland Islands, Memorandum by FCS, September 1981 [No exact day cited], TNA: FCO7/3965.
86. Ibid.
87. Fearn to Williams, 23 September 1981, TNA: FCO7/3965. Lord Carrington's decision was made at a meeting with Sir Ian Gilmour and Nicholas Ridley on 7 September 1981, according to the Franks Report. There is no official record of the meeting. *Falkland Islands Review*, 'Lord Carrington's decision' points 98–100.
88. *Falkland Islands Review*, p. 28.
89. Hunt to FCO, 11 December 1980, TNA: FCO7/3809; Record of a Call on the Minister of State by the Falkland Islands Committee on 11 March in the FCO, FCO record, TNA: FCO7/3981; and Summary Record of Meeting held in the FCO on 14 October 1981, FCO record, TNA: FCO7/3981.
90. J.M. Macgregor, to Fearn, 9 September 1981, TNA: FCO7/3965; Record of a call on Mr. Luce by Lord Buxton, 16 February 1982, FCO record, TNA: FCO7/4906.

CHAPTER 12

Conclusion

Labour's policy towards the Pinochet regime was an early example of an 'ethical' foreign policy. Other international causes such as the Spanish civil war and the anti-apartheid struggle had inspired widespread extra-parliamentary solidarity but had not been so successful in changing British government policy. The Chile solidarity movement encompassed a broad range of people and organisations including trade unions, Labour Party branches, church groups, the Communist Party, human rights organisations and students, as well as sympathetic lawyers and journalists. They captured the 'middle ground'. But the internal characteristics of the Chile solidarity movement were not the only reason for its success; Labour ministers were broadly sympathetic to its objectives and the campaign, which included many Labour MPs and Labour-affiliated trade unions, had institutional leverage over key policy-makers. Labour ministers were under continuous pressure from their own supporters to take a moral stance on Chile and ministers believed that the political and moral advantages of imposing an arms embargo and withdrawing export credits outweighed the potential costs to British businesses. However, ministers never went as far as campaigners wanted; they refused to break existing contracts or impose comprehensive sanctions on trade and investment with Chile. Furthermore, it should be borne in mind that Chile was a small market for Britain and ministers might have made a different judgement if a larger percentage of British trade had been at stake.

Nevertheless, the 'ethical' policies of Wilson and Callaghan towards the Pinochet regime were in stark contrast to those of the Conservative Heath and Thatcher governments. It is clear that domestic considerations, and in particular, party political and ideological considerations, were central to policy-making on Chile. Conservative politicians shared with the Foreign Office a pro-business outlook and a Cold War-influenced suspicion of socialists. Both Conservatives and Foreign Office officials criticised the 'chaos' of the Allende regime and thought the Chilean military regime provided a better environment for British business. Some Conservatives on the right of the party, including Margaret Thatcher, enthusiastically praised Pinochet's free-market economic policies and downplayed the regime's gross violations of human rights. Neither the Heath nor the Thatcher government had sympathy for the Chile solidarity movement and the campaigners had no institutional links to the Conservative party; they therefore had virtually no leverage over Conservative governments. The broad support that the Chile campaign achieved forced Conservative politicians and Foreign Office officials to think about the presentation of their policy and the pace with which they introduced measures, but ultimately the campaign did not succeed in changing the substance of Conservative policy. The Thatcher government overturned all Labour's 'ethical' measures towards Chile: it lifted the arms embargo, restored export credits, reinstated a British ambassador, ended the Latin America refugee programme, sent government ministers to visit the regime and sought to mute international criticism of the Pinochet regime in the United Nations.

In contrast, Labour and Conservative policy towards the Argentine junta was broadly similar. Neither government imposed an arms embargo or any other type of trade sanction. Both governments sold military hardware to the regime and sought to promote British investment in Argentina. Indeed, the lengths to which both governments went in order to persuade the Argentine military regime to buy British weapons have been revealed in this study. The Labour governments were not under the same sort of pressure, as they had been in the case of Chile, to take punitive measures against the Argentine military regime. To the British left, Chile appeared to be a clear case of democracy versus fascism. While many had been inspired by the election of the socialist Salvador Allende and horrified by his removal, most British left-wingers were suspicious of Peronism and did not mourn the overthrow of Isabel Perón's increasingly violent government. It took some time to realise that the scale of the atrocities committed by the new Argentine regime far surpassed those committed by any previous government in the country's history. Furthermore, the Soviet Union's failure to condemn the Argentine junta disorientated Communist parties abroad and this meant, in Britain, that the Argentine solidarity campaign lacked the experience and connections of a crucial layer of party and trade-union activists. The Argentina campaign, therefore, remained small with little influence in the Labour party, the Communist party or the trade unions, and membership was largely confined to those with a prior interest in Latin America, human rights groups, religious organisations and exiles. As awareness of the abuses grew, the Labour government, in its last twelve months of office extended the refugee programme to include Argentines and introduced guidelines on arms sales. However, the refugee programme was ended by the incoming Conservative government and the arms-sales guidelines were interpreted loosely and, at times, violated.

This study has considered how far politicians have the freedom to implement policies and to what degree they are constrained by the civil service. It has shown that Foreign Office officials tried to moderate the policies of the Labour government towards Chile, repeatedly warning of the risks to British trade and investment in Latin America. Nevertheless, the Labour government succeeded in introducing a set of radical policies that were starkly different from those of its Conservative predecessor, indicating that politicians did have authority over officials and suggesting that a determined government, under pressure from its own supporters, can implement its programme in the face of bureaucratic opposition. However, British policy towards the other Southern Cone dictatorships in this period—Brazil, Uruguay, Paraguay, as well as Argentina—was very different. No sanctions of any type were imposed, while trade and investment were encouraged. This suggests that politicians may have agency if they come to office determined to introduce a particular set of policies, but if they lack a clear vision and do not come under public scrutiny or extra-parliamentary pressure, the Foreign Office's traditional, pro-business approach is likely to be adopted and trade and investment will be promoted regardless of regime type.

This study has also considered whether the Foreign Office pursued 'leaseback' of the Falkland Islands without the backing of its political masters. It is true that the Foreign Office shared the concern of British businesses that the Falklands dispute was harming Britain's commercial interests, an anxiety also expressed by the Department of Trade and the sales department of the Ministry of Defence. It is also true that some British diplomats socialised with Argentine military officers and downplayed the abuses of the regime. Certainly, most officials believed that, in the face of Argentine impatience, it was becoming increasingly urgent to resolve the dispute. But it is unsustainable to argue that the Foreign Office acted without the knowledge or consent of the politicians. Margaret Thatcher and other ministers discussed and approved the leaseback initiative. The Foreign Office repeatedly presented the politicians with two alternatives: either reach a negotiated settlement or improve the defences of the Islands; under pressure from their own supporters, the Conservative government drew back from a negotiated settlement but crucially, failed to take any contingency military measures. This was not a failure of the bureaucratic machine but of the politicians.

A determined government can drive its policies through an unenthusiastic civil service. A determined government, with a large majority, can also resist the demands of pressure groups, even when these groups have institutional links to the governing party. The Falkland Island Committee, whose supporters included Tory backbenchers, peers and Establishment figures, had sufficient leverage with the Thatcher government to dissuade it from signing a leaseback deal—because the government underestimated the risk of invasion and therefore thought inaction was a low-cost option. However, despite the Falkland Islands Committee's broad-based support and its institutional links to the Conservative party, it could not persuade the administration to abandon its commitment to public spending cuts, and in particular, cuts to the naval surface fleet, because fiscal tightening was central to the government's overall strategy. Although more than a hundred Tory MPs called on the government not to withdraw *HMS Endurance*, the Falklands issue did not risk spilling over into a backbench revolt on any other element of government policy, so ministers were able to withstand the pressure.

This study has suggested that the social class of Foreign Office officials was, in part, responsible for their pro-business, conservative views. In the nineteenth century, British manufacturing elites were socially separate from the 'gentlemanly capitalist' southern-based elite, comprising landowners, professionals and the top echelons of the civil service, church and military, but after the Second World War, Britain's landed, manufacturing and financial elites became socially intertwined. The ethos of 'gentlemanly capitalism' pervaded the Foreign Office. Top officials, in the latter half of the twentieth century, not only shared a similar socio-economic, educational and cultural background with many Conservative politicians, banking executives and business leaders, they were also often part of the same informal social nexus, belonging to the same clubs, attending the same seminars or lunches and reading the same newspapers. Business leaders had numerous informal opportunities to influence Foreign Office policy, because they mixed in the same social milieu, spoke a similar language and shared a similar world outlook. In Chile and Argentina, British diplomats moved within even more restricted social circles, comprising the right-wing British expatriate business community and upper-class Latin Americans and military officers.

The nineteenth-century Foreign Office affected a disdainful aloofness from the world of commerce, while accepting that the security of British trading routes was a central aim of policy. But in twentieth-century post-war Britain, successive governments explicitly urged diplomats to promote the export of manufactured goods and financial services. It became the hegemonic view that promoting British exports was in the national interest, a view that was usually accepted by the Labour Party and trade unionists. There was therefore little tension between the Foreign Office and the Labour government on the question of arms sales to Argentina; indeed, the Labour ministers of trade, industry and employment vigorously promoted the sale of warships on the grounds of safeguarding jobs. In the case of Chile, however, when a class-conscious, militant trade union movement demanded an end to arms sales to the Pinochet regime, there was a clear contrast with the views of the Foreign Office, which can be ascribed to differing class perspectives. There was also an ideological component to the Foreign Office's position on Chile, which was heavily influenced by the Cold War; many British diplomats were critical of Allende's socialist government and suspicious of solidarity campaigners in Britain. This antagonism towards the international and domestic Left was common in British upper-class and corporate circles. Repeated social encounters between officials and business executives and other elite figures consolidated partisan views. The social class and the informal social networks of state officials are not the only factors to consider when analysing decision-making processes and the motivations of policy-makers, but they are issues that should not be overlooked by theorists of foreign policy-making and social movements.

However, a simple binary opposition between working class and upper-class perspectives has not proved sufficient to explain political divisions over the Falklands. Neither the British trade union movement nor the Labour left had a coherent or unified position on the Falklands in the years before the Argentine invasion. The political debates on the Falklands during the 1970s and 1980s are best ascribed to divisions within the elite, between those who prioritised Britain's commercial interests in Latin America, and those who took a broader, sometimes nostalgic, view of Britain's geo-strategic interests, which might include the need for strategic outposts and remnants of empire, or the desire to protect Britain's interests in Antarctica. Corporate perspectives on the Falklands dispute were shifting and over-lapping. British oil companies, for example, were strongly in favour of a rapid negotiated settlement in the 1970s that would allow them to pursue Anglo-Argentine oil exploration around the Falklands. But during the early 1980s their enthusiasm waned as North Sea oil took priority and geological data showed that advanced deep-sea technology would be needed to explore hydrocarbon deposits around the Islands. The Department of Energy therefore advised caution on a leaseback deal, concerned that Britain should not sign away its rights to oil and that any agreement should be on a timescale that suited British companies. Britain's military victory in the Falklands war, however, united all sections of the Establishment behind a reassertion of British military power abroad and the consolidation of a free-market, corporate-friendly government at home. British companies with interests in Latin America today still hope for a resolution of the Falklands dispute, but Latin America accounts for such a small share of British trade that this corporate lobby remains weak.

This study has looked closely at Britain's strategic, economic and commercial interests in the Falkland Islands. It has concluded that, while the defence Establishment did not regard the Islands as having strategic military value, the British government and British companies were interested in oil and mineral deposits in both Falklands waters and Antarctica. Although domestic political considerations were uppermost in politicians' minds and were the primary reason successive governments failed to reach a negotiated settlement with Argentina, the desire to protect Britain's rights to potential oil deposits was discussed by officials and included in government papers at every stage of the deliberations over the Falklands. It was also a clearly articulated aim of British policy to defend its access to Antarctic oil and minerals. However, in

12 CONCLUSION 239

the years before the Falklands war, officials believed that the best way to protect its territorial claim in Antarctica was to form an alliance with other claimant states such as Argentina and Chile. Before the 1982 war, officials believed that Britain's claim to territory in Antarctica was legally protected under the terms of the Antarctic Treaty and therefore would not be jeopardised if Britain ceded sovereignty over the Falkland Islands. However, this study has provided evidence that, following the Argentine invasion of 1982, ministers clearly saw a link between the two issues and expressed concerns that a British defeat in the Falklands could jeopardise its claim to Antarctica. While accepting the traditional British view that domestic factors are crucial to understanding Britain's policy towards the Falklands, this study has shown that a more comprehensive account ought to include Britain's strategic, commercial and economic interests in the South Atlantic and Antarctica.

This book has also presented empirical evidence detailing British arms sales to the Argentine military regime. It has given details of visits to Britain by Argentine military officers, who included some of the highest-ranking officials in the Argentine armed forces. It has also described how the junta's finance minister was fêted by British ministers and business leaders. But it may never be possible to present a complete picture of pre-1982 Anglo-Argentine relations because, as this study has revealed, 322 FCO files relating to Argentina during the period 1976–1982 have been destroyed by the British government, including many of the files relating to military visits. It may be impossible to keep all government documents, but deciding what to preserve should be the subject of wider discussion. Particularly after a war, when recrimination, political point-scoring, propaganda and jingoism cloud debate, it is vital that the records are preserved in the archives for future generations of historians to consult.

Appendix A

See Table A.1.

Table A.1 Career destinations of graduates of Oxford University (1917–2004) % of graduates *Source* Annual Reports of the Appointments Committee, University of Oxford

	1917	1920	1930	1940	1950	1958	1962	1975–1976	1980–1981	1998	2004
Education	67	54	62	39	39	28	30	40	40	41	48
Government (including public services)	33	24	14	29	17	8	7	9	9	8	9
Industry	0	12	20	11	33	50	46	20	25	24	27
Publishing	0	0	0	0	3	3	4	4	2	2	3
Accountancy/Law	0	0	0	0	0	0	5	16	15	7	3
Other	0	10	4	21	8	11	7	11	10	18	10

Appendix B

Table B.1 Educational background of diplomatic service and Foreign and Commonwealth Office (FCO) officials (in order of diplomatic rank for period under study 1973–1982) (Source *Who's Who* and *Who Was Who*)

Name	Education[a]	Position in FCO	Club membership
Michael Palliser	Wellington College Merton College, Oxford	1975–1982: Permanent Under Secretary of FCO and Head of Diplomatic Service 1982: Special Advisor to Prime Minister during Falklands Campaign	Bucks
Reginald Secondé	Beaumont College Kings College, Cambridge	1973–1976: Ambassador to Chile	Cavalry and Guards
Derick Ashe	Bradfield College Trinity College, Oxford	1975–1977: Ambassador to Argentina	Travellers, Beefsteak

(continued)

Table B.1 (continued)

Name	Education[a]	Position in FCO	Club membership
Anthony Williams	Oundle School Trinity College, Oxford	1980–1982: Ambassador to Argentina	Beefsteak, Canning
John Hickman	Tonbridge School Trinity Hall, Cambridge	1982–1987: Ambassador to Chile	Garrick
Anthony Parsons	Kings School, Canterbury Balliol College, Oxford	1979–1982: UK Permanent Representative to the United Nations	Royal Overseas League
Anthony Acland	Eton College Christ Church, Oxford	1972–1975: Principal Private Secretary to Foreign and Commonwealth Secretary	Brooks's
Duncan Watson	**Bradford Grammar School (direct grant grammar school)**[b] New College Oxford	1972–1975: Deputy Under Secretary of State	Travellers, Royal Commonwealth Society, Leander
Donald Maitland	George Watson's College Edinburgh University	1974–1975: Deputy Under Secretary of State December 1979–June 1980: Deputy to the Permanent Under Secretary of State	
Derek Day	Hurstpierpoint College St Catharine's College, Cambridge	1979: Assistant Under Secretary of State, FCO 1980: Deputy Under Secretary of State, FCO	Hawks
Donald Keith Haskell	**Portsmouth Grammar School (direct grant grammar school)**[b] St Catharine's College, Cambridge	1975–1978: Chargé d'Affaires and Consul General, Santiago	Hawks

(continued)

APPENDIX B   245

Table B.1 (continued)

Name	Education[a]	Position in FCO	Club membership
John Shakespeare	Winchester College Trinity College, Oxford	1973–1975: Counsellor and Consul-General, Buenos Aires 1976–1977: Chargé d'Affaires, Buenos Aires	Garrick
Hugh Carless	Sherborne School SOAS, London Trinity Hall, Cambridge	1973–1977: Head of Latin America Department, FCO 1977–1980: Chargé d'Affaires Buenos Aires	Travellers, Royal Mid Surrey Golf
Eric Anglin	**No information**	1976–1978: Consul-General, Buenos Aires 1978–1979: Chargé d'Affaires, Santiago	
Henry Hankey	Rugby School New College, Oxford	1969–1974: Assistant Under Secretary of State	
Robert H. G. Edmonds	Ampleforth College Brasenose College, Oxford	1974–1977: Assistant Under Secretary of State	Turf
George Hall	**Highbury County School (grammar)** Trinity Hall, Cambridge	1977–1979: Assistant Under Secretary of State	Bucks
John Ure	Uppingham School Magdalene College, Cambridge Harvard Business School	1977–1979: Head of South American Department, FCO 1981–1984: Assistant Under Secretary of State for the Americas	White's, Beefsteak, Pilgrims
George William Harding	Aldenham School St John's College, Cambridge	1979–1981: Assistant Under Secretary of State	

(continued)

Table B.1 (continued)

Name	Education[a]	Position in FCO	Club membership
Richard Dales	Chigwell School St Catherine's College, Cambridge	1973: FCO 1974–1977: Assistant Private Secretary to the Foreign and Commonwealth Secretary	Oxford and Cambridge
Roderic Lyne	Highfield School, Hants Eton College Leeds University	1979: Assistant Private Secretary to Secretary of State for Foreign and Commonwealth Affairs	Travellers
John Chick	**School not cited** St John's College, Cambridge	1978–1981: Commercial Counsellor and Consul General, Buenos Aires	
Peter Summerscale	Rugby School New College, Oxford Harvard University	1971–1975: First Secretary and Head of Chancery, Santiago, Chile	
Andrew Murray	Glenalmond College Edinburgh University	1979–1981: Head of Chancery, Buenos Aires	
John Murray Hunter	Fettes College Clare College, Cambridge	1971–1973: Head of the Latin America Department, FCO	
Robin Fearn	Ratcliffe College University College, Oxford	1979–1982: Head of South America Department, FCO 1982: Head of Falkland Islands Department, FCO	Oxford and Cambridge
Adrian Sindall	**Battersea Grammar School** Did not go to university	1976–1979: Assistant Head of Latin America Department, FCO 1982–1985: Head of South America Department, FCO	English-Speaking Union

(continued)

Table B.1 (continued)

Name	Education[a]	Position in FCO	Club membership
Arthur Collins	**Purley Grammar School**	1974–1977: Assistant Head of Latin America Department	Hove
Christopher Hulse	**Woking Grammar School** Trinity College, Cambridge	1981–1982: Assistant Head of Defence Department, FCO	
Robert John Chase	Sevenoaks School St John's College, Oxford	1982–1983: Assistant Head, South America Department, FCO.	Oxford and Cambridge
David Joy	**Hulme Grammar School, Lancs, (direct grant grammar school)**[b] St Catharine's College, Cambridge	1982–1984: Counsellor, Buenos Aires	Oxford and Cambridge
Dennis Amy	**Southall Grammar School**	1978–1983: First Secretary (Commercial), Santiago	
Robert A. E. Gordon	King's School, Canterbury, Magdalen College, Oxford	1978–1983: First Secretary, Santiago	
David Spedding	Sherborne School Hertford College, Oxford	1972–1973: Embassy, Chile	
John Illman	**Reading School (grammar)** St Andrews University	1975–1979: Embassy, Buenos Aires	Royal Commonwealth Society, Candlewick Ward
Dudley Ankerson	Hereford Cathedral School Sidney Sussex College, Cambridge	1978–1981: Second Secretary, Buenos Aires 1982–1985: Falkland Islands Department, FCO	Athenaeum, MCC, Penguins International Rugby Football

(continued)

Table B.1 (continued)

Name	Education[a]	Position in FCO	Club membership
Howard Pearce	City of London School Pembroke College, Cambridge	1975–1978: Third Secretary, Embassy, Buenos Aires	
Richard Gozney	Magdalen College School St Edmund Hall, Oxford	1978–1981: Embassy, Buenos Aires	
Christopher Crabbie	Rugby School Newcastle University Liverpool University Corpus Christi College, Oxford	1973–1975: FCO	
Kay Coombs	**School not cited** University of Newcastle upon Tyne	1974–1975: Latin American Department, FCO	
Susan Binns	Keighley Preparatory School Harrogate College, London School of Economics (LSE)	1975–1978: FCO	
Thomas Malcomson	**School not cited** University of Glasgow	1978–: FCO	
Gordon Duggan	**Liverpool Collegiate School (grammar)** Lincoln College, Oxford	1979–1980: FCO	United Oxford and Cambridge University
Colin Bright	Christ's Hospital St Andrew's University	1979–1983: FCO	
Roland Hedley Smith	**King Edward VII School (grammar)** Keble College, Oxford	1980: FCO	

[a]Schools which accepted non-fee paying pupils are highlighted in bold
[b]Direct grant grammar school at the time when the official attended, now independent school

Appendix C

Table C.1 Britain and 'ethical' foreign policy: unilateral action taken by Britain on arms sales

	Action taken by United Kingdom	*United Nations action*
South Africa (1961)	Arms sales guidelines introduced: licences should not be granted for weapons that could be used for internal repression	
South Africa (1964)	Arms embargo imposed	1963 UN Security Council votes for voluntary arms embargo (UK abstains) 1977: UN mandatory arms embargo

(continued)

250 APPENDIX C

Table C.1 (continued)

	Action taken by United Kingdom	United Nations action
Rhodesia (1965–1966)	Ban on all exports and most imports, following Universal Declaration of Independence for a white minority regime led by Ian Smith (1965)	1965: UN Security Council calls on UK to take all necessary action to prevent a Universal Declaration of Independence Dec. 1966: UN Security Council imposes mandatory selective sanctions, including oil and arms
Vietnam/US (1966–1967)	British government restricts sales of lethal weapons and herbicides to the United States that could be used in Vietnam	
India and Pakistan (1965)	Restrictions on arms sales, during Indo-Pakistan war (1965)	
Chile (1974–1980)	Arms embargo on Pinochet regime	
Uganda (1972–1979)	1972: suspends most aid, following Uganda's expulsion of 49,000 Asians 1976: breaks diplomatic relations 1979: suspends shipment of luxury goods for Ugandan military	
1978 El Salvador	British government cancels export licence for 15 armoured vehicles for El Salvador on human rights grounds and fears that they could pose a threat to neighbouring British territory, Belize. (Only example of British government breaking an existing arms contract)	

(continued)

Table C.1 (continued)

	Action taken by United Kingdom	United Nations action
Argentina (1979)	Arms sales guidelines introduced: licences should not be approved for weapons that could be used for internal repression or pose a threat to the Falklands	
Iran (1979–)	Arms embargo after Iranian revolution	
Argentina (1982)	Full trade sanctions after Argentine invasion of the Falkland Islands	
Iraq (1984–1988)	Restrictions on arms sales to regime of Saddam Hussein	

[a]The UK has imposed arms sales restrictions on other countries multilaterally through the UN or EU

Bibliography

Primary Sources

The National Archives (TNA), London
Cabinet Office Records: CAB 128, 129, 130, 148, 292.
Department of Energy Records: EG 14, POWE 63.
Department of Trade Records: BT 241.
Foreign and Commonwealth Office Records: FCO 7, 40, 46, 58, 76, 96.
Ministry of Defence Records: DEFE 24, 68.
Prime Minister's Office Records: PREM 16, 19.
Treasury Records: T 383.

Other Archives
Labour History Archive, Manchester, Chile Solidarity Campaign papers.
Peter Shore Archives, London School of Economics.
Senate House Archives, University of London, Pamphlet collection, N320.

Interviews with the Author
Alan Angell, Academics for Chile, 22 August 2017.
Alan Charlton, former ambassador to Brazil, 3 December 2014.
Ann Wright, Argentina Support Movement, 25 March 2015.
Bob Sommerville, fomer trade unionist at Rolls Royce, East Kilbride, 9 April 2014.
Bob Waugh, Committee for Human Rights in Argentina, 10 May 2017.
Christopher Roper, Argentina Support Movement, 27 March 2017.
David Michael, former businessman in Argentina, 27 April 2015.
David Stephen, former advisor to David Owen, 26 November 2014.

Former British embassy official in Buenos Aires who prefers not to be named, 17 December 2014.
Former minister in Margaret Thatcher's government, 3 June 2015.
Gordon Hutchison, Joint Working Group for Refugees, 6 October 2014.
Jimmy Burns, journalist, 3 March 2015.
John Keenan, former trade unionist at Rolls Royce, East Kilbride, 9 April 2014.
Julia Napier, Cambridge Committee for Human Rights in Argentina, 17 November 2014.
Mike Gatehouse, Chile Solidarity Campaign, 13 June 2013.
Richard Gozney, former embassy official in Buenos Aires, 20 March 2015.
Roy Broughton, Argentina Support Movement, 30 April 2017.
Stan Newens, former Labour MP, 17 June 2015.
The Rt Hon. Frank Dobson MP, 9 October 2013.
The Rt Hon. Lord Owen, former foreign secretary, 3 November 2014.
Vicky Grandon, Argentina human rights campaigner, 28 March 2017.
Wendy Tyndale, Chile Committee for Human Rights, 7 January 2015.

Other Interviews

Interviews with former diplomats and officials from the British Diplomatic Oral History Programme (BDOHP), Churchill Archives Centre, University of Cambridge.

British Government Publications

Britain and Latin America (London: Central Office of Information), published in the years 1968, 1973 and 1989.

Business Monitor MO4, Census of Overseas Assets (London: HMSO, 1984).

Falkland Islands Review, Report of a Committee of Privy Counsellors, Chairman: The Rt Hon. The Lord Franks (London, HMSO: 1983).

Overseas Transactions, Business Monitor (London: HMSO), published in the years 1979, 1982 and 1984.

Report of the Committee on Representational Services Overseas, chaired by Lord Plowden (London: HMSO, 1964).

Report of the Review Committee on Overseas Representation, chaired by Sir Val Duncan (London: HMSO, 1969).

Review of Overseas Representation, Report by the Central Policy Review Staff (London: HMSO, 1977).

Publications by Other Governments and International Organisations

Covert Action in Chile 1963–1973, US Senate, Staff Report of the Select Committee to Study Governmental Operations with Respect to Intelligence Activities, 18 December 1975, 94th Congress, 1st Session.

Direction of Trade Statistics (Washington: International Monetary Fund) published in the years 1978, 1979, 1980 and 1981.

Memoirs and Speeches

Benn, Tony, *Against the Tide: Diaries 1973–1976* (London: Hutchinson, 1989).
Benn, Tony, 'Obstacles to Reform', in Ralph Miliband, Leo Panitch and John Saville (eds.), *The Socialist Register 1989* (London: Merlin Press, 1989).
Benn, Tony, *Conflict of Interest, Diaries 1977–1980* (London: Hutchinson, 1990).
Benn, Tony, *The End of an Era, Diaries, 1980–1990* (London: Hutchinson, 1992).
Callaghan, James, *Time and Chance* (Glasgow: Collins/Fontana, 1988).
Carrington, Peter, *Reflect on Things Past* (London: Fontana, 1988).
Cassidy, Sheila, *Audacity to Believe* (London: Fount, 1978).
Castle, Barbara, *The Castle Diaries, 1964–1976* (London: Macmillan, 1990).
Cripps, Stafford, Hugh Dalton, Harold Laski, S.K. Ratcliffe, A.L. Rowse, and Bernard Shaw, *Where Stands Socialism Today?* (London: Rich and Cowan Ltd., 1933).
Crossman, Richard, *The Diaries of a Cabinet Minister. Volume 1, Minister of Housing, 1964–1966* (London: Hamish Hamilton & Jonathan Cape, 1975).
Dalyell, Tam, *One Man's Falklands* (London: Cecil Woolf Publishers: 1982).
Dell, Edmund, *Brazil: The Dilemma of Reform* (London: The Fabian Society, June 1964).
Donoughue, Bernard, *Downing Street Diary with Harold Wilson in No. 10* (London: Jonathan Cape, 2005).
Douglas-Home, Alec, *The Way the Wind Blows: An Autobiography* (Glasgow: Fontana, 1978).
Healey, Denis, *The Time of My Life* (London: Michael Joseph, 1989).
Heath, Edward, *The Course of My Life: My Autobiography* (London: Hodder & Stoughton, 1998).
Heffer, Eric, *Never a Yes Man* (London: Verso, 1991).
Livingstone, Ken, *You Can't Say That* (London: Faber and Faber, 2011).
Luard, Evan, *Human Rights and Foreign Policy* (Oxford: Pergamon, 1981).
Luce, Richard and John Ranelagh, *Human Rights and Foreign Policy* (London: Conservative Political Centre, 1977).
Luce, Richard, *Ringing the Changes, A Memoir* (Norwich: Michael Russell, 2007).
Mason, Roy, *Paying the Price* (London: Robert Hale, 1999).
Nott, John, *Here Today, Gone Tomorrow: Recollections of an Errant Politician* (London: Politicos, 2002).
Owen, David, *Human Rights* (London: Jonathan Cape, 1978).
Owen, David, *Time to Declare* (London: Penguin, 1991).
Owen, David, *Time to Declare: Second Innings* (London: Methuen, 2009).
Ridley, Nicholas, *My Style of Government: The Thatcher Years* (London: Hutchinson, 1991).
Thatcher, Margaret, *Margaret Thatcher: The Autobiography* (London: Harper Press, 2013).
Thatcher, Margaret, *Statecraft* (London: Harper Collins, 2011).
Thatcher, Margaret, *The Downing Street Years* (London: Harper Collins, 1993).
Thatcher, Margaret, *The Path to Power* (London: Harper Collins, 2012).
Wilson, Harold, *The Governance of Britain* (London: Weidenfeld and Nicolson, 1976).

Secondary Sources

Books About Argentina and the Falklands/Malvinas

Abudara Bini, Oscar, et al., *Malvinización y Desmentirización: Un Aporte Económico, Político y Cultural en el Marco de la Patria Grande* (Buenos Aires: Ediciones Fabro, 2013).

Abel González, Martín, *The Genesis of the Falklands Malvinas Conflict: Argentina, Britain and the Failed Negotiations of the 1960s* (Basingstoke: Palgrave Macmillan, 2013).

Anderson, Duncan, *The Falklands War 1982* (Oxford: Osprey, 2002).

Arancibia Clavel, Patricia, and Isabel de la Maza Cave, *Matthei: Mi Testimonio* (Santiago: La Tercera-Mondadori, 2003).

Arévalo, Oscar, *El Partido Comunista* (Buenos Aires: Centro Editor de América Latina, 1981).

Armony, Ariel C., *Argentina, the United States and the Anti-Communist Crusade in Central America 1977–1984* (Athens, OH: Ohio University Press, 1997).

Balmaceda, Rodolfo, *La Argentina Indefensa: Desmalvinización y Desmalvinizadores* (Buenos Aires: Editorial Los Nacionales, 2004).

Beck, Peter, *The Falklands Islands as an International Problem* (London: Routledge, 1988).

Berasategui, Vicente E., *Malvinas: Diplomacia y Conflicto Armado, Comentarios a la Historia Oficial Británica* (Buenos Aires: PROA AMERIAN Editores, 2011).

Betts, Alexander, *La Verdad Sobre Las Malvinas: Mi Tierra Natal* (Buenos Aires: Emece Editores, 1987).

Biangardi Delgado, Carlos Alberto, *Cuestión Malvinas, A 30 Años de la Guerra del Atlántico Sur* (Buenos Aires: Editorial Dunken, 2012).

Bicheno, Hugh, *Razor's Edge: The Unofficial History of the Falklands War* (London: Weidenfeld & Nicholson, 2006).

Borón, Atilio, and Julio Faúndez, *Malvinas Hoy: Herencia de un Conflicto* (Buenos Aires: Puntosur, 1989).

Boyce, George, *The Falklands War* (Basingstoke: Palgrave Macmillan, 2005).

Burns, Jimmy, *The Land that Lost its Heroes* (London: Bloomsbury, 2002).

Canclini, Arnoldo, *Malvinas - su Historia en Historias* (Buenos Aires: Instituto de Publicaciones Navales, 2008).

Canclini de Figueroa, Judith Ana, and Silvia Ruth Jalabe (eds.), *Década de Encuentro, Argentina y Gran Bretaña 1989–1999* (Buenos Aires: Consejo Argentino para las Relaciones Internacionales, 2001).

Castro Sauritain, Carlos, *Las Relaciones Vecinales de Chile y La Guerra del Atlántico Sur* (Santiago: Editorial Mare Nostrum, 2006).

Christie, Clive, *Nationalism and Internationalism: Britain's Left and Policy towards the Falkland Islands, 1982–1984* (Hull: University of Hull, Hull Papers in Politics, No. 37, April 1985).

Chubrétovich, Carlos, *Las Islas Falkland o Malvinas: Su Historia, La Controversia Argentina-Británica y la Guerra Consiguiente* (Santiago: Editorial La Noria, 1987).
Cresto, Juan José, *Historia de las Islas Malvinas: Desde su Descubrimiento hasta Nuestros Días* (Buenos Aires: Editorial Dunken, 2011).
Dale, Iain, *Memories of the Falklands* (London: Biteback Publishing, 2002).
Danchev, Alex, *International perspectives on the Falklands Conflict: A Matter of Life and Death* (Basingstoke: Macmillan, 1992).
Del Paso, Fernando, *El Va y Ven de las Malvinas* (Buenos Aires: Fondo de Cultura Económica, 2012).
Dodds, Klaus, *Pink Ice: Britain and the South Atlantic Empire* (London: IB Tauris, 2002).
Donaghy, Aaron, *The British Government and the Falkland Islands, 1974–1979* (Basingstoke: Palgrave Macmillan, 2014).
Escudé, Carlos, and Andrés Cisneros, *Historia General de Las Relaciones Exteriores de la República Argentina, Tomo XII, La Diplomacia de las Malvinas, 1966–1989* (Buenos Aires: CEPE/CARI/Nuevohacer, 2000).
Escudé, Carlos, and Andrés Cisneros, *Historia General de Las Relaciones Exteriores de la República Argentina, Tomo XIV* (Buenos Aires: CEPE/CARI/Nuevohacer, 2000).
Ferns, H.S., *Britain and Argentina in the Nineteenth Century* (Oxford: Clarendon Press, 1960).
Freedman, Lawrence, and Victoria Gamba-Stonehouse, *Signals of War: The Falklands Conflict of 1982* (London: Faber and Faber, 1990).
Freedman, Lawrence, *The Official History of the Falklands Campaign*, Volume 1 (London: Routledge, 2005).
Freedman, Lawrence, *The Official History of the Falklands Campaign*, Volume 2 (London: Routledge, 2005).
Fox, Robert, *Eyewitness Falklands: A Personal Account of the Falklands Campaign* (London: Mandarin, 1992).
Galasso, Norberto, *Aportes Críticos a la Historia de la Izquierda Argentina, Tomo II, 1961–2001* (Buenos Aires: Nuevos Tiempos, 2007).
Gamba, Virginia, *Malvinas Confidencial* (Buenos Aires: Comité Pro-Soberanía de las Malvinas, 1982).
García, Diego F. and Mike Seear, *Hors de Combat: The Falklands-Malvinas Conflict in Retrospect* (Nottingham: CCCP, 2009).
Gilly, Adolfo, and Alan Woods, Alberto Bonnet, *La Izquierda y la Guerra de Malvinas* (Buenos Aires: CEICS Ediciones RYR, 2012).
Graham-Yooll, Andrew, *The Forgotten Colony: A History of English-Speaking Communities in Argentina* (Buenos Aires: LOLA, 1999).
Graham-Yooll, Andrew, *Imperial Skirmishes: War and Gunboat Diplomacy in Latin America* (Oxford: Signal Books, 2002).

Grant, Ted, *Falklands Crisis: A Socialist Answer* (London: Militant Pamphlets, 1982).

Gustafson, Lowell, *The Sovereignty Dispute over the Falkland (Malvinas) Islands* (Oxford: Oxford University Press, 1988).

Hastings, Max, and Simon Jenkins, *The Battle for the Falklands* (London: Pan Books, 2010).

Hill, Christopher, and Stelios Stavridis (eds.), *Domestic Sources of Foreign Policy: West European Reactions to the Falklands Conflict* (Oxford: Berg, 1996).

Hennessy, Alistair, and John King, *The Land that England Lost: Argentina and Britain, a Special Relationship* (London: British Academic Press, 1992).

Honeywell, Martin, and Jenny Pearce, *Falklands/Malvinas: Whose Crisis? Latin America Bureau Special Brief* (London: LAB, 1982).

Hunter Christie, E. W., *The Antarctic Problem* (London: George Allen & Unwin Ltd., 1951).

Jones, Charles, *European Bankers and Argentina, 1880–1890* (Cambridge: University of Cambridge, Centre of Latin American Studies Working Papers, Business imperialism series, No. 3, 1970).

King, Doreen, The *Falklands (Malvinas) War—As Told by the British Media* (Chelmsford: Opran Publications, 2009).

Laborde, Julio, and Rina Beraccini, *Malvinas en el Plan Global del Imperialismo* (Buenos Aires: Editorial Anteo, 1987).

Laver, Roberto, *The Falklands/Malvinas Case: Breaking the Deadlock in the Anglo-Argentine Sovereignty Dispute* (The Hague: Martinus Nijhoff Publishers, 2001).

Lorenz, Federico, *Las Guerras por Malvinas* (Buenos Aires: Edhasa, 2006).

Lorenz, Federico, *Malvinas: Una Guerra Argentina* (Buenos Aires: Editorial Sudamericana, 2009).

McManners, Hugh, *Forgotten Voices of the Falklands* (London: Ebury Press, 2007).

Middlebrook, Martin, *The Falklands War 1982* (London: Penguin, 2001).

Moro, Rubén Oscar, *La Trampa de Malvinas: Historia del Conflicto de Atlántico Sur* (Buenos Aires: Edivérn, 2005).

Nadra, Fernando, *La Religión de Los Ateos: Reflexiones sobre el Estalinismo en el Partido Comunista Argentina* (Buenos Aires: Puntosur, 1989).

Norden, Deborah, *The United States and Argentina: Changing Relations in a Changing World* (New York: Routledge, 2002).

Ollier, María Matilde, *De la Revolución a la Democracia: Cambios Privados, Públicos y Políticos de la Izquierda Argentina* (Buenos Aires: Siglo Veintiuno, 2009).

Palermo, Vicente, *Sal en las Heridas: Las Malvinas en la Cultura Argentina Contemporánea* (Buenos Aires, Sudamericana, 2007).

Phipps, Colin, *What Future for the Falklands?* Fabian Tract 450 (London: Fabian Society, July 1977).

Richardson, Louise, *When Allies Differ: Anglo-American Relations during the Suez and Falklands Crises* (New York: St Martin's Press, 1996).
Rock, David, *Argentina 1516–1987: From Spanish Colonization to Alfonsín* (Berkeley, CA: University of California Press, 1987).
Rock, David, *State Building and Political Movements in Argentina, 1860–1916* (Redwood City, CA: Stanford University Press, 2002).
Sheinin, David, *Argentina and the United States: an Alliance Contained* (Athens, GA: University of Georgia Press, 2006).
Silenzi de Stagni, Adolfo, *Las Malvinas y El Petróleo*(Buenos Aires: Editora Theoría SRL, 1983).
Smith, Wayne, *Toward Resolution? The Falklands/Malvinas Dispute* (London: Lynne Rienner Publishers, 1991).
Till, Geoffrey, *Understanding Victory, Naval Operations from Trafalgar to the Falklands* (Santa Barbara, CA: Praeger, 2014).
Tulchin, Joseph S., *Argentina and the United States: A Conflicted Relationship* (Boston, MA: Twayne, 1990).
Vargas Otto, et al., *La Trama de Una Argentina Antagónica: Del Cordobazo al fin de la Dictadura* (Buenos Aires: Editorial Agora, 2006).
Verbitsky, Horacio, *Malvinas: La Ultima Batalla de la Tercera Guerra Mundial* (Buenos Aires: Editorial Sudamericana, 2002).
West, Nigel, *The Secret War for the Falklands: The SAS, MI6 and the War Whitehall Nearly Lost* (London: Little, Brown & Company, 1997).
The New Argentina: Planning for Profits in the 1980s (New York: Business International Corp., 1984).

Books About Chile

Alegria, Vicente, *The General and his Nemesis: The Struggle for Human Rights and the Arrest of General Pinochet in London* (London: Escaparate Ediciones, 2001).
Altman, David and Sergio Toro, Rafael Piñeiro, *International Influences on Democratic Transitions: The Successful Case of Chile* (Stanford, CA: Stanford University Center on Democracy, Development and the Rule of Law, Working Paper No. 86, 2008).
Beckett, Andy, *Pinochet in Piccadilly: Britain and Chile's Hidden History* (London: Faber and Faber, 2002).
Blakemore, Harold, *British Nitrates and Chilean Politics 1886–1896* (London: Athlone Press, 1974).
Brody, Reed, and Michael Ratner, *The Pinochet Papers: The Case of Augusto Pinochet in Spain and Britain* (The Hague: Kluwer Law International, 2000).
Chavkin, Samuel, *Storm over Chile, The Junta Under Siege* (New York: Lawrence Hill, 1985).

Christiaens, Kim, Goddeeris, Idesbald & Rodríguez García, Magaly (eds.), *European Solidarity with Chile, 1970s–1980s* (Frankfurt: Peter Lang, 2014, pp. 187–207.

Couyoumdjian, Juan Ricardo, *Chile y Gran Bretaña: Durante la Primera Guerra Mundial y la Posguerra: 1914–1921* (Santiago: Editorial Andrés Bello, 1986).

Davis, Madeleine (ed.), *The Pinochet Case, Origins, Progress and Implications* (London: Institute of Latin American Studies, 2003).

Del Pozo Artigas, José (ed.), *Exiliados, Emigrados y Retornados, Chilenos en América y Europa, 1973–2004* (Santiago: Ril Editores, 2006).

Dinges, John, *The Condor Years: How Pinochet and his Allies brought Terrorism to Three Continents* (New York: New Press, 2005).

Dorfman, Ariel, *Exorcising Terror: The Incredible Unending Trial of General Augusto Pinochet* (London: Pluto Press, 2002).

Edmundson, William, *A History of the British Presence in Chile: From the Bloody Mary to Charles Darwin and the Decline of British influence* (New York: Palgrave Macmillan, 2009).

Edmunson, William, *The Nitrate King: A Biography of Colonel John Thomas North* (New York: Palgrave Macmillan, 2011).

Falcoff, Mark, Arturo Valenzuela and Susan Kaufman Purcell, *Chile: Prospects for Democracy* (New York: Council on Foreign Relations, 1988).

Fermandois, Joaquín, Mundo y Fin de Mundo, *Chile en la política mundial 1900–2004* (Santiago: Universidad Católica de Chile, 2005).

Garcés, Joan E. et al., *La Intervención de Estados Unidos en Chile* (Santiago: Editorial 30 Años, 2003).

Garretón, Manuel Antonio, *Transición Hacia la Democracia en Chile y Influencia Externa: Dilemas y Perspectivas*, Kellogg Institute Working Paper 56 (Notre Dame, IN: Kellogg Institute, 1986).

Gustafson, Kristian, *Hostile Intent: US Covert Operations in Chile* (Washington, D.C.: Potomac Books, 2007).

Harmer, Tanya, *Allende's Chile and the InterAmerican Cold War* (Chapel Hill, NC: University of North Carolina Press, 2011).

Haslam, Jonathan, *The Nixon Administration and the Death of Allende's Chile: A Case of Assisted Suicide* (London: Verso, 2005).

Huneeus, Carlos, *The Pinochet Regime* (London: Lynne Rienner, 2007).

Jones, Ann, *No Truck with the Chilean Junta!* (Canberra: Anu Press, 2014).

Kornbluh, Peter, *The Pinochet File: A Declassified Dossier on Atrocity and Accountability* (New York: New Press, 2003).

Kay, Diana, *Chileans in Exile. Private Struggles, Public Lives* (London: Macmillan, 1987).

Mayo, John, *British Merchants and Chilean Development 1851–1886* (Boulder, CO: Westview Press, 1987).

Moss, Robert, *Chile's Marxist Experiment* (Newton Abbot: David & Charles, 1973).
Muñoz, Heraldo, *The Dictator's Shadow: Life under Augusto Pinochet* (New York: Basic Books, 2008).
Muñoz, Heraldo, and Carlos Portales, *Elusive Friendship: A Survey of US-Chilean Relations* (Boulder, CO: Lynne Rienner Publishers, 1991).
O'Brien, Thomas, *The Nitrate Industry and Chile's Crucial Transition 1870–1891* (New York: New York University Press, 1982).
O'Shaughnessy, Hugh, *Pinochet: The Politics of Torture* (London: LAB, 2000).
Petras, James, and Morris Morley, *The United States and Chile: Imperialism and the Overthrow of the Allende Government* (New York: Monthly Review Press, 1975).
Petras, James, and Fernando Ignacio Leiva, *Democracy and Poverty in Chile: the Limits to Electoral Politics* (Boulder, CO: Westview Press, 1994).
Purcell, Fernando, and Alfredo Riquelme (eds.), *Ampliando Miradas: Chile en un Tiempo Global* (Santiago: RiL Editores/Instituto de Historia, Pontifica Universidad Católica de Chile, 2009).
Puryear, Jeffery, *Thinking Politics: Intellectuals and Democracy in Chile, 1973–1988* (Baltimore, MD: Johns Hopkins University Press, 1994).
Ramírez Necochea, Hernán, *Historia del Imperialismo en Chile* (Santiago: Editora Austral Ltda, 1960).
Sigmund, Paul E., *The United States and Democracy in Chile* (Baltimore, MD: Johns Hopkins University Press, 1993).
Uribe, Armando, *The Black Book of American Intervention in Chile* (Boston, MA: Beacon Press, 1975).
A Study in Exile: A Report on the WUS (UK) Chilean Refugee Scholarship Programme (London: World University Service, 1986).
Inversión Extranjera y Empresas Transnacionales en la Economía de Chile (1974–1989), Estudios e Informes de la Cepal, 86 (Santiago: ECLAC, 1992).

Other Books

Adonis, Andrew, and Stephen Pollard, *A Class Act: The Myth of Britain's Classless Society* (London: Penguin, 1998).
Alden, Chris, and Amnon Aran, *Foreign Policy Analysis: New Approaches* (Abingdon, Oxon: Routledge, 2012).
Aldous, Richard, *Reagan and Thatcher: The Difficult Relationship* (London: Arrow, 2012).
Ashworth, Lucian, *International Relations and the Labour Party: Intellectuals and Policy Making from 1918–1945* (London: Tauris, 2007).
Baylis, John and Steve Smith (eds.), *The Globalization of World Politics* (Oxford: Oxford University Press, 2005).
Blasier, Cole, *The USSR and Latin America* (Pittsburgh: University of Pittsburgh Press, 1983).

Baumann, Fred E. (ed.), *Human Rights and American Foreign Policy* (Gambier, OH: Public Affairs Conference Center, Kenyon College, 1982).

Beck, Peter, *The International Politics of Antarctica* (London: Crook Helm, 1986).

Belton, Neil, *The Good Listener* (London: Phoenix, 1999).

Bethell, Leslie, *George Canning and the Independence of Latin America* (London: The Hispanic and Luso Brazilian Councils, 1970).

Bonsor, Nicholas, *Britain and Latin America: Economic Prospects* (London: Institute of Latin American Studies, University of London, Occasional Papers 13, 1996).

Bieler, Andreas, and Werner Bonefeld, Peter Burnham, Adam David Morton (eds.), *Global Restructuring, State, Capital and Labour: Contesting Neo-Gramscian Perspectives* (London: Palgrave Macmillan, 2006).

Brzoska, Michael, and George A. Lopez (eds.), *Putting Teeth in the Tiger: Improving the Effectiveness of Arms Embargoes* (Bingley: Emerald Group, 2009).

Brown, Matthew (ed.), *Informal Empire in Latin America: Culture, Commerce and Capital* (Oxford: Blackwell, 2008).

Budd, Adrian, *Class, States and International Relations* (London: Routledge, 2013).

Bulmer-Thomas, Victor (ed.), *Britain and Latin America: A Changing Relationship* (Cambridge: Cambridge University Press, 1989).

Bulmer-Thomas, Victor, *British Trade with Latin America in the Nineteenth and Twentieth Centuries* (London: Institute of Latin American Studies, University of London, Occasional Papers No. 19, 1998).

Burk, Kathleen, *Old World, New World: The Story of Britain and America* (London: Abacus, 2007).

Burnham, James, *The Managerial Revolution* (New York: Putnam, 1942).

Busby, Joshua, *Moral Movements and Foreign Policy* (Cambridge: Cambridge University, Press, 2010).

Byrne, Paul, *Social Movements in Britain* (London: Routledge, 1997).

Callaghan, John, *The Labour Party and Foreign Policy* (Abingdon, Oxon: Routledge, 2007).

Cain, P. J., and A. G. Hopkins, *British Imperialism 1688-2000* (London: Pearson, 2001).

Cannadine, David, *The Decline and Fall of the British Aristocracy* (London: Papermac, 1996).

Cannadine, David, *Class in Britain* (London: Penguin, 2000).

Cardoso, Fernando Henrique, and Enzo Faletto, *Dependency and Development in Latin America* (Berkeley, CA: University of California Press, 1979).

Carlsnaes, Walter and Stefano Guzzini (eds.), *Foreign Policy Analysis* (London: Sage, 2011).

Chandler, David, and Volker Heins, *Rethinking Ethical Foreign Policy* (London: Routledge, 2006).
Chomsky, Noam, *Human Rights and American Foreign Policy* (Nottingham: Spokesman, 1978).
Coker, Christopher (ed.), *The United States, Western Europe and Military Intervention Overseas* (London: Macmillan, 1987).
Cockett, Richard, *Thinking the Unthinkable: Think-tanks and the Economic Counter-revolution, 1931–1983* (London: Harper Collins, 1995).
Corthorn, Paul, and Jonathan Davis (eds.), *The British Labour Party and the Wider World: Domestic Politics, Internationalism and Foreign Policy* (London: Tauris, 2008).
Cox, Robert, *The New Realism: Perspectives on Multilateralism and World Order* (London: Macmillan, 1997).
Cox, Robert, and Timothy Sinclair, *Approaches to World Order* (Cambridge: Cambridge University Press, 1996).
Crozier, Brian, '*We Will Bury You*', *Studies in Left-Wing Subversion Today* (London: Tom Stacey Ltd., 1970).
Crozier, Brian, *A Theory of Conflict* (London: Hamish Hamilton, 1974).
Crozier, Brian, *Strategy of Survival* (London: Temple Smith, 1978).
Crozier, Brian, *The Minimum State: Beyond Party Politics* (London: Hamish Hamilton, 1979).
Deo, Nandini, and Duncan McDuie-Ra, *The Politics of Collective Advocacy in India: Tools and Traps* (Sterling, VA: Kumarian Press, 2011).
Dickie, John, *Inside the Foreign Office* (London: Chapmans, 1992).
Dinges, John, and Saul Landau, *Assassination on Embassy Row* (London: Writers and Readers, 1981).
Dodds, Klaus, *The Antarctic: A Very Short Introduction* (Oxford: Oxford University Press, 2012).
Dudley Edwards, Ruth, *True Brits: Inside the Foreign Office* (London: BBC Books, 1994).
Dumbrell, John, *The Making of US Foreign Policy* (Manchester: Manchester University Press, 1990).
Dumbrell, John, *A Special Relationship: Anglo-American Relations in the Cold War and After* (Basingstoke: Macmillan Press, 2001).
Engstrom, Par, 'The Inter-American Human Rights System and US–Latin American Relations', in Juan Pablo Scarfi & Andrew Tillman, *Cooperation and Hegemony in US–Latin American Relations* (New York: Palgrave Macmillan, 2016).
Fairlie, Henry, edited by Jeremy McCarter, *Bite the Hand that Feeds you: Essays and Provocations* (Newhaven, CT: Yale University Press, 2009).

Fawcett, Louise, and Eduardo Posada-Carbo, *Britain and Latin America: Hope in a Time of Change?* (London: Institute of Latin American Studies, University of London, Research Papers, No. 44, 1996).

Foweraker, J., *Theorizing Social Movements* (London: Pluto Press, 1995).

Ferguson, James, and Jenny Pearce, *The Thatcher Years: Britain and Latin America* (London: LAB, 1988).

Flood, Patrick James, *The Effectiveness of UN Human Rights Institutions* (Westport, CT: Praeger, 1998).

Freedman, Lawrence, *The Politics of British Defence, 1979–1998* (London: Macmillan, 1999).

Fukuyama, Francis, *The End of History and the Last Man* (London: Penguin, 2012).

Gamble, Andrew, *The Free Economy and the Strong State: The Politics of Thatcherism* (Basingstoke: Macmillan, 1988).

Gamble, Andrew, and Steve Ludlam, Andrew Taylor, Stephen Wood, *Labour, the State, Social Movements and the Challenge of Neo-Liberal Globalisation* (Manchester: Manchester University Press, 2007).

Gaskarth, Jamie, *British Foreign Policy* (Cambridge: Polity Press, 2013).

Giugni, Marco, *Social Protest and Policy Change* (Oxford: Rowman & Littlefield, 2004).

Giugni, Marco, and Doug McAdam, Charles Tilly (eds.), *How Social Movements Matter* (Minneapolis, MN: University of Minnesota Press, 1999).

González, Francisco, *Dual Transitions from Authoritarian Rule: Institutionalized Regimes in Chile and Mexico, 1970–2000* (Baltimore, MD: Johns Hopkins University Press, 2008).

Grandin, Greg, *Empire's Workshop: Latin America, the United States and the Rise of the New Imperialism* (New York: Metropolitan Books, 2006).

Grabendorff, Wolf, and Riordan Roett (eds.), *Latin America Western Europe and the US: Re-evaluating the Atlantic Triangle* (New York: Praeger, 1985).

Gunder Frank, Andre, *Capitalism and Underdevelopment in Latin America*, rev. edn (Harmondsworth: Penguin, 1971).

Guttsman, W. L., *The British Political Elite* (London: MacGibbon & Kee, 1968).

Guttsman, W. L. (ed.), *The English Ruling Class* (London, Weidenfeld and Nicolson, 1969).

Hennessy, Peter, *The Great and the Good: An Inquiry into the British Establishment* (London: Policy Studies Institute, 1986).

Hill, Christopher, *Cabinet Decisions on Foreign Policy* (Cambridge: Cambridge University Press, 1991).

Hill, Christopher, *The Changing Politics of Foreign Policy* (London: Palgrave Macmillan, 2003).

Hill, Dilys, *Human Rights and Foreign Policy: Principles and Practice* (Basingstoke: Macmillan, 1989).

Hirst, Paul, and Graham Thompson, *Globalization in Question* (Cambridge: Polity Press, 2009).
Hitchens, Christopher, *The Trial of Henry Kissinger* (London: Verso, 2001).
Hudson, Valerie, *Foreign Policy Analysis: Classic and Contemporary Theory* (Lanham, MD: Rowman & Littlefield, 2014).
Hufbauer, Gary Clyde, and Jeffrey J. Schott, Kimberly Ann Elliot, *Economic Sanctions Reconsidered: History and Current Policy* (Washington, D.C.: Institute for International Economics, 1990).
Humphreys, R. A., *Latin America and the Second World War: 1939–1942* (London: Continuum International Publishing Group, 1981).
Jenkins, Simon, and Anne Sloeman, *With Respect, Ambassador: An Inquiry into the Foreign Office* (London: BBC Books, 1985).
Jones, Charles, *International Business in the Nineteenth Century: The Rise and Fall of a Cosmopolitan Bourgeoisie* (Brighton: Wheatsheaf, 1987).
Jones, Owen, *The Establishment and How They Get Away With It* (London: Penguin, 2015).
Jones, Ray, *The Nineteenth Century Foreign Office, An Administrative History* (London: Weidenfeld and Nicolson, 1971).
Keck, Margaret, and Kathryn Sikkink, *Activists Beyond Borders: Advocacy Networks in International Politics* (Ithaca, NY: Cornell University Press, 1998).
Knox, K., and T. Kushner (eds.), *Refugees in an Age of Genocide: Global, National and Local Perspectives during the Twentieth Century* (London: Frank Cass, 1999).
Laski, Harold, *The Labour Party and the Constitution* (London: Socialist League, 1933).
Little, Richard, and Mark Wickham-Jones, *New Labour's Foreign Policy: A New Moral Crusade* (Manchester: Manchester University Press, 2000).
Livingstone, Grace, *America's Backyard: The US and Latin America from the Monroe Doctrine to the War on Terror* (London: Zed Books, 2009).
Louis, W. R., *The Robinson and Gallagher Controversy* (New York: New Viewpoints, 1976).
Lowenthal, Abraham F. (ed.), *Exporting Democracy: The United States and Latin America* (Baltimore, MD: Johns Hopkins University Press, 1991).
McAdam, Doug, and Sidney Tarrow, Charles Tilly, *Dynamics of Contention* (Cambridge: Cambridge University Press, 2001).
Meisel, James, *The Myth of the Ruling Class: Gaetano, Mosca and the Elite* (Ann Arbor, MI: University of Michigan Press, 1958).
Miller, Nicola, *Soviet Relations with Latin America* (Cambridge: Cambridge University Press, 1989).
Miller, Rory, *Britain and Latin America in the Nineteenth and Twentieth Centuries* (London: Longman, 1993).

McKercher, B. J. C. (ed.), *Routledge Handbook of Diplomacy and Statecraft* (London: Routledge, 2012).
McKercher, B. J. C. and D. J. Moss (eds.), *Shadow and Substance in British Foreign Policy, 1895–1939* (Edmonton: University of Alberta Press, 1984).
Moorhouse, Geoffrey, *The Diplomats: The Foreign Office Today* (London: Jonathan Cape, 1977).
Mosca, Gaetano, *The Ruling Class* (New York: McGraw-Hill, 1939).
Moss, Robert, *The Collapse of Democracy* (London: Abacus, 1977).
Muñoz, Heraldo, *El Fin del Fantasma: Las Relaciones InterAmericanas después de la Guerra Fría* (Santiago: Hachette, 1992).
Nel, Philip, and Janis van der Westhuizen, *Democratizing Foreign Policy? Lessons from South Africa* (Lanham, MD: Lexington Books, 2004).
O'Donnell, Guillermo, and Philippe Schmitter, Laurence Whitehead, *Transitions from Authoritarian Rule: Prospects for Democracy, Latin America* (Baltimore, MD: The Johns Hopkins University Press, 1986).
Otte, T. G., *The Foreign Office Mind: The Making of British Foreign Policy 1865–1914* (Cambridge: Cambridge University Press, 2011).
Pareto, Vilfredo, *The Mind and Society* (New York: Harcourt-Brace, 1935).
Parry, Geraint, *Political Elites* (Colchester: ECPR Press, 2005).
Phythian, Mark, *The Politics of British Arms Sales Since 1964* (Manchester: Manchester University Press, 2000).
Phythian, Mark, *The Labour Party, War and International Relations, 1945–2006* (London Routledge, 2007).
Platt, D.C.M., *Finance, Trade and Politics in British Foreign Policy, 1815–1914* (Oxford: Clarendon Press, 1968).
Platt, D.C.M. (ed.), *Business Imperialism, 1840–1930, An Inquiry Based on British Experience in Latin America* (Oxford: Clarendon Press, 1977).
Roberts, Kenneth M., *Deepening Democracy? The Modern Left and Social Movements in Chile and Peru* (California: Stanford University Press, 1998).
Rowe, Cami, *The Politics of Protest and US Foreign Policy: Performative Construction of the War on Terror* (New York: Routledge, 2013).
Sampson, Anthony, *Anatomy of Britain* (London: Hodder and Stoughton, 1962).
Sampson, Anthony, *The New Anatomy of Britain* (New York: Stein and Day, 1972).
Sanders, David, *Losing an Empire, Finding a Role: British Foreign Policy since 1945* (London: Macmillan, 1990).
Schoultz, Lars, *National Security and United States Policy toward Latin America* (Princeton, NJ: Princeton University Press, 1987).
Skidmore, David, and Valerie Hudson, *The Limits of State Autonomy, Societal Groups and Foreign Policy Formulation* (Boulder, CO: Westview Press, 1993).
Smith, Karen, and Margot Light (eds.), *Ethics and Foreign Policy* (Cambridge: Cambridge University Press, 2001).

Steiner, Zara, *The Foreign Office and Foreign Policy, 1898–1914* (Cambridge: Cambridge University Press, 1969).
Snyder, Richard, and H. W. Bruck, Burton Sapin, *Decision Making as an Approach to the Study of International Politics* (New York: Free Press of Glencoe, 1962).
Theakston, Kevin, *The Labour Party and Whitehall* (London: Routledge, 1992).
Theakston, Kevin (ed.) *British Foreign Secretaries since 1947* (London: Routledge, 2004).
Tsebelis, George, *Veto Players: How Political Institutions Work* (Princeton, NJ: Russell/Sage Foundation, University Press, 2002).
Vincent, Raymond John, *Human Rights and International Relations* (Cambridge: Cambridge University Press, 1986).
Vital, David, *The Making of British Foreign Policy* (London: George Allen and Unwin, 1968).
Walldorf, William, *Just Politics: Human Rights and the Foreign Policy of the Great Powers* (London: Cornell University Press, 2008).
Watt, D. C., *Personalities and Policies: Studies in the Formulations of British Foreign Policy in the Twentieth Century* (London: Longmans, 1965).
Whitehead, Laurence (ed.), *International Dimensions of Democratization* (Oxford: Oxford University Press, 2001).
Wright, Thomas C., *State Terrorism in Latin America: Chile, Argentina and International Human Rights* (Lanham, MD: Roman & Littlefield, 2007).
Wright Mills, Charles, *The Power Elite* (New York: Oxford University Press, 1966).
Wyn Jones, Richard (ed.), *Critical Theory and World Politics* (Boulder, CO: Lynne Rienner, 2000).
Britain and Latin America: An Annual Review of British-Latin American Relations (London: Latin America Bureau, 1978).
Britain and Latin America: An Annual Review of British-Latin American Relations (London: Latin America Bureau, 1979).
Europe and Latin America: An Annual Review of European-Latin American Relations (London: Latin America Bureau, 1980).

Journal Articles
Alemán, Eduardo, 'Policy Gatekeepers in Latin American Legislatures', *Latin American Politics and Society*, 48 (2006), 125–155.
Amunátegui Solar, Domingo, 'Orígenes del comercio inglés en Chile', *Revista Chilena de Historia y Geografía*, 103 (1943), 83–95.
Angell, Alan and Susan Carstairs. 'The Exile Question in Chilean Politics', *Third World Quarterly*, 9 (1987), 148–167.
Bawden, John R., 'Cutting off the Dictator: The United States Arms Embargo of the Pinochet Regime 1974–1988', *Journal of Latin American Studies*, 45 (2013), 513–543.

Cain, P. J., and A. G. Hopkins, 'Gentlemanly Capitalism and British Expansion Overseas I. The Old Colonial System, 1688–1850', *Economic History Review*, 39 (1986), 501–525.

Cain, P. J., and A. G. Hopkins, 'Gentlemanly Capitalism and British Expansion Overseas II: New Imperialism, 1850–1945', *Economic History Review*, 40 (1987), 1–26.

Denzau, Arthur, and Robert Mackay, 'Gatekeeping and Monopoly Power of Committees: An Analysis of Sincere and Sophisticated Behavior', *American Political Science Review*, 27 (1983), 740–761.

Friedman, Max Paul, 'Retiring the Puppets, Bringing Latin America Back in: Recent Scholarship on United States-Latin American Relations', *Diplomatic History*, 27 (2003), 621–636.

Fry, Geoffrey, 'The British Diplomatic Service: Facts and Fantasies', *Politics* (1982), 4–8.

Gallagher, John, and Ronald Robinson, 'The Imperialism of Free Trade' *Economic History Review*, 6 (1953), 1–15.

Gaskarth, Jamie, 'Where would we be without rules?, A virtue ethics approach to Foreign Policy Analysis', *Review of International Studies*, 37 (1) (2011), 393–415.

Gaskarth, Jamie, 'Interpreting Ethical Foreign Policy: Traditions and Dilemmas for Policy Makers', *The British Journal of Politics and International Relations*, 15 (2013), 192–209.

Giugni, Marco, 'Political Opportunities from Tilly to Tilly', Swiss Political Science Review, 15 (2009), 361–368.

Goldsmith, Jack, and Eric Posner, 'International Agreements: A Rational Choice Approach', *Virginia Journal of International Law*, 44 (2003), 113–143.

Hildebrandt, Timothy, and Courtney Hillebrecht, Peter Holm, Jon Pevehouse, 'The Domestic Politics of Humanitarian Intervention: Public Opinion, Partisanship and Ideology', *Foreign Policy Analysis*, 9 (2013), 243–266.

Hoffman, Stanley, 'Reaching for the Most Difficult: Human Rights as a Foreign Policy Goal', *Daedalus*, 112 (4) (1983), 19–49.

Hyam, Ronald, 'The Colonial Office Mind, 1900–1914', *Journal of Imperial and Commonwealth History*, 8 (1979), 30–55.

Joly, Daniele, 'Britain and its Refugees: The Case of Chileans', *Migration* (1987), 91–108.

Jones, Charles, '"Business Imperialism" and Argentina, 1875–1900: A Theoretical Note', *Journal of Latin American Studies*, 12 (1980), 437–444.

Ortega, Alejandro, 'International Effects on the Democratic Onset in Chile', *Stanford Journal of International Relations*, 6 (2010), 28–39.

Patrick William Kelly, 'The 1973 Chilean Coup and the Origins of Transnational Human Rights Activism', *Journal of Global History*, 8 (1) (2013), 165–186.

Roniger, Luis, and Mario Sznajder, 'Comunidades del exilio y su dinámica institucional diferenciada: un análisis comparativo de las diásporas políticas chilenas y uruguayas', *Revista de Ciencia Política*, 27 (1) (2007), 43–66.

Tripodi, Paolo, 'General Matthei's Revelation and Chile's Role during the Falklands War: A New Perspective on the Conflict in the South Atlantic', *The Journal of Strategic Studies*, 26 (2003), 108–123.

Von Stein, Jana, 'Do Treaties Constrain or Screen? Selection Bias and Treaty Compliance, *American Political Science Review*, 99 (2005), 611–622.

Wilkinson, Michael D., 'The Chile Solidarity Campaign and British Government Policy towards Chile, 1973–1990', *European Review of Latin American and Caribbean Studies*, 52 (1992), 57–74.

Unpublished Conference Papers and Dissertations

Bayle, Paola, '*La Diáspora de una Población Calificada: el Exilio Académico Chileno en el Reino Unido*', unpublished doctoral thesis, Universidad Nacional de Cuyo, Argentina, 2010.

Burk, Kathleen, 'The Relationship between Great Britain, the United States, Argentina and the Falkland Islands/Las Malvinas', paper delivered at a colloquium 'The Falklands/Malvinas War Thirty Years After', at the Institut des Amériques, Paris, and the University of Pau, 16–19 October 2012.

Gideon, Jasmine, 'Health and Wellbeing among Chilean exiles in London: A research Agenda', Birkbeck College, 2015. https://ageingandmigration.files.wordpress.com/2013/10/gideon-ageing-and-migration-pp.pdf.

Parsons, Michael, 'The Falklands/Malvinas War and the United States,' paper delivered at a colloquium 'The Falklands/Malvinas War Thirty Years After', at the Institut des Amériques, Paris, and the University of Pau, 16–19 October 2012.

INDEX

A

Academics for Chile, 41, 48
Aid
   to Chile, 21, 35–38, 40, 46, 48, 49, 53, 58–61, 64, 79, 86, 92, 93, 100, 106, 115, 129, 135, 148
Alginate Industries, 173, 212
Allara, Rear-Admiral Walter, 194
Allende, Hortensia Bussi de, 76, 101, 102, 112
Allende, Salvador, 4, 35, 38, 49, 74, 76, 101, 234
Ambassador
   Restoration of British ambassador to Argentina (1979), 122, 152, 181
   Restoration of British ambassador to Chile (1980), 36, 40, 85, 88, 89, 91–94
   Social background of British ambassadors, 6, 8, 57; Argentine Ambassador to the United Kingdom, *see* Carlos Ortiz de Rozas; British ambassadors to Chile, *see* John Hickman (1982–87); John Heath (1980–82); Reginald Secondé (1973–76); British Ambassador to Argentina, *see* Anthony Williams (1980–82)
   Withdrawal of British ambassador to Argentina (1976), 164
   Withdrawal of British ambassador to Chile (1975), 2, 9, 35, 40, 71–73, 115
Amery, Julian, 45, 54
Amnesty International, 18, 48, 93, 94, 101, 103, 104, 117, 135, 140, 144, 151, 199
Amy, Dennis, 93, 96, 247
Angell, Alan, 31, 41, 44, 48
Anglo-Argentines in Argentina
   attitudes to the military regime, 135–136
Anglo-Chileans in Chile
   attitudes to Pinochet regime, 52, 70–73
Antarctica
   British interest in oil and minerals in Antarctica, 24, 217–220

272 INDEX

links to Falklands claim, 2, 206, 218, 220, 227
see also Antarctic Treaty; British Antarctic Territory (BAT)
Antarctic Treaty, 61, 217–220, 239
Apartheid, 215, 233
Aquitaine, 166
Argentina Support Movement (ASM), 139, 140, 172
Arms embargo
   on Chile, 2, 35, 36, 38–41, 85, 89, 91, 94, 96–97, 106, 115, 122, 131, 233, 234
   on South Africa, 18, 41, 249–251
   unilateral British arms embargos, 249–251
Arms sales
   to Argentina, 21, 25, 122, 145–147, 150–153, 181, 188–189, 191–198, 227, 234–235, 237, 239
   to Chile, 8, 9, 21, 25, 35–36, 38–40, 47–49, 79, 85, 93–95, 98–99, 106, 108, 122, 153, 194, 198, 234, 237
   to El Salvador, 250
   restrictions on sales to Argentina, 151–153
   violations of guidelines on arms sales to Argentina, 123, 153, 189–198, 195–198
   violations of guidelines on arms sales to Chile, 108
Ashland Oil, 164, 176
Avebury, Eric [Lord], 151, 198

B
Bader, Sir Douglas, 190, 202
Bamber, Helen, 101
Barclays, 134
Baring Brothers, 100, 134
Barlow, Sir John, 175
Beagle channel, 105
Beausire, William, 74, 92, 103
Belgrano, The, 107, 113
Bell, Tim, 88
Bennett, Frederic, 94
Benn, Tony, 4, 7, 24, 26, 33, 45, 57, 58, 63, 65, 80, 121, 161, 166, 168, 172, 178, 223
Berrill, Kenneth, 210, 218, 229
Bevin, Ernest, 7
Bindman, Geoffrey, 75
Binns, Susan, 75, 248
Black, Conrad, 88, 110
Blair, Tony, 2
Board of Trade, 69, 184
Booth, Albert, 147
Braine, Bernard, 198
Brazil, 9, 13, 15, 36, 75, 132, 154, 179, 215, 216, 235
Bright, Colin, 186, 229, 248
British Aerospace (BAE), 99, 150, 184, 192, 193
British Antarctic Survey, 135, 219
British Antarctic Territory (BAT), 70, 184, 218–220
British Argentina Campaign, 140, 156, 172, 179, 198
British Broadcasting Company (BBC), 50. *See also Panorama*
British-Chilean Chamber of Commerce, 52
British Embassy in Buenos Aires, 129, 144–145, 191, 223. *See also* John Shakespeare; Hugh Carless; Anthony Williams
   attitudes to Argentine dictatorship, 129–132, 133, 135, 140–142, 144–45, 153, 181–182, 187–188
   attitudes towards refugees, 136, 141, 144

divisions within the Embassy, 144–145
human rights reporting, 145, 182-183
response to Panorama broadcast on torture in Argentina, 136–137
British Embassy in Santiago, 39, 73, 85, 92. *See also* Amy, Dennis; Heath, John; Secondé, Reginald
  attitude to Pinochet coup, 85
  relations with Anglo-Chilean community, 73
  social ties with Pinochet regime officials, 39, 92
British Nationality Bill, 1981, 125, 205, 225
British Nationality Bill, 1983, 225
British National Oil Corporation (BNOC), 209, 213, 229
British Petroleum (BP), 9, 100, 134, 135, 163–166, 177, 209
  and Falklands oil, 165, 170, 209, 210
British Shipbuilders, 146, 147, 150, 190
Brown, Gordon, 47, 54
Buenos Aires Herald, 136, 156
Bunster, Alvaro, 50
Buxton, Lord, 219, 226, 231, 232

C
Callaghan, James, 2, 23, 58, 59, 72, 80, 83, 115, 123, 125, 126, 131, 140, 146, 154, 164, 177
Canberra bomber planes, 108, 191
Canning, George, 13, 29
Canning House, 17, 116, 162, 185, 208
Carless, Hugh, 49, 54, 59–61, 69, 72, 78, 80, 83, 117, 132, 136, 140, 143, 145, 150, 154, 167, 174, 176, 177, 181, 184, 186, 200, 216, 228, 245
Carrington, Lord (Peter Carrington), 24, 80, 85, 89–91, 93, 100, 126, 182, 185, 191, 198, 207, 208, 210, 211, 218, 219, 222, 226
Carter, Jimmy, 18, 21, 38, 90
Cassidy, Sheila, 64, 71–73, 83, 92, 93
Castle, Barbara, 24, 33, 58, 80
Catholic Agency for Overseas Development (CAFOD), 48, 117, 140
Catholic Institute for International Relations (CIIR), 48
Chapman Pincher, Harry, 190
Charted Consolidated, 100
Chevron, 166
Chilean armed forces, 40, 61, 87, 97, 107, 113
Chilean navy, 60, 61, 64, 99, 107
Chilean Supporters Abroad, 87, 88
Chile Committee for Human Rights (CCHR), 38, 39, 48, 58, 109
Chile Solidarity Campaign (CSC), 11, 22, 32, 48, 49, 54, 58, 68, 76, 77, 99, 102, 117, 118, 121, 138, 139, 175
Christian Aid, 48
Christians for a Just World, 49
Class
  of FCO officials, 6–8, 57, 117, 174, 175, 206, 220
  relevance to foreign policy-making, 3, 5, 237
Committee for Human Rights in Argentina, 140, 156, 172, 179, 198
Commonwealth Parliamentary Association (CPA), 53, 171
Communist Party. *See* Euro-communism
Communist Party of Argentina (*Partido Comunista de la Argentina*), 121, 156

Communist Party of Great Britain (CPGB), 139
Conlan, Bernard (MP), 171
Conservative Party, 12, 35, 42, 52, 89, 90, 181, 185, 187, 201, 221, 234, 236
Consolidated Goldfields, 100
Cox, Robert, 5, 26, 136, 156. *See also Buenos Aires Herald*
Crabbie, Christopher, 51, 76, 248
Cran, Bill, 50
Cripps, Stafford, 4, 26, 57
Crossman, Richard, 4, 26, 57, 78
Crozier, Brian, 87, 110
Cubillos, Hernán, 73, 94, 110

D

Daily Mail, 70, 88, 93, 111
Daily Telegraph, 66, 70, 109, 150, 159
Dalyell, Tam, 172, 223
Day, Derek, 192, 203, 244
De Castro, Sergio, 94
 meeting with Parkinson, Cecil, 94
Defence attaché, British, 85, 98, 203
 appointment to Chile, 85, 98
 in Argentina, 105
Dell, Edmund, 65, 69, 81, 133, 147, 149, 158
Department of Energy, 124, 134, 164–169, 177, 206, 209–211, 213, 214, 218, 227, 238
Department of Trade, 64–66, 89, 117, 134, 147, 149, 185, 188, 235
Dependencies of Falkland Islands (South Georgia and Sandwich Islands), 167, 219
Desire Petroleum, 166, 170
Douglas-Home, Alec, 46, 53, 80
Duncan Report, 15, 27, 30, 117

E

East Kilbride dispute. *See* Rolls Royce, aero-engine dispute
Economist, The, 25, 86, 100
Edmonds, Robin, 154, 175, 176
Ejercito Revolucionario del Pueblo (ERP), 138
Elections, 4, 35, 46, 53, 57, 58, 88, 89, 91, 106, 131, 152, 171, 181, 182, 184, 185, 199, 201, 234
 general election 1979, 91
 general election February 1974, 46, 53, 58
 general election October 1974, 58
Elf, 166
Elites, 6, 10, 28, 37, 38, 125, 191, 236
Escuela de Mecánica de la Armada (ESMA) [Naval Mechanical School, Argentina], 148
Esso, 134, 209
Ethical foreign policy, 18, 19, 30, 35
Euro-communism, 20
European Economic Community (EEC), 21, 39, 89, 141, 183
Evans, Moss, 65, 94
Exocet missiles, 151
Export Credit Guarantee Department (ECGD), 44, 91
Export Credit Guarantees, 85, 91
Export Guarantee Advisory Council, 91

F

Fairlie, Henry, 9, 28
Falkland Islands, 1, 2, 5, 11, 23–25, 32, 33, 60, 61, 122–127, 132, 142, 146, 147, 151, 152, 158, 161–167, 169–171, 173, 175–178, 180, 184, 187, 190–193, 200, 208, 210–217, 219, 221, 227–232, 238, 239, 246, 247, 251

INDEX 275

Anglo-Argentine sovereignty talks, 24, 163, 164
Argentine military threat to, 1, 147
British economic and strategic interest in, 2, 23, 24, 124, 238
Labour left position on, 172
and oil, 2, 24, 25, 124, 161, 163–167, 169, 170, 176, 210–214, 219, 220, 227, 238
Falkland Islands Committee (FIC), 11, 171–173, 175, 179, 206, 223, 224, 226, 236
Falkland Islands Company, 162
Falklands War, 1, 2, 22–25, 32, 36, 39, 85, 88, 105–109, 113, 123, 146, 148, 151, 166, 169, 170, 179, 181, 189, 190, 200, 205, 214, 220, 221, 223, 225, 227, 228, 231, 238, 239
Chile's support to UK during, 41
FCO. *See* Foreign Office/Foreign & Commonwealth Office
Fearn, Robin, 96, 97, 105, 107, 183, 191, 192, 197, 201, 213, 229, 246
Flannery, Michael (MP), 198
Foot, Michael, 63
Ford, Gerald, 21, 67, 73
Foreign Office/Foreign & Commonwealth Office
  attitude towards campaigners, 9, 49, 50, 53, 99, 101–103, 117
  educational background of recruits, 6–8, 10, 243
  membership of private clubs, 9, 243–248
  relations with the media, 50, 78, 136–138, 174–175, 183
  response to coup in Argentina, 21, 129–132, 138
  response to coup in Chile, 46–53
Foreign Policy Analysis, 5, 25, 26

France, 20, 31, 40, 41, 46, 67, 106, 217
Freedman, Lawrence, 23, 32, 105, 113, 126, 175, 178, 232
Friends of the Falklands, 175
Frow, Brian (Air Commodore), 226

G
Galtieri, Leopoldo (General), 181, 205
Game theory, 11, 12, 28
Gatehouse, Mike, 48, 76, 179, 204
Gate-keepers, 11, 28, 119, 138. *See also* Veto-players
GEC, 10, 69, 135, 145, 148, 184, 186, 202, 208
Germany, 38, 40, 41, 46, 67, 109
Gibraltar, 127, 170, 215, 225
Gilmour, Ian (Lord Privy Seal), 90, 91, 95, 202, 232
Griffin, Anthony. *See* British Shipbuilders
Griffiths, D.H., 163, 165
Griffiths report on Falklands oil, 163, 165
Guerrillas, 130, 136–138. *See also Ejercito Revolucionario del Pueblo* (ERP); Montoneros

H
Hall, David, 174, 175
Hankey, Henry, 50, 51, 54, 60, 80, 245
Harris, Robin, 87
Hart, Judith, 48, 53, 59, 76, 78, 80, 94, 172, 198
Hart, Steve, 48
Hawker Hunter aircraft, 47, 52, 64. *See also* Rolls Royce, aero-engine dispute
Hawker Siddeley, 149, 186

Heath, Edward, 4, 35, 46, 80
Heath, John (British Ambassador to Chile 1980–82), 94–97, 99, 103
Heffer, Eric, 45, 63, 81
Hickman, John, 244
HMS Endurance, 60, 125, 126, 176, 205, 224, 226, 232, 236
Howell, David, 210, 211, 229
Hunter Christie, Bill, 174
Hunt, Rex, 203, 224, 225, 230, 232
Huntrods, Guy, 134, 155, 208
Hutchison, Gordon, 156, 157, 179

I

Imperialism, 14, 37, 172
Informal empire, 13, 14, 29
Informal social networks, 3, 5, 9, 12, 42, 73, 100, 116, 135–136, 184, 237
Institute of Economic Affairs (IEA), 86, 100
Investment
 British investment in Argentina, 14, 131, 135, 145–146, 183–184, 187, 208, 234
 British investment in Chile, 40, 61, 68, 70, 100, 119
 British investment in Latin America, 13, 16, 124
 international investment in Chile, 39, 40, 68

J

Jack, James (Scottish TUC head), 54
Johnson, Paul, 88
Joint Working Group for Refugees, 41, 44, 48, 144, 157, 179
Jones, Jack, 63, 76, 81
Joseph, Keith, 94

K

Kast, Miguel, 100
Kelvin Resources, 164
Kent, Bruce, 49
Kent, Sir Peter, 163
Kissinger, Henry, 21, 43, 143

L

Labour Party, 2, 4, 6, 7, 9, 21, 26, 45–47, 50, 52, 53, 57–59, 63, 66, 67, 77, 80, 90, 95, 102, 115, 117–119, 121, 131, 138, 140–142, 144, 151, 152, 157, 160, 172, 173, 179, 198, 233, 235, 237
 National Executive Committee, 58, 118, 144, 172, 199
 views on Argentine dictatorship, 121–122, 132, 138–140, 144, 173
 views on Falklands dispute, 125–126, 170–173
 views on Pinochet regime, 35, 39, 41, 45, 47–48, 58–60, 63–64, 121, 138–140
Lamont, Norman, 2, 88
Lancaster House Agreement. *See* Rhodesia
Lapsey, Sir John, 175
Laski, Harold, 4, 6, 26, 57
Latin America Bureau (LAB), 17, 30
Latin American Newsletter, 17, 139
Lawson, Nigel, 214, 219, 230
Leaseback, 123, 124, 163, 165, 167, 168, 175, 206–210, 212–214, 216, 221–227, 235, 236, 238
Letelier, Orlando, 38, 93
Lewin, Admiral Sir Terence, 150
Livingstone, Ken (MP), 102
Lloyds Bank, 68, 99, 134, 155, 162, 208

London Metal Exchange, 100
London School of Economics (LSE), 48, 139, 248
Love, Colonel Stephen, 193
Luce, Richard, 18, 24, 30, 33, 100, 103, 193, 199, 204, 206, 208, 226, 228, 231
Lynx helicopters, 108, 123, 193, 196

M
Mandelson, Peter, 2
Martínez de Hoz, José, 133, 155, 201
　meeting with Margaret Thatcher, 122, 186
　visits to Britain, 185
Massera, Admiral Emilio, 148
Matthei, Fernando (General), 105, 109
Midland, 134
Military sales. *See* Arms sales
Military training, 9
Military visits, 25, 149, 150, 158, 159, 239
　of Argentine officers to Britain, 148–150, 188–189
　of British officers to Argentina, 25, 149, 150, 205
　of Chilean officers to Britain, 99
　destruction of British files containing military visits, 25, 148, 149, 239
Millan, Bruce, 143, 147, 158
Ministry of Defence, 7, 16, 60, 64, 89, 94, 97–99, 117, 123, 147, 158, 184, 189, 193, 216, 227, 236
Mobil, 166
Montgomery, Viscount, 162, 185, 208
Montoneros, 130, 137, 138
Moore, Charles, 222, 231
Morgan Grenfell, 99, 100
Moss, Robert, 86, 109, 110

Mothers of the Plaza de Mayo, 198
Movimiento Peronista Montonero. See Montoneros
Mulley, Fred, 147, 152, 158

N
National Association for Freedom (NAFF), 66, 86, 87
NATO, 215, 216
Natwest, 134
Newens, Stan, 19, 63, 154, 172, 179, 198
Nixon, Richard, 21, 37

O
Ogden, Eric (MP), 171
Oil
　in Antarctica, 2, 24, 25, 124, 206, 218–220, 227, 238, 239
　around the Falkland Islands, 2, 23–25, 123, 124, 161–170, 175, 209–214, 219, 221, 227, 238, 239
Oil companies, 209, 213. *See also* British National Oil Corporation (BNOC); British Petroleum (BP); Shell
Ortiz de Rozas, Carlos, 24, 208, 212
O'Shaughnessy, Hugh, 51, 55, 187
Owen, David, 7, 18, 23, 30, 65, 78, 81, 104, 125, 127, 147–149, 151, 152, 158, 167, 168, 170, 171, 179, 226
OXFAM, 48, 117

P
Palliser, Michael, 149, 159, 225, 243
Panorama, 50, 51, 136

278 INDEX

Parkinson, Cecil, 85, 93, 94, 97, 111, 181, 185, 186, 190, 202
Parsons, Anthony, 90, 184, 200, 244
Perón, Isabel, 122, 129, 132, 138, 139, 234
Peronism, 9, 129, 138, 234. *See also* Montoneros; Perón, Isabel
Labour Party view on, 9, 138
Pettifer, Julian, 50
Phipps, Colin (MP), 166, 177, 209
Piñera, José, 100
Pinochet, Augusto, 2, 31
  arrest in London, 15, 22, 85, 87
  coup, 2
  meeting with Cecil Parkinson, 97
  meeting with Mrs. Thatcher, 181
  regime, 2
Plessey, 96, 184, 186, 195
Pucara planes, 190
Pym, Francis, 108, 190, 191, 202, 230

R

Reagan, Ronald, 21, 38, 217
Rees, Peter, 100, 109
Refugees, 20, 35, 39–41, 44, 73, 79, 85, 115, 122, 136, 141, 144, 199. *See also* Academics for Chile; Joint Working Group for Refugees; World University Service (WUS)
  from Argentina, 122, 136, 139, 141, 144
  from Chile, 20, 35, 39, 41, 47, 61, 79, 85, 122, 144, 234
  Latin America refugee programme, 122, 144, 234
  policy towards Chilean refugees under Edward Heath, 35, 39, 47
  policy towards Chilean refugees under Thatcher, 41, 85, 122
  policy towards Chilean refugees under Wilson and Callaghan, 35, 39, 41, 61, 79, 144, 234
Rhodesia, 18, 41, 88–91, 93, 215, 250
Ridley, Nicholas, 80, 88, 91–95, 98, 100, 101, 103, 117, 182, 183, 190, 192, 199, 203, 207, 208, 211, 212, 218, 221, 222, 225, 232
Roca-Runciman pact, 15
Rockhopper Exploration PLC, 170
Rolls Royce, 64–66, 69, 70, 78, 79, 81, 99, 119, 149, 184, 189
  aero-engine dispute, 64. *See also* Hawker Hunter aircraft
Rothschild, 9, 100, 116, 184
Rowlands, Ted, 72, 77, 83, 132, 133, 142, 151–153, 165, 170, 174, 177
Royal Navy, 60, 125, 147, 148, 173, 195, 216, 224
Royal Ordnance, 113, 197
RTZ, 100
Russia. *See* Union of Soviet Socialist Republics (USSR)

S

Samuel Montague, 100
Sandelson, Neville, 7
Sandwich Islands. *See* Dependencies of Falkland Islands (South Georgia and Sandwich Islands)
SAS, 107, 113
Scargill, Arthur, 102
Secondé, Reginald, 43, 47, 51, 52, 59–60, 65, 67, 71–73, 81, 243
Shackleton, Lord, 164, 175, 219, 226, 231
Shakespeare, John, 126, 130, 132, 137, 145, 154, 156, 245
Shell, 70, 99, 134, 162, 164, 184, 209

Smith, Knight, 102
Social class. *See* Class
Social movements, 3, 11, 19, 28, 42, 58, 117, 118, 122, 237. *See also* Gate-keepers; Veto-players
  political opportunity structures, 11
  political process theory, 11
Social networks. *See* Informal social networks
Solari Yrigoyen, Hipólito, 199, 204
Soref, Harold, 45
South Africa, 18, 41, 44, 78, 152, 215, 249, 216, 249
South Georgia. *See* Dependencies of Falkland Islands (South Georgia and Sandwich Islands)
Spain, 2, 20, 39, 46, 86
Spanish Civil War, 35, 63, 233
Standard Chartered Bank, 100
Stingray Torpedo, 189, 196
Straw, Jack, 25, 86
Submarines (sales to Chile), 19, 47, 62–64, 98, 190

T
Tate & Lyle, 184
Tebbit, Norman, 101, 112
Thatcher, Margaret, 2, 4, 23, 24, 32, 36, 41, 47, 54, 85–88, 94, 98, 100, 105, 109–111, 122, 123, 125, 126, 181, 182, 184–187, 191, 200, 201, 205–207, 210, 212, 221, 222, 228, 229, 231, 234, 236
The Times, 86, 110, 137, 156
Torture, 36, 50–52, 64, 71, 73, 74, 85, 92, 101, 103, 136, 149, 182, 189
  of Sheila Cassidy, 64, 71, 72, 92, 93
  of William Beausire, 74, 92, 103
Total, 14, 16, 37, 44, 62, 101, 119, 170, 172, 221

Trade
  British trade with Argentina, 8, 9, 13–15, 122–123, 131, 135, 138, 145–152, 182, 183–187, 189–198, 207–208, 224, 227
  British trade with Chile, 13, 15, 39, 40–41, 52, 58, 59, 61, 68–70, 76, 85, 89–90, 92
  British trade with Latin America, 13–15, 16, 162, 170, 221, 227
  international trade with Chile, 39–40
Trades Union Congress (TUC), 47, 140
Trade unions, 11, 17, 20, 36, 42, 47, 48, 52, 58, 65, 66, 68, 70, 76, 78, 90, 93, 117, 119, 138, 139, 153, 156, 179, 185, 233, 235. *See also* Rolls Royce, aero-engine dispute; Trades Union Congress (TUC); Transport and General Workers Unions (TGWU)
  attitude to arms sales in Argentina, 153
  attitude to arms sales in Chile, 47
  response to coup in Chile, 20, 48, 138
Transport and General Workers Unions (TGWU), 63, 65. *See also* Jones, Jack
Tyndale, Wendy, 48, 54
Type 42 frigates, 123, 146, 150, 190, 193, 195

U
Union of Soviet Socialist Republics (USSR), 91, 215
  relations with Argentina, 215
United Nations, 18, 39, 41, 75, 85, 108, 109, 123, 141, 162, 166, 183, 234, 244, 249

British attempts to soften UN stance on Chile, 109
Convention on the Law of the Sea, 166
Resolution on Falklands dispute, 123
Special Rapporteur on Chile, 39, 109
UN Commission for Human Rights, 109, 141
UN General Assembly, 109
and the United States, 38
United States, 13, 15, 16, 18, 21, 22, 37–39, 42, 43, 46, 67, 79, 90, 125, 139, 215–217, 230, 250. *See also* Carter, Jimmy; Ford, Gerald; Kissinger, Henry; Letelier, Orlando; Nixon, Richard; Reagan, Ronald
Ure, John, 77, 91, 92, 104, 107, 117, 120, 137, 152, 177, 182, 225, 245
Uruguay, 9, 75, 132, 154, 235

V

Varley, Eric, 147, 158
Veto-players, 12
Videla, Jorge Rafael (General), 139
Viscount Boyd of Merton, 175
Visits, 134, 145, 149, 200, 207, 239. *See also* Martínez de Hoz, José; Military visits
of Argentine politicians to Britain, 133–135, 184–186
of British business representatives to Argentina, 10, 69, 99, 133, 135, 145–150, 184, 186, 190, 194–197, 208
of British defence sales officials to Argentina, 147, 150
of British politicians to Argentina, 85, 93, 94, 97, 181, 185–187, 190
of British politicians to Chile, 85, 93, 94, 97, 99, 181, 186, 190
of Chilean politicians to Britain, 94, 100
Vosper Thorneycroft, 133, 146
Vulcan bomber, 192, 193, 196

W

Wallace, Stuart (Falkland Islands councillor), 212
Walters, Alan, 86, 100
Williams, Anthony, 145, 187–188, 201, 225, 244
William Whitelaw
Wilson, Harold, 2, 18, 57, 58, 63, 80, 81, 115, 131, 177
Wimpey, 186
World Cup 1978, 140, 142, 198
World in Action, 50, 51
World University Service (WUS), 41, 44

Y

YPF, 166, 209

Z

Zimbabwe. *See* Rhodesia

The manufacturer's authorised representative in the EU is Springer
Nature Customer Service Centre GmbH, Europaplatz 3, 69115 Heidelberg,
Germany. If you have any concerns regarding our products, please
contact ProductSafety@springernature.com

Printed and bound by CPI Group (UK) Ltd, Croydon, CR0 4YY
23/03/2026
02076739-0005